ANCIENT INDIAN WARFARE

ANCIENT INDIAN WARFARE

WITH SPECIAL REFERENCE TO THE VEDIC PERIOD

SARVA DAMAN SINGH

Foreword by
SIR MORTIMER WHEELER, C.I.E

MOTILAL BANARSIDASS PUBLISHERS
PRIVATE LIMITED • DELHI

First Edition: Leiden, 1965
Reprint: Delhi, 1989, 1997

ISBN: 81-208-0486-4

Also available at:

MOTILAL BANARSIDASS
41 U.A. Bungalow Road, Jawahar Nagar, Delhi 110 007
8 Mahalaxmi Chamber, Warden Road, Mumbai 400 026
120 Royapettah High Road, Mylapore, Chennai 600 004
Sanas Plaza, Subhash Nagar, Pune 411 002
16 St. Mark's Road, Bangalore 560 001
8 Camac Street, Calcutta 700 017
Ashok Rajpath, Patna 800 004
Chowk, Varanasi 221 0011

PRINTED IN INDIA
BY JAINENDRA PRAKASH JAIN AT SHRI JAINENDRA PRESS,
A-45 NARAINA, PHASE I, NEW DELHI 110 028
AND PUBLISHED BY NARENDRA PRAKASH JAIN FOR
MOTILAL BANARSIDASS PUBLISHERS PRIVATE LIMITED,
BUNGALOW ROAD, DELHI 110 007

TO PROFESSOR A. L. BASHAM

CONTENTS

FOREWORD

Regarded unemotionally, war would appear to be a natural condition of mankind; only its proportional importance varies with period and place. In pre-literate ages it was a primary vehicle of expression, liable always to be a major preoccupation amongst any folk whose wits had not been dulled by bucolic contentment. And it must be confessed that the advent of literacy, in an elementary and restricted sense, has not yet effected any fundamental change in this violent form of mass-fulfilment. Half-educated millions are still prepared to express themselves in terms of mutual slaughter without intelligent calculation and at incalculable cost. Ultimately, no doubt, a fuller education will provide a proper substitute for these cruder forms of self-realization, but that is still a long way ahead.

This gloomy preamble is designed merely to re-emphasize the human quality which is the underlying importance of the warring of history, and to re-affirm the essential "oneness" of that warring whether its mechanism be based upon slingstones, arrows or high explosive. But varying and evolving mechanism has, like an evolving language structure, given a varying shape and significance to the social aspects of warfare; reflecting and at the same time helping to create the policies and classifications in which man has sought satisfaction from one age to another. In the present book Dr. S. D. Singh, dealing primarily with the military apparatus of the great formative age traditionally associated with the *diaspora* of the Aryan-speaking peoples, is fully conscious of these wider implications. The class distinctions, for example, introduced or shaped by the introduction of the horse and the chariot to the battlefield, seemingly at that time (whatever that time may have been), are suitably recognized. And, in a more general sense, the relationship of commander to commanded, of conqueror to captive, are of the essence of history; so that the current trend to isolate "economic" and "cultural" history from the marchings and countermarchings of armies must be regarded rather as a reaction than as a revelation.

It is of the highest importance, moreover, that our understanding of warfare and its meaning be founded upon exact knowledge of its nature, its mechanism, at any given period. It is not enough to put coloured squares on a map and to call the result a "battle". Details of equipment, of manoeuvrability, of chains of command, of formations and units, and of course of terrain (reconstructed) are vital to the intelligent student of mankind, whether of the 20th century B.C. or the 20th century A.D. For his clear statement of many such details in relation to the Indian subcontinent of the protohistoric and early historic era, Dr. Singh has set a pattern for which we are his debtors.

London, 1964 MORTIMER WHEELER

ACKNOWLEDGEMENTS

This book embodies the thesis that I submitted to the University of London in October 1962 for the Degree of Doctor of Philosophy, with a few additions rendered necessary by reports of the later archaeological discoveries.

Sir Mortimer Wheeler, who was one of the examiners of this thesis, has very graciously written the *Foreword*; I am fully conscious of the honour he has done me, and gratefully acknowledge his generous encouragement.

To Professor A. L. Basham, who kindly supervised the progress of this work, I owe a deep debt of gratitude. Of his time and talents he gave unstintingly, and his affectionate encouragement no less than his valuable comments and suggestions, sustained me through my labours. It is at once a privilege and a pleasure to be his student, and I take this opportunity to put on record my sincere gratitude and appreciation.

I am also indebted to Dr. H. W. F. Saggs for his kind advice and help and for his translations of old Assyrian texts. I must also thank Dr. J. G. de Casparis who was good enough to read some of my chapters and offer a few suggestions. And I must add that the award of a postgraduate studentship by the School of Oriental and African Studies, University of London, made this work possible.

My thanks are also due to my publisher; and to the Government of Uttar Pradesh, India, for financial assistance.

New Hyderabad,
Lucknow.

SARVA DAMAN SINGH

ABBREVIATIONS

AĀ.	Aitareya Āraṇyaka.
AB.	Aitareya Brāhmaṇa.
ABORI.	Annals of the Bhandarkar Oriental Research Institute.
AL.	Altindisches Leben.
Aṅguttara.	Aṅguttara Nikāya.
ASI.	Archaeological Survey of India.
AV.	Atharva Veda.
BDCRI.	Bulletin of the Deccan College Research Institute.
Br.	Brāhmaṇa.
BU.	Bṛhadāraṇyaka Upaniṣad.
CHI.	Cambridge History of India.
CHU.	Chāndogya Upaniṣad.
DA.	Sumaṅgala Vilāsinī, 3 vols. PTS.
Dīgha.	Dīgha Nikāya.
DhA.	Dhammapada aṭṭhakathā, 5 vols. PTS.
Ed.	Edited by, edition.
Edn.	Edition.
ERE.	Encyclopaedia of Religion and Ethics.
HOS.	Harvard Oriental Series.
IA.	Indian Antiquary.
IHQ.	Indian Historical Quarterly.
JAOS.	Journal of the American Oriental Society.
Jāt.	Jātaka.
JB.	Jaiminīya Brāhmaṇa.
JBBRAS.	Journal of the Bombay Branch of the Royal Asiatic Society.
JBORS.	Journal of the Bihar and Orissa Research Society.
JCS.	Journal of Cuneiform Studies.
JDL.	Journal of the Department of Letters, Calcutta University.
JRAI.	Journal of the Royal Anthropological Institute.
JRAS.	Journal of the Royal Asiatic Society.
JUB.	Jaiminīya or Talavakāra Upaniṣad Brāhmaṇa.
KB.	Kauṣītaki Brāhmaṇa.
Kapisthala KS.	Kapisthala Kaṭha Saṁhitā
Kauṣ. Up.	Kauṣītaki Upaniṣad.
KS.	Kāṭhaka Saṁhitā.
Majjhima.	Majjhima Nikāya.
MA.	Majjhima aṭṭhakathā.
MASI.	Memoirs of the Archaeological Survey of India.
Mbh.	Mahābhārata. Cr. Ed. = Critical Edition. Cal. Ed. = Calcutta Edition.
MBU.	Maitrāyaṇa Brāhmaṇa Upaniṣad.
MS.	Maitrāyaṇī Saṁhitā.
MU.	Muṇḍaka Upaniṣad.
NBP.	Northern Black Polished Ware.
OIP.	University of Chicago, Oriental Institute, Publications.

OST.	Oriental Sanskrit Texts.
PB	Pañcaviṁśa Brāhmaṇa.
PGW.	Painted Grey Ware.
PTS.	Pāli Text Society.
Rām.	Rāmāyaṇa.
RV.	Ṛgveda.
Saṁyutta.	Saṁyutta Nikāya.
SBB.	Sacred Books of the Buddhists.
SBE.	Sacred Books of the East.
St. Petersb. Dic.	St. Petersburg Dictionary.
SV.	Sāma Veda.
SVB.	Sāma Vidhāna Brāhmaṇa.
ŚB.	Śatapatha Brāhmaṇa.
ṢVB.	Ṣaḍviṁśa Brāhmaṇa.
TA.	Taittirīya Āraṇyaka.
TB.	Taittirīya Brāhmaṇa.
Tr.	Translated by.
TS.	Taittirīya Saṁhitā.
TU.	Taittirīya Upaniṣad.
Up.	Upaniṣad.
Vinaya.	Vinaya Piṭaka.
VS.	Vājasaneyi Saṁhitā.
ZDMG.	Zeitschrift der deutschen morgenländischen Gesellschaft.

INTRODUCTION TO THE SECOND EDITION

It is a matter of great gratification that Motilal Banarsidass are bringing out an Indian edition of my book on ancient Indian warfare. Professor Basham, to whom I dedicated this work remarked not long before his death that this book had never been easily available in India, and that there was a crying need for an Indian edition. That need is now being met, thanks to the enthusiasm of my friend, Mr. N.P. Jain.

Almost everything I wrote during 1960-62, has been vindicated by later archaeological discoveries; and I can happily hold my thesis without any revision. The wheels of time, though, know no rest; and the continuing work of exploration and excavation in different parts of the Indian sub-continent in the years past has significantly enlarged the horizons of Indian archaeology. The antiquity of the earliest kind of human settlement at Chopani-Mando on a terrace of the Belan river near Allahabad in north India goes back beyond the ninth millennium B.C., which is the date of the later period there with some suggestion of an incipient agriculture.[1] Only three kilometres from Chopani-Mando, each on opposite banks of the Belan river, are the twin sites of Mahagara and Koldihwa. The remains of rice impressions in potsherds at Koldihwa represent a domesticated variety; and radiocarbon dates push back the cultivation of rice in India to the seventh, sixth and fifth millennia B.C.[2] Increasingly sedentary settlements pose hitherto unknown problems of protection and self-preservation.

As Mahagara on the opposite bank of the river reveals, neolithic villages were permanent villages with an economy based on agriculture. The discovery of sling balls and a cattle-pen at the end of the village close to the river bank clearly illustrates a new awareness of danger. The area was surrounded by wooden posts certainly to support fencing of some kind, with three openings facing the river; and four house-unit clusters around the cattle-pen added to the measure of protection provided to the cattle. We can see the beginnings of primitive fortification in these prehistoric fences.

---

1 Cf. Durrans, Brian, and Robert Knox, *India Past Into Present*, British Museum Publication, London, 1983, pp. 15-17.

2 *Ibid.*, p. 18; *Indian Archaeology—A Review*, 1975-76, p. 43.

3 *Ibid.*, pp. 18-19.

Neolithic villages in Baluchistan now go as far back as the eighth millennium B.C. The vast site of Mehrgarh in Sibi District presents an unbroken sequence of occupation from the eighth millennium B.C. to a period synchronous with the Harappan civilization in its maturity in the middle of the third millennium B.C.[1] The years between 3500 B.C. and 3000 B.C. witnessed the steady growth of cultural elements that culminated in the full-blown Harappan civilization. Settlements of considerable size, such as those at Rahman Dheri and Gumla in the North-west Frontier Province, Kot Diji near Khairpur, and Tarakai Qila in Waziristan, provide impressive evidence of "planning and monumental architecture, often including massive city walls".[2] These ancient fortifications provide a tradition of defensive architecture that reaches new heights in the haughty citadels of the Harappan cities.

On my interpretation of the literary and archaeological evidence I had concluded that iron was introduced into India around 1000 B.C., if not earlier. Sir Mortimer Wheeler, who had earlier proposed c. 500 B.C. as the date for the introduction of this metal into India through the Achaemenids, recognised the correctness of that conclusion and honoured me with a gracious *Foreword* to the first edition. I take this opportunity to pay my tribute to the memory of a truly great man, whose exacting standards of scholarship brooked no compromise.

New archaeological discoveries have pushed back the date for the use of iron in India beyond 1000 B.C. The earliest radiocarbon dates for iron come from Eran in Madhya Pradesh, and range between 1339 and 1040 B.C. In Malwa and northern Maharashtra, Nagda, Eran, Prakash and Bahal have yielded a considerably thick deposit of an immediately post-chalcolithic Black and Red ware with iron. A seven foot thick deposit of this level at Nagda contained fiftynine identifiable objects divisible into ten tool types, such as a double-edged dagger, socket of an axe, spoon, flat axe with a broad cutting edge, ring, nail, arrowhead, spear-head, knife and sickle. There is a distinct element of continuity between this and the preceding chalcolithic level. It is indeed significant that the chalcolithic culture of Malwa came to an end around 1300 B.C., giving way to the use of iron in this part of India.[3] By about 1000 B.C., the use of iron was widespread in India, undoubtedly in Madhya Pradesh

---

[1] *Ibid.*, p. 24.

[2] *Ibid.*, p. 25. Also Kalibangan I in Rajasthan; *cf. The Cambridge Encyclopedia of Archaeology*, Edited by A. Sherratt, Cambridge University Press, Cambridge, 1980, pp. 162-163.

[3] *Cf.*, Chakrabarti, Dilip, "The Beginning of Iron in India", *Antiquity*, Vol. 50, 1976, p. 119; Allchin, B. and R., *The Rise of Civilization in India and Pakistan*, Cambridge University Press, Cambridge, 1982, p. 356.

and in the Karnataka plateau in the south.[1] Hallur in Karnataka produced iron at the very beginning of the first millennium B.C. There is no proof of the diffusion of iron from West Asia to peninsular India; and the only credible conclusion is an indigenous development of iron-smelting techniques in this part of the country. The rich ore deposits in central and southern India and the conspicuous continuity between the early and the contemporary pre-industrial traditions of iron metallurgy in this country alike attest the great probability of a local evolution.[2]

In the north, Atranjikhera in District Etah of U.P., presents a continuous sequence of two different cultures preceding that of the Painted Grey Ware, which is followed by two others. The first three in the sequence may be distinguished from one another by the use of Ochre-Coloured Pottery, Black and Red Ware and Painted Grey Ware. The users of OCP were early agriculturists who lived in well-made houses and also occasionally used burnt bricks. The authors of PGW were fully familiar with iron, which is regularly found in association with that ware. The material has been thoroughly classified and illustrated in R.C. Gaur's *Excavations at Atranjikhera.* On the basis of c. 14 dates, Gaur credits both the Painted Grey Ware and iron to the Ṛgvedic Aryans, around 1200 B.C.[3]

At Jakhera, also in District Etah, an iron rod was found in association with Black and Red Ware in Period II A; and Period II B yielded a fine variety of Painted Grey Ware and a plain grey ware, and many iron objects such as an axe, spearhead, fragment of a sickle, tanged arrowheads, dagger, chisels, nails and slag.[4] The same sequence is attested by the evidence from Noh, in Bharatpur District of Rajasthan, where Period II is characterized by a plain Black-and-Red Ware, a distinct phase between deposits yielding OCP and PGW. And this period records the presence of shapeless pieces of iron, which thus predates the advent of PGW here.[5]

Thus the excavations at Atranjikhera and Jakhera in Etah District, Noh in Bharatpur District, Lal Kila in Bulandshahar District, Saipai in

---

1 *Ibid.*

2 Many scholars have expressed reservations regarding the hypothesis of a single centre of the origin of iron-smelting, first dominated by the Hittites. *Cf.*, Snodgrass, A.M., *The Dark Age of Greece*, Edinburgh, 1971; Pleiner, R., and J. Bjorkman, "The Assyrian Iron Age," *Proceedings of the American Philosophical Society*, c xvii, 1974, pp. 283-313. The scarcity of copper might have triggered the transition to iron.

3 *Cf.*, also *Indian Archaeology—A Review*, 1963-64, pp. 45-46, and Plate XXXII A.

4 *Ibid.*, 1975-76, pp. 50-51.

5 *Ibid.*, 1971-72, pp. 41-42.

Etawah District, and Ahicchatra in Bareilly District, and at many other places have revealed a pottery sequence consisting of OCP, followed by a short period of Black-and-Red Ware. The earliest evidence of iron in the north comes from this period. This is followed by PGW, which is associated with the earliest appearance of iron at several sites. Thermoluminescence dates available for Atranjikhera, Lal Kila, Nasirpur and Jhinjina indicate the beginning of the iron age around 1180 B.C.[1]

The iron tools found at places like Hastinapur, Atranjikhera and Noh are arrowheads, spearheads, knife-blades, daggers, hoes, fish-hooks, tongs, adzes and nails. And the horse is also known and used.

Elsewhere, the dates for iron in Baluchistan are c. 800 B.C.; at Swat representing the Gandhara Grave Culture c. 1000 B.C.; at Mahishdal and Chirand in eastern India c. 750 B.C.[2]

The excavations at Bhagwanpura in Haryana, and Dadheri, Kotpalon and Nagar in Punjab have revealed an interlocked phase between the late Harappans and users of the Painted Grey Ware. And at Manda, in District Akhnoor of Jammu-Kashmir, Grey Ware, affined to the Painted Grey Ware, has been found overlapping with the late Harappans. We now know that the Harappans did encounter the "Aryans or users of PGW". Dr. Ghurye contends that the Indo-Aryans, as well as the Indo-Europeans, should now be dated much earlier than 1500 B.C., particularly after the decipherment of the Linear B. Script as Greek; and that they entered India about 2200 B.C.[3] And scholars such as S.R. Rao[4] read a language related to later Sanskrit in the Harappan script. We cannot be sure; but if that were truly so, our history would have to be drastically revised.

We may now visualize a complex continuity, not exactly linear, from the late Harappan in the Punjab through to the Painted Grey Ware period, which witnessed the emergence of the iron age in north India. Even though the earliest Indo-Aryans may not have known iron, and

1 *Cf.*, Allchin, B. and R., *op. cit.*, pp. 255-256. The validity of C. 14 dates has been called into serious question in recent years. Comparative studies of C. 14 dates and dendrochronology reveal that the former need an addition of fifty years at 300 B.C. to 650 years at 2700 B.C. Cf. Ralph, E.K., "Carbon 14 Dating" in *Dating Techniques for the Archaeologists*, Eds., Michael and Ralph, London, 1971, pp. 1-48; M. Lal, "The Date of Painted Grey Ware Culture", *BDCRI*, Vol. 40, 1979-40, pp. 65-77.

2 Cf. *The Cambridge Encyclopedia of Archaeology*, p. 167; *Indian Archaeology—A Review*, 1966-67, p. 72.

3 Cf. Ghurye, G.S., *Vedic India*, Popular Prakashan, Bombay, 1979, and its review by H.D. Sankalia in *BDCRI*, Vol. 40, 1979-80.

4 Cf. Rao, S.R. *Lothal and the Indus Civilization*, Asia Publishing House, Bombay, 1973, Chapter X.

ayas in the *Ṛgveda* may at places mean copper or bronze, there are passages in that text strongly suggesting a knowledge of iron. By the middle of the first millennium B.C., many small iron age villages in the Ganges valley grew into large urban centres of population, usually on the banks of rivers, fortified with massive defensive walls of burnt brick pierced by gates at regular intervals. Their remains stand even today, damaged but not totally destroyed by the fell hand of time, silent sentinels of jealous polities and royal rivalries.

The foregoing lines, I hope, bring us abreast of the researches undertaken since the book was first published in 1965. I must now put on record my indebtedness to my sisters Priyam Vadā, Madhuram Vadā, Manju, Pushpā, Māyā, and neice Mālavikā for all kinds of help in preparing the book for a new edition.

SARVA DAMAN SINGH

INTRODUCTION TO THE FIRST EDITION

The first rapid advances in human civilization followed the discovery of metals and the domestication of cattle, among them ridden and draught animals. The growth of populations beyond their means of subsistence in given areas intensified the struggle for survival; fresh pastures beckoned to the adventurous spirit of man. It is precisely in these dim and distant beginnings of civilization that we are interested. In the pages that follow, an attempt has been made to study the earliest forms of Indian warfare; the domestication of the horse and the elephant and their use for military purposes; the invention of wheeled vehicles and the battle-chariot; the use of metals for the manufacture of weapons; the nature of ancient arms and armour, forts and fortifications; military order and organisation; and the uneasy birth of a moral consciousness evidenced in the development of a code of war.

We have pieced together all the available archaeological data and made a thorough study of the entire range of Vedic literature in a bid to present for the first time as complete a picture of warfare as these sources permit. Our task has been rendered easier by the many Vedic scholars who, though not directly interested in the military aspect of the Vedic Aryans' lives, have nevertheless said something here and there about warfare and other related matters during the course of their writings. To all of them we are indebted for help and guidance.

For the archaeological data, we are indebted to authorities such as Sir John Marshall, E. J. H. Mackay, M. S. Vats, Sir Mortimer Wheeler, Gordon Childe, Stuart Piggott, B. B. Lal, G. R. Sharma, and the publications of the Archaeological Survey of India.

Other historians before us, such as E. W. Hopkins, G. T. Date, V. R. R. Dikshitar, P. C. Chakravarti, and B. K. Majumdar, have worked on ancient Indian warfare. But none of them studied the problems that form the main burden of our thesis; the prehistoric and the Vedic periods were given short shrift in a few lines here and there and treated with an attention at best perfunctory. We stop where virtually all of them began.[1] Much more archaeolo-

[1] Cf. Chakravarti, The Art of War in Ancient India, Introduction, II.

gical material has come to light in recent years enabling us to interpret the Vedic evidence with a certainty and clarity that was hitherto unattainable.

Hopkins alone among the old historians studied the Epic evidence in detail in an essay that was masterly for its day.[1] But we have gone straight to the sources and scanned the new *Critical Edition* of the *Mahābhārata*. Our opinions are based on this independent study, and not infrequently we have found it necessary to disagree with that learned scholar. The Epic material provides depth to the picture that we have gleaned from our Vedic sources. The nature of the Vedic literature precludes the possibility of the graphic descriptions of warfare which we can find in the Epics. The echoes of the Mahābhārata war can be detected in the Vedic literature[2] and, as we have pointed out time and again in our text, some of the Epic tradition is indeed very ancient. Chariots in the Epic are the invincible instruments of battle; elephants and cavalry play a role of comparative insignificance. That this state of affairs was earlier than the days of the Buddha and the centuries that followed, will be amply demonstrated by the study of the *Nikāyas* and *Vinaya*—good evidence for the 6th—4th century B. C.[3] By the time Alexander came to India, things had changed; the chariots were there of course, but the real responsibility of attack and defence had shifted to the elephants and the cavalry. Again, the election and consecration of the commander on the field of battle as evidenced in the Epic at once reminds one of the Vedic king's coronation;[4] it is doubtless earlier than the Buddhist period. We are aware that much of the Epic was compiled later,[5] but we emphasize, nevertheless, the genuine antiquity of its tradition. Recent archaeological discoveries attest the rich efflorescence of the Ganges civilization in the first half of the first millennium B. C., in which 'we may recognise. . . the general urban background of the Mahābhārata without too much labouring of detail: a picture

---

[1] Hopkins, The Social and Military Position of the Ruling Caste in Ancient India, as represented by the Sanskrit Epic, JAOS, 13, pp. 57ff.

[2] H. C. Raychaudhuri, Political History of Ancient India, pp. 7,40.

[3] Cf. Cambridge History of India, vol. I, pp. 192-197; Dialogues of the Buddha, S. B. B. vol. II, Preface, xx; vol. IV, Introduction, vii.

[4] See below, pp. 146-148.

[5] For some opinions on the subject see Winternitz, History of Indian Literature, 1927, vol. I, pp. 454-475, 500-517; Hopkins, CHI, vol. I, p. 258; Macdonell, History of Sanskrit Literature, London, 1928, pp. 285-7, 309 etc.

of wealthy and jealous dynasties and polities, based upon a limitless and fertile soil and serviceable river-communications.' [1]

The descriptive portions of the *Mahābhārata* reveal a social and political structure recognisably earlier and less elaborately organised than that described in the accounts of Megasthenes and the *Artha-śāstra* of Kauṭilya. We have, however, exercised great caution in the treatment of the didactic portions of the Epic, which are generally agreed to be late. The *Śānti parva* has been used as little as possible, and so also the later *parvas* of the great Epic. The *Rāmāyaṇa* has been used with the greatest reserve and only in so far as it corroborates the information derived from the *Mahābhārata*. The Epic testimony is generally accepted only when it agrees with the Vedic, Buddhist or archaeological evidence.

Scholars before us tried to sift the evidence of the *Jātakas*, but no notice was taken of the earlier and vital information contained in the *Nikāyas* and the *Vinaya*. We have carefully studied these texts and culled all the relevant data bearing on the domestication of animals and their use for warfare, the arms of the army and the other allied points of interest. Despite the greater antiquity of the Epic military tradition, we have put the Buddhist evidence earlier than the Epic in our text, for the *Nikāyas* and the *Vinaya* were compiled earlier than the *Mahābhārata* and the *Rāmāyaṇa*.

The warfare of the Vedic Aryans has been thoroughly studied. The Epic and Buddhist material has been used to support, elucidate and complete the picture of the early period. The archaeological evidence on the domestication of animals, use of metals, arms and armour, and forts and fortifications, has been utilised as fully as possible to add the weight of material proof to literary testimony. All the sources have been used in their proper chronological order in a topical treatment of the subject to bring out the growth and development in different directions. Events and parallels in foreign history have often been cited in the text or foot-notes for the sake of interest as well as of explanation. It was deemed unnecessary to inflate the text of the thesis with criticisms of obsolete opinions which have been ignored in silence. Current opinions are however challenged whenever found necessary in the text; generally, though, these are referred to in the foot-notes. We may perhaps claim a

[1] Wheeler, Early India and Pakistan, p. 132. Cf. also G. J. Held, The Mahabharata, An Ethnological Study, London, 1935, p. 345.

measure of originality for the first detailed study of Indian warfare prior to the fourth century B. C.; for the synthesis of the archaeological material and the literary; and for new conclusions on many aspects of the problems discussed.

TABLE OF CHRONOLOGY

c. 4th and 3rd millennia B.C.	Early peasant communities of Western India.
c. 2700—± 141 B.C.	Kot Dijian Culture.
c. 2500—1500 B.C.	Harappan Civilization.
c. 1600—1000 B.C.	Composition of the hymns of the *Ṛgveda* and the earlier parts of the later *Saṁhitās*.
c. 1100—800 B.C.	Painted Grey Ware. Associated with the Aryans.[1]
c. 1000—900 B.C.	Mahābhārata War.[2]
c. 1000—600 B.C.	Later *Vedas*, *Brāhmaṇas* and the early *Upaniṣads*.
c. 600—200 B.C.	Northern Black Polished Ware in the Ganggeṣ Valley.[3]
c. 600—400 B.C.	The Epics in existence as popular poems before they were finally revised. They contain a military tradition that harks back to the Vedic days.
c. 563—483 B.C.	The Buddha. (Kings Bimbisāra and Ajātaśatru of Magadha, Udayana of Kauśāmbī, and Prasenajit of Kośala, were his contemporaries.)
c. 500—300 B.C.	The compilation of the *Nikāyas* and the *Vinaya* more or less complete. Aśoka's Bhabru Edict cites passages from the *Sutta Piṭaka*.

---

[1] See Ancient India, Nos. 10 and 11, pp. 2-3, 23; 138ff. Cf. also G.R. Sharma, The Excavations at Kauśāmbī (57-59), p. 9. For Wheeler's opinion, see Early India and Pakistan, pp. 26ff.

[2] Cf. Raychaudhuri, Political History of Ancient India, pp. 7, 8.

[3] Cf. Ancient India, Nos. 10 and 11, pp. 22, 23; also Wheeler, loc. cit., pp. 30, 31.

CHAPTER ONE

THE INFANTRY

Man found his feet on land, and on foot he first fought. Our palaeolithic ancestor was parasitic on nature; he hunted and killed animals as he roamed about the forests in search of food. Rude implements of wood, and of stone, chipped and flaked, added to the strength of bone and sinew against the depredations of man and beast. The clash of interests and of wills often fanned the flame of primitive bellicosity; but duels rather than battles were fought in the food-gathering stage of human evolution. The neolithic age, however, marked the beginning of cooperation with nature. Man cultivated the land and domesticated the cattle. As life thus became more sedentary, small settlements sprang into existence. The quality of tools and weapons improved; they were now ground and polished. But still, speaking with reference to India, there were no organised armies, and there was no organised warfare. Hordes of men must have frequently fought their rivals for the prize of land and booty in cattle. In those early struggles of acquisitive and greedy man, his rough and ready weapons of stone must have played their part, besides clubs of wood and the brute force of muscle.

Big strides were made in the chalcolithic age. Fortified settlements came into being, and the Indus Valley civilization reached its full flower. The many fortified sites of Baluchistan and Sind are eloquent reminders of organised life and defence; mighty citadels such as those of Harappā and Mohenjodaro, provided with watchmen's quarters, suggest the presence of standing garrisons to man the defences.[1] Fighting, then, must have already become a profession, and the army, such as it was, an important factor in the life of these wealthy communities. The Ṛgvedic references to the forts [2] and large armies [3] of the native inhabitants of India lend support to the evidence of archaeology. Foot-soldiers must

---

[1] See the chapter on forts and fortifications.

[2] RV. I. 53.7; I. 33.12; I. 61.5; I.63.7; I.103.3; IV. 16.13, etc.

[3] Ibid., I. 53.9; II. 14.7; IV. 16.13; IV. 30.21; cf. Muir, OST., vol. V, p. 471.

have protected these fortifications, fighting from rampart and parapet, tower and bastion. Indeed, direct evidence for mounted warriors in the Indus valley is strangely lacking, and we are led to believe that their fighting forces must have largely opposed their enemies on foot. Their weapons included dirks and swords,[1] knives and daggers,[2] flat axes without the shaft-hole,[3] spears and lances,[4] maces,[5] and bows and arrows [6] tipped with copper heads.[7] Slings were used as in Sumer and Anau in Turkestan.[8] The prehistoric warrior of India appears to have usually fought on foot and made use of such weapons as barbed spears and harpoons, flat axes and swords of copper, as suggested by the finds of the Gangā-Yamunā valley, the region around the uplands of Ranchi, and also Kallur in Hyderabad, Deccan.[9] The deposition of hoards, such as that of Gungeria tools and weapons, betokens a time of trouble and turmoil; perhaps the Aryan invader had arrived, and the conquest of the north-west spurred him on to the valley of the Gangā.

Infantry doubtless formed the most numerous arm of the Aryan forces, but, like the Hittite foot-soldiers,[10] played a role subordinate to the chariots in open battle. Thus, according to the *Ṛgveda*, the Aryans win treasures with hosts on foot and chariots.[11] The *Ṛgveda*, as already remarked,[12] mentions very large armies resisting the Aryan advance; some of the figures range from 30,000 up to 100, 000. A literal acceptance of the latter inflated figures would indeed be open to question; but an acquaintance with armies of consider-

---

1 ASI, Annual Report, 1930-34, I, p. 58; Mackay, Further Excavations at Mohenjodaro, I, p. 466.

2 Ibid., p. 465.

3 Ibid., pp. 453-454; Marshall, Mohenjodaro and the Indus Civilization, II, pp. 494-495.

4 Mackay, loc. cit., p. 459; Marshall, loc. cit., pp. 497, 498.

5 Mackay, loc. cit., p. 397.

6 Ibid., p. 461. The Vedic Age, pl. VII, fig. 7, depicts a horned archer of the Indus valley.

7 Marshall, loc. cit., II, p. 499; Childe, New Light on the Most Ancient East, p.178.

8 Marshall, loc. cit., p. 466. For a full treatment of the Indus Valley weapons, see below, pp. 85-91.

9 V. A. Smith, The Copper Age and Prehistoric Bronze Implements of India, IA., 1905, vol. 34, pp. 230ff.; Stuart Piggott, Antiquity, vol. 18, 1944, pp. 173-182; Prehistoric India, pp. 236-238.

10 O. R. Gurney, The Hittites, p. 106.

11 RV. I.100.10, *sa grāmebhiḥ sanitā sa rathebhir. . . .*

12 See above, p. 7, n. 3.

able size would alike be undeniable. And the available evidence suggests that most of these non-Aryans must have stood their ground on foot.

The willing and able-bodied members of the various tribes must have constituted the infantry of the Ṛgvedic Aryans, while the king and his nobility usually rode in chariots and commanded the army. The *Ṛgveda* refers to the gathering of tribes on the day of trial;[1] there is the warrior, and there also his son on the field of battle. Even three generations together [2] brave the foe in defence of their property.[3] The armies carry banners as they march to the fateful encounter. Flag unites with flag in battle,[4] as band on band and troop following troop invoke divine favours;[5] brave men, impetuous, march on, like flames of fire in form, with pointed arrows and sharp weapons.[6] Passages such as these hint at some kind of a marching order as well as battle formation. The Maruts, likened to the people in the Vedic literature, are in the *Ṛgveda* like brothers, among whom none is the eldest or the youngest; [7] they are equal in age,[8] of one mind,[9] and look alike, with golden mantles,[10] helmets,[11] and armlets.[12] They move about in fixed formations—thrice sixty [13] or thrice seven.[14] Though most of them, however, usually ride on horseback or in chariots, it is noteworthy that the poet can visualise the form of a well ordered army that must have included warriors both mounted and on foot. Terms like *śardha*, *vrāta*, and *gaṇa*,[15] cannot, therefore, be summarily dismissed as signifying no 'distinct series of divisions'.[16] Zimmer [17]

---

1 RV. VI.26.1.2; VII.79.2.
2 Ibid., VIII. 23.12
3 Ibid., X.42.4.
4 Ibid., I.103.1; VII. 83.2; X. 103.11.
5 Ibid., III. 26.6, *vrātaṁ vrātaṁ gaṇaṁ gaṇaṁ*.
6 Ibid., X. 84.1, . . . *abhi pra yantu naro agnirūpāḥ*
7 Ibid., V.59.6; 60.5.
8 Ibid., I.165.1.
9 Ibid., VIII.20.1,21.
10 Ibid., V. 55.6.
11 Ibid., V.54.11.
12 Ibid., II. 34.2.
13 Ibid., VIII.85.8.
14 Ibid., I.133.6; cf. R.N. Dandekar, Vṛtrahā Indra, ABORI, vol. 31, 1950, p. 50.
15 RV.V.53.11; *vrāta* in RV.I.163.8; III.26.2; IX.14.2, etc.
16 Vedic Index, II, pp. 341, 342; cf. CHI, vol. I, p. 98.
17 Zimmer, AL, p. 162.

deduced from these terms that the clan (*viś*), the village (*grāma*) and the family constituted the units of the military organisation. We cannot be positive as to the nature of these divisions,[1] though tribes and relations not infrequently fought side by side. And in the later Epic, too, we find relations fighting beside each other.[2] Outside India, Homer refers to the tribal organisation of the army,[3] and so does Tacitus in his *Germania*.[4]

The *vrājapati*[5] and the *grāmaṇī*[6] were officials of more or less equivalent status, who commanded the village contingents in battle. The *Ṛgveda* explicitly refers to the people (*viś*) fighting;[7] they must have formed the bulk of the infantry. In one passage, though, the people and wars are contrasted;[8] the desire for peace and security seems to break like sunshine through the clouds and clamour of war.

The chief weapon of the infantry, as also of the chariotry, was the bow and arrow. Arrows were tipped with metal or horn, and sometimes poisoned.[9] Flaming arrows[10] were shot presumably in order to set fire to the enemy strongholds. Lances, spears, swords, axes, and slingstones were also used by the Ṛgvedic foot-soldier.[11] Those among the infantrymen who could afford it, and few perhaps could, may have worn armour,[12] or at least the hand-guard called *hastaghna*, against the friction of the bowstring. Instruments like the *dundubhi* and *bakura*[13] provided the music of war. The warriors charged with loud shouts to keep up their animation and ardour, so that the word *krandas*[14] became synonymous with a 'shouting host.' No doubt, the infantry of the day could achieve little against the chariots, which invariably stole the thunder in open battle. Nevertheless, the foot-soldier was still indispen-

---

1 Apte in 'The Vedic Age', p. 355, infers battle arrays of different types from these terms, which denote different military units.

2 Hopkins, JAOS, 13, p. 193.

3 Iliad, II, 362.

4 Germania, p. 275 (ch. 7).

5 RV. X. 179.2; Vedic Index, II, p. 341; CHI, I, p. 95.

6 See p. 142.

7 RV. I.69.3; 126.5; IV. 24.4; VI. 26.1; VII. 79.2, etc.

8 Ibid., VI. 41.5; cf. Vedic Index, I, p. 204.

9 RV. VI.75.11,15.

10 Ibid., I.66.4.

11 CHI, I, p. 98.

12 Cf. RV. VI.75.1,18.

13 Vedic Index, II, p. 418.

14 RV. II.12.8; compare Germania, pp. 267, 269 (ch.3).

sable. He must have won battles for the Aryans in hilly and difficult terrain, inaccessible to their chariots; he must have stormed the enemies' forts, scaled the walls and fought inside to wrest the advantage. And he must have later protected the Aryan strongholds. He fought under the over-all command of the king [1] and the *senānī*,[2] and the immediate control of the *grāmaṇī* or the *vrājapati*. If the chariots routed the armies of the non-Aryan opponents, the foot-soldiers secured possession of the enemy property. But their casualties were often heavy; the figures of the opposing armies quoted in the *Ṛgveda* furnish an approximate idea of the immense slaughter that was the concomitant of victory. Those that fled from the field of battle, 'ran like cows unherded from the pasture, each clinging to a friend as chance directed'.[3] The archers, though formidable from a distance, could achieve little at close quarters. The chariots, therefore, as well as the cavalry, found themselves at an advantage. Horses trampled and destroyed an army.[4] Battles were frequently fought on the banks of rivers;[5] the Paruṣṇī witnessed the famous battle of the ten kings, and the Yamunā the encounter between Sudās and Bheda. Clouds of dust arose as the battle raged;[6] the defeated host was driven into the river to drown and perish.[7] So much about the wars of defence and aggression. Raids for cattle and booty formed part of the normal business of life.[8] The king shared the prize with his people;[9] indeed, the allurement of loot must have been an incentive to popular military service.

The *Atharva Veda* mentions the army as a regular institution of the state, like the *sabhā* and the *samiti*.[10] The *Taittirīya Saṁhitā* refers to the army and its commander (*senānī*).[11] The infantry is

---

1 RV. X.75.4; U.N. Ghoshal, Kingship in the Ṛgveda, IHQ, 20, 1944, p.40; CHI, I, p. 98.

2 CHI., I, p. 95..

3 RV. VII.18.10.

4 Ibid., VI.75.7.

5 CHI, I, p.98.

6 RV. VII.83.3.

7 CHI, I, p. 82.

8 Cf. RV. X.142.4; Vedic Index, II, p. 212.

9 Ibid.

10 AV. XV. 9.2, *sabhā ca samitiśca senā ca*; cf. K. P. Jayaswal, Hindu Polity, p. 20.

11 TS. IV.5.4.1.

alluded to in various passages of the later *Saṁhitās*;[1] the *Atharva Veda* uses the term *patti* to denote a foot-soldier.[2] The *Vājasaneyi Saṁhitā* calls Śiva 'the lord of footmen.'[3] The people still constituted the rank and file; an AV. passage speaks of 'sharpening up clan on clan (*viś*)', in order to fight.[4] The *Taittirīya Saṁhitā* refers to the Maruts as the people of the gods; they are organised in seven troops; and in troops does a king win his people.[5] The passage reinforces the idea of popular participation in warfare, besides suggesting some order in the organisation of the army. It was not a mere multitudinous horde without any form or divisions; *gaṇa* and *vrāta* and the chariots mentioned in a TS. passage,[6] and repeated elsewhere, seem to indicate separate divisions. A certain measure of orderliness is again suggested by the mention of the lines of enemies;[7] of thought and design in the context of warfare;[8] of those who come to fight, having made their ensigns, in troops;[9] and of the armies of enemies going conquered in troops.[10] The *Sāma Veda* possibly refers to some kind of a battle formation through the word *yukteṣu*.[11] And banners,[12] presumably, point to the same conclusion. The troop-leaders were the *grāmaṇī*,[13] the *gaṇapati*, and the *vrātapati*.[14] The *grāmaṇī* came from the ranks of the people (*viśaḥ*).[15]

The more well-to-do among the foot-soldiers may have used articles of armour and protection.[16] The bow and arrow was still the best beloved of all the weapons of offence and defence. Says the *Atharva Veda*:[17]

---

1 AV. XI.10.24; VII.62.1; XIX.15.2; TS.IV.5.4.1. etc.
2 AV. VII.62.1.
3 VS. XVI.19, *pattināṁ pati*.
4 AV. IV.31.4.
5 TS. V.4.7.7; cf. IV.3.13.4.
6 Ibid., IV.5.4.1.
7 AV. XI.10.20, *amitrāṇāmamūḥ sicaḥ*; cf. XI.9.8.
8 Ibid., XI.9.1.
9 Ibid., VI. 103.3.
10 Ibid., V.21.9; cf. III.1.6.
11 SV. I.IV.1.5.6.
12 AV. V.21.12; XIX.13.11; TS. IV.6.4.3.
13 AV. III.5.7.
14 TS. IV.5.4.1.
15 KS. VIII.4; XV.4; MS. I.6.5; TB. I.1.4.8; 7.34; ŚB. V.3.1.5.
16 AV. VII.118.1; TS. IV.6.4.5; VS. XXIX.38.
17 AV. I.19.2; cf. VI.66.2; XI.9.1.

'Dispersing from us let the shafts fly, those that are hurled
and·that are to be hurled;
ye divine arrows of men pierce my enemies'.

And the *Taittirīya Saṁhitā*:[1]

'By the bow cows, by the bow the contest may we win, by
the bow dread battles may we win;
the bow doth work displeasure to the foe;
by the bow let us win in all the quarters'.

The other weapons used were swords (*asi*), axes (*paraśu*),[2] and spears.[3] Snares, nets and traps are also mentioned.[4] The smoke of burning putrid rope was used to strike terror into the enemies' hearts.[5] An awful smell, added to the fear of a wild fire, perhaps turned the enemy back. The warriors were asked to don their armour and hold their flags in readiness for a fight;[6] the war drum shouted as the herald of victory.[7]

The desire to kill,[8] to give no quarter and ask for none, animated the heart of every fierce warrior; for, then, the victor did not have to fear the vengeance of the defeated. Indeed, the carnage must have been great, and the infantry must have borne the brunt of it; the poet does not shudder at the sight of the battlefield, bestrewn with corpses, a place of feasting for vultures and beasts.[9] This implacable hatred of the foe is best illustrated in the grim verse:

'Let ravens and strong pinioned
birds pursue them; yea, let
that army be the food of vultures.
Indra, let none escape. . . .'[10]

That the infantry was invariably rated below the chariotry in an encounter is proved by the reference to Agni conquering opponents as a combatant on a chariot overcomes men fighting on foot.[11]

---

1 TS.IV.6.6.1; cf. IV.6.4.3.
2 AV. XI.9.1; cf. TS. IV.5.3.1.
3 TS. IV.5.11.2.
4 AV. VIII.8.5.7; VIII.8.18.
5 Ibid., VIII.8.2.
6 Ibid., IX.10.1, *uttiṣṭhata saṁ nahyadhvaṁ udārāḥ ketubhiḥ saha.*
7 Ibid., V.20.9.
8 Ibid., VIII.8.1.
9 AV. XI.9.9.
10 SV. II.IX.3.6.1.
11 AV. VII.62.1.

But there were other uses for the foot-soldiers, even away from the field of battle; they guarded the paths and fords with spears and weapons.[1]

Even though the people still fought as the need arose, and the infantry in particular represented their strength, the backbone of the armies was formed by the warrior community, who had by this time arrogated to themselves the right to protect as to rule. Fighting was their profession, and the defence of the people their obligation. The masses began to be averse to war. The *Atharva Veda* pictures a happy family under the benign rule of king Parīkṣit. 'Mounting his throne, Parīkṣit, best of all, has given us peace and rest',[2] says the husband to his wife. While the king performed the imperial sacrifices, and there was victory and territorial agglomeration abroad, the common people enjoyed a measure of peace and rest they had not known before. An increasing tendency to follow peaceful avocations as opposed to the perils of a warrior's life appears here to be in evidence. Functions tended to be hereditary and thus conducive to the growth of classes that solidified into castes as the years passed.

The pursuit of peaceful tasks did not, however, entirely damp the military ardour of the people. The *Brāhmaṇas* still affirm their inclusion in the ranks of the army. They could even rise against the oppressions of the nobility and smite the lordly power.[3] A passage of the *Śatapatha Brāhmaṇa* speaks of a refractory peasantry as equal to the nobility.[4] The people of the gods,[5] the Maruts, are the most numerous in their army. Indra calls on them saying, 'Do you join me, so that with you as my force, I may smite Vṛtra'.[6] Elsewhere, Indra and Agni represent the *kṣatra*, and the All-gods the *viś*; wherever *kṣatra* conquers, *viś* is allowed to share.[7]

It may be that in some cases the *Brāhmaṇas* look back to the past, for the opposite view is also not far to seek. We are told that the peasantry is less powerful than the nobility, and unlike the latter in its thought and speech.[8] The people are devoid of energy,

1. TS. IV.5.11.1,2.
2. AV. XX.127.7-10.
3. AB.III.19; cf. PB. II.10.4.
4. ŚB. X.4.3.22; cf. II.5.2.34.
5. Ibid., II.5.2.27; II.5.2.34.
6. Ibid., IV.3.3.6,7.
7. Ibid., II,4.3.6.
8. Ibid., VIII.7.2.3.

and hence likened to the female, the symbol of frailty.[1] The peasant, according to a passage of the *Pañcaviṁśa Brāhmaṇa*, is lived upon by his superiors; he is rich in cattle.[2] There is no reference here to his participation in war. Commoners, however, continued to serve in the army till much later, despite the growing specialisation of functions; they were probably fewer than before, but still many, and by far the largest part of the infantry.

That the army was not a mere rabble without any attempt at order and organisation, is again suggested by various passages. Agni goes to battle in three rows, and the Asuras are in three columns.[3] Another passage refers to the Asuras beaten off on the north, running round to the front in battle array (*anīka*).[4] The *Śatapatha Brāhmaṇa* speaks of aggressive armies, onrushing with drawn up lines.[5]

The *Aitareya Brāhmaṇa*[6] indicates that night attacks and surprises were rampant, and the infantry must have doubtless played a major part in such engagements. The army should always keep alert and awake, if the enemy is awake.[7] Ordinarily, however, a troop of men rested for a day and night, if they had journeyed for a day and night.[8] The infantry played an indispensable, if subordinate, role in early and later Vedic warfare. The superiority of the mounted warrior, and of the charioteer in particular, was still unquestionable. Says the *Śatapatha*: '. . . whatever turns away from the warrior (*rājanya*) that he overtakes with his chariot'.

Indra took *soma*,[9] and the *rājanya surā*;[10] the foot-soldier must have had his dose of intoxicating beverages to boost his morale and whip up his courage.

The *Nikāyas*[11] and the *Vinaya*[12] alike refer to the infantry as

---

[1] Ibid., II.5.2.36.
[2] PB. VI.1.10.
[3] AB, III.39, *triśreṇirbhūtvā tryanīko 'surān yuddhamupaprāyad. . . .*
[4] Ibid., VI.4, *purastātparyadravantsamanīkataste. . . .*
[5] ŚB. VI.6.3.10. Armies are mentioned in KB. XXVIII.6; ŚB. VIII.6.1.16; IX.1.1.18.
[6] AB. VIII.28.
[7] Ibid.
[8] ŚB. VI.7.4.10.
[9] Ibid., I.6.4.7.
[10] Ibid., XII. 8.1.6.
[11] Majjhima, III. pp. 173, 174, 176; Saṁyutta, I.73, *pattikāyo*, 83,84; Aṅguttara, III, pp. 151, 157-158, 161-162, 397, etc.
[12] Vinaya, I, 241,342; II,182; IV.105.

part of the army. Ever loyal and alert to the command of the ruler, the four divisions of the forces remained the main instrument of his power and authority.[1] Thus the army had a measure of stability and permanence, as also implied by another reference.[2] That people from the various ranks of society occasionally fought or even chose a soldier's career, is demonstrated by an interesting dialogue between the Buddha and king Pasenadi of Kosala.[3] The Buddha asks him whether, while at war, he would employ a noble youth (*khattiya kumāro*), untrained and unskilled, unpractised and undrilled, timid and trembling, affrighted and sure to fly from the press of battle.[4] 'No', says Pasenadi. Would he accept such a man if he were a brāhmaṇa, or the son of a merchant or labourer? 'No', says the king once again. What would then his opinion be if, irrespective of class, the youth were trained and skilled, expert and practised, drilled and bold, of steady nerve and undismayed, and incapable of cowardly flight? Pasenadi would gladly accept any man of such qualifications. We may reasonably infer that the main body of the infantry still depended on the people in general for its recruitment as well as for its numerical superiority over the other divisions of the army. Hereditary vocations, though, were manifestly on the increase. The *asibandhakaputta* of the *Saṁyutta Nikāya*[5] seems to represent the community of mercenary foot-soldiers; a section of the people showed a predilection for the hazards of war, formed into a group in a given locality, and bequeathed to their children property and profession.

Yet another point arising out of the Buddha-Pasenadi dialogue is the evidence it gives on the training and discipline of the warrior. Soldiers must have usually had a training in conformity with the standards of the time, in the handling of weapons and developing the right temperament in the face of danger. Sham fights were organised; the army was disposed in arrays of battle and reviewed.[6] There is an interesting reference to a fourfold army standing on level ground, arrayed and armoured, for the ceremony of the washing

---

[1] Aṅguttara, III, p. 151.

[2] Ibid., III, 369.

[3] Saṁyutta, I, 98ff.

[4] Ibid., I, 98ff. *atha āgaccheyya khattiya-kumāro asikkhito akatahattho akata-yoggo akat-upāsano bhīrū chambhī utrāsī palāyī.*

[5] Ibid., IV. 312, 314. Also see below, p. 67.

[6] Vinaya, IV.107, *uyyodhika, balagga, senābyūha, anīkadassana.*

of the swords.[1] The *Vinaya* refers to infantrymen with arrows in their hands (*sarahatthā*).[2] But other weapons were also used.

Drill and discipline, and the formations of battle enable men to hold out longer under pressure and subordinate fear to the sense of duty. The essential man, however, remains lonely at heart and instinctively afraid of real danger. So the Buddha says that one warrior may lose heart at the cloud of dust, another at the uplifted standard; the third at the tumult and the fourth at the conflict; but the fifth goes forth to victory.[3]

In size, if not in importance, the infantry looms large in the Epic story; the mass fills the canvas of poetic imagination and provides the bulk of the ornate yet ineffectual arrays as an apposite setting for the exploits of the chariotry. A chariot and an elephant, three horses and five foot-soldiers together form a *patti*; three *pattis* make a *senāmukha*, three *senāmukhas* a *gulma*, three *gulmas* a *gaṇa*, three *gaṇas* a *vāhinī*, three *vāhinīs* a *pṛtanā*, three *pṛtanās* a *camū*, three *camūs* an *anīkinī* and ten *anīkinīs* constitute an *akṣauhiṇī*.[4] Elsewhere, we are told that 500 chariots, and as many elephants, (1500 horses and 2500 foot-soldiers) form a *senā* (army).[5] Another verse assigns ten elephants to every chariot, ten horses to every elephant, and ten foot-soldiers to every horse.[6] Yet another speaks of a force in reserve to repair broken ranks, consisting of chariots, to each of which were assigned fifty elephants, to each elephant a hundred horses, and to each horse as many as seven foot-soldiers.[7] Some of these impossible figures perpetrate an outrage on easy credulity; the relative equations of the different arms and their artificial arrangement are alike belied by the dispositions of battle as elsewhere described in the Epic; but significant, despite the contradictions, remains the numerical superiority of the infantry. This superiority is pathetically matched by their inability to tip the scales of victory. They serve only as fodder

---

[1] Vinaya, I, 342. The pregnant wife of the Kosala king expresses a desire to drink at the washing of the swords. That such water eased obstructed delivery according to popular belief, is attested by authorities in India as well as Europe. See I.B. Horner, SBB., vol. XIV, p. 490, n.4.

[2] Ibid., IV, 105, 107-108.

[3] Aṅguttara, III, 89,90.

[4] Mbh. 1.2.15-18.

[5] Ibid., 5.152.21.

[6] Ibid., 5.152.19.

[7] Ibid., 5.152.20, *bhinnasandhānakāriṇaḥ*.

in the holocaust of war, to applaud a hero's deeds and lament another's fall.

Nevertheless, the art of fighting on foot was an obligatory part of military education which even a charioted knight could ignore at his own peril. Thus Droṇa teaches Arjuna how to fight on the bare ground.[1] And so must all the princes learn from their teacher. King Duḥṣanta of old was skilled in the four modes of mace-fight;[2] and Bhīma and Duryodhana decide the fate of the kingdom in a duel with the mace.[3] The *Śalya parva* describes their fight and manoeuvres like the *kauśika* or jumping up, *yamaka* or turns to the right and left, and *gomūtraka* or zigzag movements.[4] All the charioted knights carried swords and shields which they used if they were deprived of their cars; [5] Nakula is praised as a consummate swordsman.[6] Wrestling was developed to the pitch of the modern free-style with no holds barred. Bhīma's marathon bout with Jarāsandha is well known;[7] he whirls Jarāsandha round a hundred times and throws him down with a fatal force to win a gruelling duel.[8] Again, Bhīma breaks a *rākṣasa* in two by applying the 'bow-and-arrow' hold,[9] and kills another by giving him the 'aeroplane spin' and hurling him down with a terrific thud.[10] Even Arjuna is a great wrestler, as we learn from the account of his fight with the Kirāta.[11]

The might of the heroes and the poet's partiality notwithstanding, the importance of the foot-soldiers is revealed by the fact that they form part of a regularly paid military organisation,[12] and are often paid in advance before they march.[13] Bhīṣma speaks of

---

1 Mbh.1.123.7.

2 Ibid., 1.62.12; also see pp. 111-12.

3 Ibid., 1.1.152.

4 Ibid., 9.55.ff.; 57.16,ff. Cal. Ed.

5 See pp. 50, 51.

6 Mbh. 3.255.10.

7 Ibid., 2.21.17ff.

8 Ibid., 2.22.6. For wrestling in the ancient world, see H. W. F. Saggs, The Greatness that was Babylon, p. 393; pl.51B.

9 Mbh. 1.151.22,23. The 'bow-and-arrow' hold, practised in present day American free-style wrestling, answers the description of the text.

10 Ibid., 3.12.59. 'Aeroplane spin', also a modern term, corresponds with the textual description.

11 Ibid., 3.40.43.

12 Ibid., 3.16.21,22; 12.41.11; cf. 2.5.38,39; Rāmāyaṇa, Ayodhyā, 100. 32,33.

13 Mbh. 2.5.48.

mercenaries as well as irregulars, and their functions, arrangement and withdrawal from the field of battle.[1] Dhṛtarāṣṭra describes the qualities of his soldiers, neither very young nor very old, neither lean nor fat, free from drunkenness and lechery, and efficient and devoted to their masters.[2] They take all kinds of armed exercises, and march and retreat in order. Duly examined, they are duly paid.[3] And, what is more, they are not recruited for the sake of lineage or favour, or connections of birth and blood.[4] Thus, the ranks of the infantry were filled in particular by people of ordinary and sometimes low extraction.

The equipment of the infantry included arms as well as armour. Bows and arrows, swords and shields, javelins and lances, axes and pikes, clubs and maces, were all pressed into service.[5] It seems that the archers did not carry any shields, as their hands were already full, with their bows and arrows. The sculptures of Bharhut and Sānchī furnish the earliest visual evidence of a foot-soldier's equipment in ancient India, and depict swordsmen and javelin-bearers carrying shields, but the archers without them.[6] Soldiers from a hilly country, according to an Epic passage, fought with stones as missiles.[7] Some of the infantrymen carried conches, drums, cymbals, horns and such other musical instruments.[8]

Various verses suggest a marching order in divisions,[9] and the battle arrays are meticulously formed before the commencement of the day's fight.[10] Superior, middling and inferior troops are placed respectively in the van, centre and the rear of an army.[11] Names and badges are given to the bodies of troops for purposes of recognition during the course of a battle.[12] The bulk of the infantry fight together, except a few who support the chariots as *padānugas*

---

[1] Mbh. 5.162.8ff., *bhṛtānapyabhṛtānstathā*
[2] Ibid., 6.72.1ff.
[3] Ibid., 6.72.7-9, *parīkṣya ca yathānyāyaṁ vetanenopapāditaṁ.*
[4] Ibid. 6.72.10.
[5] Ibid., 5.197.17; 6.18.17; 6.44.13-15; 6.53.13.
[6] Maisey, Sanchi and Its Remains, London, 1892, pl. XX; Cunningham, The Stupa of Bharhut, London, 1879, pl. XXXII.
[7] Mbh. 7.97.29ff.
[8] Ibid., 6.1.15; 6.23.13; 7.38.30.
[9] Ibid., 4.29.15,24; 6.18.17.
[10] Ibid., 5.160.27, *yuktā tiṣṭhatyanīkinī*; 6.22.1,2, etc.
[11] Ibid., 5.152.2.
[12] Ibid., 6.1.12, *abhijñānāni sarveṣāṁ saṁjñāścābharaṇāni ca.*

and *anucaras* in small bodies,[1] and a few others who similarly support the elephants.[2] Despite the accent on size, the Epic tells us in one place that strength in numbers is never the cause of victory, which depends on luck and chance.[3] The authority of Bṛhaspati is invoked to advise that the few must be made to fight by condensing them into a deep formation, while the many may be extended according to pleasure.[4]

All the care and circumspection bestowed on the elaborate arrays of battle, however, proves unavailing, if the poet is to be believed; order vanishes and confusion prevails no sooner than a fight is joined. Weapons as well as fists are used,[5] and the wails and shrieks of bleeding humanity rend the air.[6] The code of morality goes unheeded in the passage of arms; the foot-soldiers fight the other divisions of the opposing army as well as opponents of their own kind.[7] A thick dust adds darkness to misery; but the battle rages unabated; the combatants guess and strike, guided by the watchwords, names and tribal distinctions of the contending forces.[8] Soldiers are pierced by javelins and cut asunder by axes, trodden by elephants and trampled by horses; the wounded moan and the parched throats cry out for water.[9]

Twice in the Epic, we come across battles at night. In the *Virāṭa parva*, dust and darkness stop the fight; the moon rises and the soldiers fight once more, hardly able to distinguish a friend from foe.[10] And in the *Droṇa parva*, foot-soldiers carry blazing torches at night, while others fight on.[11] The weary soldiers desist and rest when it gets very dark, only to resume the struggle with moonrise.[12] The *Rāmāyaṇa* also describes the monkeys and the rākṣasas grappling in the dark; they ask each other's identity before dealing their blows.[13]

---

1 See p. 50.
2 See p. 83.
3 Mbh. 6.4.35.
4 Ibid., 6.19.4.
5 Ibid., 1.17.16.
6 Ibid.
7 Ibid., 6.53.14ff.
8 Ibid., 6.53.5,6, *anumānena saṁjñābhir nāmagotraiśca saṁyuge*; cf. 4.31.24; 6.42.28,29.
9 Ibid., 6.44.34ff.
10 Ibid., 4.32.1-3.
11 Ibid., 7.138.12,24.
12 Ibid., 7.159.22ff.
13 Rām. yuddha, 44.

Never does the foot-soldier influence the outcome of a battle. His blood only helps the narrator conjure up a picture of gruesome horror. The knight in his chariot sends him flying. In the *Āraṇyaka parva*, a panic-stricken infantry implores the Pāṇḍavas for mercy before a blow has been dealt or received.[1] Warriors like Bhīṣma and Arjuna, Droṇa and Karṇa, and many more, slaughter and scatter the foot-soldiers like leaves in the wind.[2] The Pāṇḍava army broken by Bhīṣma rallies to the fight when Arjuna advances against the old warrior.[3] This is typical of the infantry on various occasions, against different warriors. Not infrequently, they merely watch the progress of an encounter between two great heroes.[4] Once or twice, however, the army fights on, unwavering and steadfast, regardless of the heroes and their might; not one soldier shows his back to his adversaries.[5]

If a mishap overtakes the king or the commander, the army, including the infantry, take to their heels. In the *Virāṭa parva*, Virāṭa's capture signals the flight of the Matsyas;[6] and the Trigartas flee when Bhīma seizes their ruler.[7] Elsewhere, the fainting Duryodhana is taken away by his charioteer for a while, which is enough to start a rout of his forces.[8] And when a great warrior or commander is slain, the army flies and does not look back.[9] Droṇa actually stops the battle by order when Bhīṣma falls, and the party opposite follow suit.[10] The mass of the infantry has no individuality; their cause is synonymous with their master; and for him they gladly give up their lives. The tragedy of the routs of mighty armies consequent on the death or disappearance of the king or commander, is a commonplace of past Indian history; the old Epic only provides a foretaste of so much misery to follow.

But shall we believe all the Epic accounts of the heroic supermen routing large armies? Shall we believe the descriptions of the

---

1 Mbh.3.254.21.

2 Ibid., 6.48.8ff.; 6.102.24,25; 6.55.78,79; 7.6.41; 7.64.59,60; 7.148.19. Whole armies are routed by these heroes.

3 Ibid., 6.102.39; cf. 6.55.48.

4 cf. Rām. yuddha, 109.1ff.

5 Mbh. 7.70.33,34; cf. 6.53.2,3.

6 Ibid., 4.32.8-10.

7 Ibid., 4.32.33.

8 Ibid., 6.54.16-18.

9 Ibid., 6.115.20ff.; 7.48.32; 7.165.55; 9.16.65; 9.17.38;

10 Ibid., 6.115.25,26. Compare the story of Ahab in the Bible, Ist. Book of Kings, ch.22, vs.34,36.

utter disorder and disarray of the battlefield, as opposed to the pictures of fastidiously arrayed troop formations? With the confusion and medley of combatants, there would be mutual extermination, but there would be no victors. How would one side recognise the other? Names and shouts would not be any sure guide. Is it possible to conceive of two mixed masses of men, where everyone fighting in front can be struck with impunity from the side or from behind? Victory would then belong only to the survivors; in the confusion, no one would know where to flee. The imagination of the poet created the melée.[1] And yet there is too much stress on the personal bravery of the commander and the principal heroes to be accordant with the unity of the army as an instrument of planned and concerted action. Reliance on numbers rather than tactics spelt defeat on many an occasion in India's chequered past.

We cannot, however, forget that the infantry must have been the decisive arm when the sheer weight of numbers told, as it sometimes did. Also, the foot-soldiers fought where the other divisions of the army failed, in forests, and hilly and inaccessible regions. The archers amongst them were formidable propositions in battle, as the Greeks under Alexander learnt to their cost. Forts were besieged and stormed, as well as defended by infantrymen; they reigned supreme in that sphere of war. Besides, they helped reconnoitre the enemy territory, as the *Rāmāyaṇa* testifies,[2] and also formed the body-guards of kings. In the *Sabhā parva*, Nārada asks Yudhiṣṭhira if soldiers, dressed in red and armed with swords, stand around him to protect his person.[3]

---

1 In ancient battles, demoralisation and flight began in the rear ranks. See Ardant Du Picq, Battle Studies, pp. 85-90.

2 Rām. yuddha, 4.106.

3 Mbh. 2.5.77.

CHAPTER TWO

CHARIOTS

The discovery of rotary motion and its application to vehicular transport, through the invention of the wheel around the end of the fourth millennium B.C., wrought a revolution in peace and war. The strength of oxen, horses and asses added to the wheel provided man with means of communication that were not superseded till the nineteenth century. Chariots in war decided the fate of nations in antiquity; the incredibly fast engines of destruction reduced opposition to a farce; the knight in his car became equal to an army.

The available evidence points to the Sumerians as the first inventors of the wheeled vehicle as early as Uruk times.[1] Light chariots drawn by asses and oxen, with two solid wheels and high fronts, are depicted on 'Scarlet Ware' vessels of E.D.I. date.[2] Four wheeled wagons were found in tombs of the *Y* cemetery at Kish.[3] And the Early Dynastic models, carvings, paintings and mosaics illustrate vehicles of a similar type.[4] All of them ran on solid wheels fashioned out of three planks held together by wooden stouts and perhaps also by leather tyres secured by copper nails.[5] The wheels turned in one piece with the axle attached by leather thongs or copper bolts to the vehicle's body;[6] and one animal on each side pulled on the yoke that was fixed to the pole. When more than two draught animals were yoked on each side, the outer ones pulled on their neighbours' collars.[7]

The civilization of the Indus was fully cognizant of the wheeled vehicle; toy-carts were found at Mohenjodaro,[8] Harappā[9] and

---

1 Childe, New Light on the Most Ancient East, p. 239.

2 Piggott, Prehistoric India, p. 274.

3 Childe, loc.cit., p.149.

4 Ibid., p. 150, fig. 84; pl. XXIV,a.

5 Ibid., p. 149.

6 Ibid., pp. 149-150; Woolley, Ur Excavations, ii, The Royal Cemetery, pp. 64,108.

7 Frankfort, More Sculpture, OIP., lx, 1943, p.13.

8 Marshall, Mohenjodaro and the Indus Civilization, vol. II, p. 554, pls. CXXXI, 38; CLIV, 7, 10, 11.

9 M. S. Vats, Excavations at Harappa, vol. I, p. 451; vol. II, pl. CXX, 1-9.

Chanhudaro;[1] some of these look like the modern Sindhi cart and other North Indian types. A copper chariot from Harappā [2] appears to have been the lineal ancestor of the present day *ekkā*. The model of a four-wheeled wagon from Chanhudaro with a high dashboard reminds one of the Sumerian chariot. The wheels in India were made of three solid planks as in Sumer and Elam,[3] which has led scholars to conclude that the knowledge of the wheeled vehicle was derived from Sumer.[4] This may well be so, if we must assume such an orderly lineal development and diffusion from only one centre. And we are aware of the close contacts of the Indus people with Sumer; the Indus merchants may even have had a colony in some Sumerian city,[5] and thus furnished a living link between the two cultures. One wonders, then, why the Indians did not yoke the ass and possibly also the horse to their carts and vehicles—the humped ox is the only positively attested draught animal; —example is said to be better than precept. And the *ekkā*-like model from Harappā is just the suitable vehicle for the equids. We may note here that at Lothal,[6] a solid wheel of a toy-chariot in alabaster carved with geometric and other designs, and three terra-cotta horses have been found; it appears that horses were yoked to the chariots. There is no proof, however, that the people of the Indus or Lothal ever made use of the wheeled vehicle as an instrument of war.

---

1 Mackay, Chanhudaro, pl. LVIII; compare Mesopotamian toy carts illustrated in Armas Salonen's Die Landfahrzeuge des Alten Mesopotamien, pls. X, XI, XV. etc.

2 Vats, op. cit., II, pl. CXXV, 35.

3 Childe, New Light on the Most Ancient East, p. 176.

4 Ibid., p. 239; Mackay in Marshall's Mohenjodaro and the Indus Civilization, II, p. 555. The chariots on the Ur 'Standard' have solid wheels made of two half-discs dowelled together against the hub, and not made of three planks of wood. Why did the Indus people not borrow the shaft-hole axe of Sumer together with the technique of wheel-construction? One would expect that the two would have been taken together, as the axe-adze would help fashion the wheel. Further, if the Tell-Halaf representation is taken as one of a wheeled vehicle, the Sumerians may not be entitled to the credit of inventing the wheel. Dr. H. W. F. Saggs of the S. O. A. S., thinks that Sumer is perhaps the ideal place for the sledge and not the wheel; the slightest rainfall provides a perfect sliding surface for the former, which must have been turned to account in antiquity. Presumably, the wheel was first invented in the gravel-plain of Tell-Halaf.

5 Childe, loc. cit., pp. 169-170.

6 A. Ghosh, Indian Archaeology 1959-60-A Review, p. 18; pls. XVB and XVE.

The idea was apparently first seized on by the Sumerians; and from them it spread to their enemies. The famous 'Standard' from the royal tombs of Ur shows the war-chariots of Sumer in vivid detail. The wheels are solid; each chariot appears to have four,[1] and is drawn by a pair of asses. Two men ride in every chariot; one of them drives the asses while the other is the warrior who hurls javelins, four of which are kept in a quiver tied to the front of the car.[2] The Sumerian war-chariot was a clumsy vehicle and extremely costly; the asses yoked were controlled by reins attached to copper rings passing through their upper lips,[3] and were specially trained to put up with the strangling harness that had been originally devised for the broad-shouldered oxen. A breastband across the animals' throats transmitted their tractive power to the yoke; the poor beasts choked themselves as they pulled. The harness went wherever the chariot did, and was not reformed until the invention of the horse-collar in the 9th century A.D.[4]

The Assyrians of Cappadocia used chariots of the old Sumerian type with four wheels and horses. Sidney Smith[5] published a seal in the British Museum depicting a chariot or wagon with four wheels and four horses. But the light horse-drawn chariot with spoked wheels marked the beginning of a new epoch and appeared more or less simultaneously (around 1600-1500 B.C.) in Kassite Babylonia, 18th Dynasty Egypt, in the new kingdom of the Mitanni,[6] and in India. The Aryans had borrowed the idea from the Sumerians around 2000 B.C., invented the spokes, done away with two of the four wheels, and substituted the horse for the ass. And the chariot thus improved posed a threat to the security of peoples;

---

1 Piggott, Prehistoric India, p. 274, cites the authority of Sidney Smith to state that the wheels are actually two, and not four as ordinarily understood, this being 'the result of a curious Picasso-like technique of representing frontal and lateral views of the same object in one convention'. See Childe, New Light on the Most Ancient East, p. 151.

2 Woolley, Ur of the Chaldees, p. 66.

3 Andre Parrot, Syria, XVI, 1935, p. 136.

4 Childe, What Happened in History, p. 83. But a sculptured *toraṇa* architrave of the 1st century B. C., from Mathura, now in the Lucknow Museum, seems to suggest the beginnings of the horse-collar beside the yoke at a much earlier date. See Bachhofer, Early Indian Sculpture, II, pl. 72, Bottom.

5 Sidney Smith, Early History of Assyria, pl. VII, fig. b.

6 Gurney, The Hittites, p. 104. It made its appearance in Greece before 1500 B.C., and in Crete about 1450 B.C., according to Piggott, Prehistoric India, p. 274.

speed and shock became the watchwords of victory. The archives of Boghaz-Köy yielded a work in four tablets by a Mitannian called Kikkuli on the training and acclimatization of horses, which helps us to trace the origin of this important development. It contains technical terms in a language that is very close to Sanskrit; we are at once reminded that the Mitanni also worshipped the Indo-Aryan gods Indra, Mitra, Varuṇa, and the Nāsatya twins.[1] Their personal names too point in the same direction. Gurney concludes that 'this Aryan clan, moving westwards, brought with them their special knowledge of horse-breeding, and that it was from them that the art was learnt by the peoples of Western Asia'.[2] The Hittite and the Egyptian chariots had six-spoked wheels; but while the latter held two men, the driver and the fighter, the former carried three with specific functions of offence and defence.[3] The lance and the bow were the chief weapons of offence. The warrior on the chariot was essentially a mighty bowman.

The dust and rumble of their chariots preceded the footsteps of the Aryan invaders on the Indian soil. With his 'all-outstripping chariot wheel',[4] Indra reduced kings and their castles; the enemy was too startled to resist, too weak to cope with the shattering force of the new arm. As their chariots rolled onwards, their poets were not slow to praise the great leveller of the foe. Numberless verses sing the glories of the chariot and mention its various parts. Indeed, the descriptions are detailed almost to a fault; for though we can reconstruct a fairly trustworthy picture of the Aryan chariot, we may not be able to explain many of the impressive array of words denoting the different parts of the vehicle.

The Ṛgvedic chariot, called *ratha*,[5] was a two-wheeled vehicle.[6] The *Ṛgveda*, however, describes the car of the Aśvins built by the

---

[1] Paul Thieme, Aryan Gods of the Mitanni Treaties, JAOS, vol. 80, no. 4, Dec., 1960, pp. 301 ff.

[2] Gurney, The Hittites, p. 105. The names of Indian deities as an element in the names of the Kassite rulers of Babylonia may be significant in this connection. We know that the Kassites had an otherwise different language.

[3] Ibid., pp. 105-106,

[4] RV., I.53.9.

[5] Piggott, Prehistoric India, p. 276, points out that *ratha* is an Indo-European word for 'wheel'; the words for axle, nave and yoke are likewise common to the whole language group.

[6] RV. VIII.5.29; cf. CHU., IV.16.5; JUB. III.16.7; Kauṣītaki Up.I.4; Vedic Index, II, p. 201; Hopkins, JAOS, 13, p. 235.

Ṛbhus,[1] as having three wheels and as triple in some other parts of its construction.[2] This chariot was in all probability a figment of imagination; the wheels as well as the accompanying sets of three seem to have had some symbolical significance.[3]

The word *kośa* denoted the box of the chariot, which must have been, like its West Asian, Mycenaean and Egyptian counterparts, a closed vehicle. The box was presumably made of wickerwork as in the Aegean and Celtic chariots, or of leather on a light wooden framework as in Egypt.[4] It was fixed on a wooden axle (*akṣa*),[5] fastened by straps of cowhide. The wheels were fixed to the ends of the axle projecting free of the vehicle's body on each side, and secured by linch-pins[6] on their outer faces. The axle, according to Piggott,[7] was fixed centrally to the chariot-floor, as in Mycenaean and earlier reliefs from Malatya in Asia Minor and Iron-Age Europe. The wheels had metal tyres,[8] besides a felly (*pradhi*), spokes (*ara*),[9] and a nave (*nābhya*). The rim and the felly together were called *nemi*. The hole in the nave was called *kha*. The number of spokes in a wheel is nowhere specified. Mycenaean, Egyptian and early Hittite chariot wheels had four; later Hittite and Assyrian wheels had six to eight; while Homeric chariots had eight spokes. The Vedic chariot wheel seems to have had four to eight spokes; more might have been added at a later date. The felloe of the wheel might have been occasionally a single piece bent

---

1 RV. X.39.12.

2 Ibid., I.34.2,9; I.47.2; I.118.1,2; I.157.3; VII.71.4; X.41.1.

3 The use of the vehicle is confined only to the Aśvins even in the *Ṛgveda*. There is no archaeological corroboration of its existence anywhere in or outside India. Cf. Zimmer, AL., p. viii. But Weber, Macdonell and Keith, and Hopkins believed that the three-wheeled chariot of the Aśvins represented a real form in human use. See Vedic Index, II, p. 201; Hopkins, JAOS, 13, p. 235.

4 Piggott, Prehistoric India, p. 276.

5 The axle made of *araṭu* wood is mentioned in RV. VIII. 46.27. Cf. Zimmer, AL., p. 247, n. RV. VIII.5.29 has *akṣo hiraṇyayaḥ*; it may not, however, denote an axle of metal.

6 It is not certain whether *āṇi* stands foı the linch-pin or the end of the axle. The use of linch-pins is common to the Celtic and Egyptian chariots.

7 Piggott, loc. cit., p. 277. Later Assyrian coach-builders moved the axle to the back of the body.

8 The word *pavi* denotes the rim of the wheel. RV. I.180.1 describes the Aśvins' car with *hiraṇyayā vāṁ pavayaḥ*. Cf. ŚB. V.4.3.16; Piggott, loc. cit., p. 278.

9 *Ara*, cf. RV. I.32.15; I.141.9; V.13.6; V.58.5; VIII.20.14; VIII. 77.3; X.78.4; KS. X.4, etc.

into circular shape as attested by a Ṛgvedic simile.[1] A wheel thus made must have required more than four spokes.

A central pole projected forwards from the bottom of the chariot, and its end was passed through a hole (*kha*,[2] *tardman*[3]) in the yoke. This pole rose at an angle with the chariot floor, usually in a curve, but perhaps sometimes also in a straight line. A stout pin (*śamyā*) or bolt was provided through the chariot pole, against which the yoke was tied with straps of leather.[4] The yoke (*yuga*) was laid across the necks of the horses on either side of the pole; they were tied by the neck, and at the shoulder, perhaps by traces[5] fastened to a bar of wood[6] at right angles to the pole. Two horses were usually yoked to a chariot, but even three or four were not infrequently pressed into service.[7] When this was done, the horses must have been yoked abreast, though occasionally an extra-horse might have been placed in front. The practice of yoking horses abreast would commend itself more in war, as the broad front would wield a greater projectile force, and if horses were used one behind the other, an injured horse in front would impede the progress of those behind. The *Ṛgveda* also attests the use of asses for drawing chariots in war,[8] which at once reminds us of the early Sumerian representations. A single horse was sometimes yoked to a chariot,[9] which was not indeed a military proposition of

---

1 RV. VII.32.20, . . . *nemiṁ taṣṭeva sudravaṁ*. Piggott, Prehistoric India, pp. 277-278, points out that the Celtic chariot wheels were thus made, and the practice still survives in Turkestan.

2 RV. VIII.91.7; cf. Vedic Index, II,p.202.

3 AV. XIV. 1.40.

4 RV. III.6.6; V. 56.4; X.60.8. Piggott, loc. cit., does not mention the hole in the yoke through which the pole was passed. The practice survives even today; the hole in the yoke and the peg in the pole are used to secure the junction of the two.

5 The words *raśmi* and *raśanā* seem to denote the traces, though they also signify the 'reins' fastened to the bit (*śiprā*) in the horse's mouth. See RV. I.163.2,5; IV.1.9; VIII.7.8; IX.87.1; X.18.14; X.79.7; X.130.7; *śiprā* in RV. I.101.10; cf. Vedic Index, II,p. 380.

6 *Vāṇī* in RV. I.119.5, presumably signifies the two bars of wood to which the traces were fastened. See Zimmer, AL., p. 249; St. Petersb. Dic., s.v.; Piggott, loc. cit., p.279; Vedic Index, II, p. 202.

7 Two horses in RV. I.5.4; I.6.2; three in X.33.5. *Praṣṭi* in RV. I.39.6 and VIII.7.28, may mean a third horse. Four horses in RV. II.18.1. *Daśābhīśu* occurs in RV. X.94.7, the ten bridles probably pointing to five horses yoked to a chariot. Cf. Vedic Index, I, p. 29.

8 RV. I. 116.2.

9 Ibid., X.101.11; 131.3.

any consequence. The draught-horses, half choked by their unsuitable harness, would need special breeding and long training.

The *Śulba Sūtra* of Āpastamba,[1] a text of late date, specifies the dimensions of the chariot as 188 *aṅgulis* or finger-breadths for the pole, 104 for the axle, and 86 for the yoke. Piggott [2] adopts a value of ½ inch for the *aṅguli*, and arrives at a pole-length of about 7 ft. 10 ins., part of which projects beyond the yoke; an axle-length of about 4 ft. 6 ins., and a yoke-width of about 3 ft. 6 ins. These details more or less agree with the proportions of chariots known elsewhere from material evidence, in Egypt and Iron-Age Europe. He further suggests that the wheel diameter was 2 ft. 6 ins. to 3 ft., on the strength of analogy;[3] the horses domesticated in antiquity were perhaps small animals like the *Przewalski* and the *Tarpan*, and those represented in the art of Western Asia. Piggott actually gives a hypothetical figure of the Ṛgvedic chariot built on a *U*—shaped plan.[4] Two cave illustrations of chariots at Morhana Pahar in Mirzapur District, one of them attacked by two men on foot with bow and arrow and shield and spear, record, according to Mrs. Allchin,[5] the reminiscence of a sortie in the early centuries B.C. from some centre in the Gangā-Yamunā Doab into the territory of hunting tribes who still used no metal. One of these chariots is drawn by two, and the other by four horses, pulling the vehicle by means of wooden yokes attached to a pole. They look like two-wheeled vehicles with long axles, square floors and high fronts, behind which the charioteers stand. It is not clear whether the two circles shown one on each side near the front of one of the chariots represent another pair of wheels or the sides of the vehicle shown in plan. One would perhaps also do well to look at the Bharhut [6] and Sānchī [7] sculptures of the

---

[1] VI.5.

[2] Piggott, Prehistoric India, p. 280.

[3] Ibid., p. 281.

[4] Ibid., p. 280, fig. 32.

[5] Mrs. B. Allchin, Morhana Pahar- A Rediscovery, Man 58, 1958, article 207, pp. 153-5 and plate M. The absence of metal in the caves provides no certain clue to the early date of these paintings, for we know well enough how various tribes in India stay primitive despite the passage of years, unruffled by the mainstream of progress in other parts of the country. Besides, do the two men attacking a chariot in one of the paintings handle only weapons of wood, such as the shield and spear and the bow and arrow? We do not know.

[6] Cunningham, The Stupa of Bharhut, 1879, pls. XIII; XXV, 4.

[7] See Marshall's 'The Monuments of Sanchi', vol. II, pls. XI, middle lintel; XV, bottom lintel; XXIII a, etc. See below, p. 30, fig. 1.

ancient Indian chariot. Piggott himself holds that the coach-builders' and wheelwrights' practice was virtually unchanged for about a thousand years over the wide area between Britain and

Fig. 1
A Sānchī chariot.

India.[1] In a country like India where old forms evince a remarkable tenacity of life, the Bharhut and Sānchī chariots might reasonably hark back to the days of the Aryan advent with but slight modifications.

Two Ṛgvedic verses[2] refer to the Bhṛgus as chariot-builders. The *Ṛgveda* associates them with the legend of the acquisition of fire by the human race. Emil Sieg[3] thinks that they probably discovered the technique of producing fire by the friction of wood This, however, is a matter of doubt and conjecture. But more important, the incidental references seem to reveal that they might have worked their way up to priesthood from the position of wood-workers and handicraftsmen. In primitive societies today, as also in the past, smiths and carpenters act as religious leaders not infrequently, and are credited by superstition with magic and supernatural powers. Others must have learnt the art as the Bhṛgus rose to intellectual eminence to disdain the job that was originally theirs, and *rathakāras* appear as a functional caste as early as the *Atharva Veda*.[4]

---

1 Piggott, op. cit., p. 281.
2 RV. IV.16.20; X.39.14.
3 Emil Sieg on Bhṛgus in the 'Encyclopaedia of Religion and Ethics', vol. II, p. 558.
4 AV. III.5.6. It may be significant that the carpenters of North India persist in calling themselves *brāhmaṇas*, even though a misguided society looks down upon them owing to a lamentable derogation of manual work.

Marvels of the carpenters' skill, and used mainly for war, chariots consolidated the authority of the chiefs and nobles who could alone afford them, as did the knights' armour in the Middle Ages of Europe. Each chariot carried a warrior and his driver.[1] The presence of two in a chariot can also be deduced from Ṛgvedic verses describing Indra and Vāyu as sharing the same car.[2] The warrior called *savyeṣṭha*[3] or *savyaṣṭhā*,[4] stands on the left, or sits if he pleases on a seat called *garta* or *vandhura*.[5] His all-important weapon is the bow and arrow,[6] though he also makes use of spears, swords and daggers, if necessary.[7] On the analogy of Middle Eastern evidence and that of later Sanskrit literature, quivers containing arrows and spears must have been tied to the box of the chariot. The warrior also wears armour;[8] Indra himself is the 'golden-helmeted hero'.[9] He is the best of charioteers;[10] none has surpassed him in his might; and none has with good steeds overtaken him. His triumphant chariot rolls on, crushing everything in its way; foremost in the fight,[11] on his car he wins treasures[12]. The Maruts are also sometimes shown as riding in chariots with breastplates, armlets and wreaths, and bows and arrows.[13] Another verse refers to the bright red mares yoked to their chariot.[14]

---

[1] RV. II.12.8.

[2] RV. IV.46.2; IV.48.2; VII.91.5. One cannot but wonder at the impossible suggestion of Dikshitar, War in Ancient India, p. 158, that the warrior in his chariot was his own driver until the functions of the two were separated about the time of the *Aitareya Brāhmaṇa*.

[3] TS. I.7.9.1, has *savyeṣṭha-sārathi*, where the warrior and charioteer are meant.

[4] AV. VIII. 8.23.

[5] The Aśvins' chariot has three seats; cf. RV. I.34.9; I.47.2; I.118.1; I.157.3; VII.71.4, etc. In I.34.2, their chariot is said to have three supports fixed in it to lay hold of (*trayaḥ skaṁbhāsaḥ skabhitāsa ārabhe*), which might have secured the rider's balance when the vehicle was at full speed. In X.53.7, a chariot with eight seats (*aṣṭāvandhuraṁ*) is mentioned. Such a cumbrous vehicle could not possibly have any military use, except perhaps as a mode of transport, if it really existed.

[6] Cf. RV. VI.75; AB. VII.19.2.

[7] See the chapter on Arms and Armour. Cf. RV.V.57.2.

[8] RV. VI.75.1.

[9] RV. VI,29.6, *hiriśipraḥ*; cf. Monier Williams Dic., s.v., *śipra*.

[10] RV. I.84.6.

[11] RV. V.35.7; I.102.9.

[12] Ibid., I.100.10.

[13] Ibid., V.53.4.

[14] Ibid., V.56.6. It is sometimes assumed from these stray references to draught mares that they were preferred for the purpose. We may perhaps speak from personal experience that mares as draught-animals fight shy

The *sārathi* or the driver stands on the right to guide his horses. He has no seat provided and is aptly called *sthātṛ*.

> 'Upstanding in the car, the skilful charioteer guides his strong horses on whithersoe'er he will.
> See and admire the strength of those controlling reins which from behind declare the will of him who guides'.[1]

This does not detract from his honourable status; he may even be a kinsman of the knight on the chariot.[2] How he manages his horses with a whip is best conveyed by the animated verse:

> 'He lays his blows upon their backs, he deals his blows upon their thighs.
> Thou, whip, who urgest horses, drive sagacious horses in the fray'.[3]

The horses neigh as they advance irrepressibly to the charge with their hoofs raining dust and their forefeet trampling the enemy.[4] The outstanding role of the war-chariot in the story of Aryan progress cannot be overestimated, and quite appositely, the *Ṛgveda* addresses a hymn to the instrument of their victories.[5]

Chariot-racing also constitutes a favourite diversion of the Ṛgvedic epoch, described by Kaegi[6] as a peaceful struggle for the decisive contest on the field of battle.

The later *Saṁhitās*, too, pay their tribute of homage to the chariot of war.[7] There is none worthy of Indra's steel, the mightiest of charioteers;[8] his car is always right in front of the battle,[9] a terror to his enemy. The god Bṛhaspati goes around in his chariot, dealing death and defeat to the hosts that oppose, and protecting

---

of muddy roads, and for that reason, horses are invariably preferred for the job.

[1] RV. VI.75.6, *rathe tiṣṭhan nayati vājinaḥ*, etc.; TS. IV.6.6.2,3; VS. XXIX.43.

[2] As in Homeric Greece and Iron-Age Ireland.

[3] RV. VI.75.13, *aśvājani* for the whip.

[4] Ibid., VI.75.7; TS.IV.6.6.3; VS. XXIX. 44.

[5] RV. VI.47.26, *vanaspate vīḍvaṅgo hi bhūyā asmatsakhā prataraṇaḥ suvīraḥ/gobhiḥ sannaddho asi vīḷayasvā 'sthātā te jayatu jetvāni*. Cf. AV. VI.125; TS. IV.6.6.5; MS. III.16.3; VS. XXIX.52.

[6] Adolf Kaegi, The Rigveda, (The Oldest Literature of the Indians), translated by R. Arrowsmith, p. 19.

[7] TS. IV.5.4.1. Also see n.l.

[8] Ibid., IV.6.3.4; cf. ŚB. VIII.7.3.7.

[9] TS. I.7.13.5.

the war-cars of the faithful.[1] Indeed, the din of the conquering chariots reaches our ears through a passage of the *Taittirīya Saṁhitā*;[2] another hymn lauds the armoured and corsleted hero with his swift car.[3] The *Vājasaneyi Saṁhitā* mentions the inviolable chariot of Agni.[4] The drum sounds as the signal of battle; the warriors invoke divine aid for victory in their chariots.[5] The *Atharva Veda Saṁhitā* refers to the chariots and the cavalry side by side.[6] The *Yajus* texts pray for the *mahāratha*, a great car-fighter, in the ritual of the *aśvamedha*.[7] The terms *rathagṛtsa* (skilled in chariot fight), *rathaujas* (mighty in chariot fight), and *rathecitra* (glorious in chariot), occur in the *Taittirīya Saṁhitā* in a symbolical passage as epithets of the chieftain and commander.[8]

The *Atharva Veda Saṁhitā*[9] mentions the chariot, chariot-lap, pole, chariot-mouth, Indra the left-stander, and the moon the charioteer. The presence of two in a chariot, i.e., the warrior and his driver, is also elsewhere attested.[10] The charioteer (*saṁgrahītṛ*, *sārathi*), it seems, wore a turban, an ornament called *niṣka*, a garland (*sraj*), with the upper part of his body naked, and probably carried no weapons[11].

VS. XXX.11, mentions the *anukṣattṛ*,[12] who is, according to Sāyaṇa, an attendant on the charioteer. The *Vrātya* hymn of the *Atharva Veda*[13] speaks of two forerunners (*puraḥ sarau*), and two footmen (*pariṣkanda*) running beside a chariot.

The chariot of the *Vrātya* is called *vipatha*, and is drawn by two beasts guided with a goad (*pratoda*).[14] A covered chariot is elsewhere alluded to.[15] There are references to the spokes of the wheels.[16]

1 TS. IV.6.4.1,2.
2 Ibid., IV.6.4.4.
3 Ibid., IV.5.6.2.
4 VS. III.36, *dūḍabho ratho*.
5 TS. IV.6.6.7; VS. XXIX.57.
6 AV. XI.10.24; cf. also AV. VI.126.3; VS. XXIX.57.
7 TS. VII.5.18.1; VS. XXII.22; cf. ŚB. XIII.1.9.2.
8 TS. IV.4.3.1; cf. ŚB. VIII.6.1.16,17.
9 AV. VIII.8.23, *Indraḥ savyaṣṭhāścandramāḥ sārathi*
10 Ibid., III.21.3; ŚB. V.2.4.9; V.4.3.17; AB. II.25.
11 Wilhelm Rau, Staat und Gesellschaft im Alten Indien, p.101. He could, however, always help himself to a weapon from his chariot, if necessary.
12 Cf. VS. XXX.73; TB. III.4.9.1.
13 AV. XV.2.1, et seq.; *pariṣkanda* also in VS. XXX.13.
14 AV. XV.2.1, et seq.; PB. XVII.1.14.
15 TS. III.5.11.1. Such a chariot could have little use in war.
16 PB. VII.7.13; CHU. VII.15.1.

Many parts of the chariot are mentioned in the later Vedic literature, with meanings more or less obscure.[1] The *Śatapatha Brāhmaṇa* tells us that two smashed chariots can be united into one, which will then be serviceable.[2] The chariot is trimmed up and looks beautiful, enveloped with cords.[3] Two, three, four, or even five horses are yoked to chariots as before.[4] Asses and mules are also used as draught animals.[5] Relays of horses for a long journey are known to the *Aitareya Brāhmaṇa*.[6]

The *Atharva* and *Yajur Veda Saṁhitās* mention the *rathakāra* or the chariot-maker as the representative of an important class of the industrial population.[7]

The horse-chariot is indeed one of the attributes and weapons of the lordly power,[8] which alone can afford to own it. The chieftain and commander is described as *rathaprota* (fixed on a chariot) and *asamaratha*, possessing a matchless chariot.[9] And the charioteer figures as one of the *ratnins*[10].We learn from an interesting passage in the *Aitareya Brāhmaṇa* that the charioteers claim one fourth of the booty when the Bharatas sack the property of the Satvants.[11] Indra received one fourth of the prize in days of yore, acting as Agni's charioteer, and established the precedent. The *Chāndogya Upaniṣad* [12] refers to a mule-car laden with slaves and jewels, which, presumably, formed the prize of victory.

The wheels of the battle-chariot spin fast and far in the wake of Aryan progress; but they operate effectively only with a vast plain before them, and would serve little practical purpose in an inhospitable terrain. Chariot-racing continues as a popular sport, and forms an important part of the *vājapeya* ritual. Hillebrandt saw in it a lingering relic of an old national festival, reminiscent of the Olympic. [13]

---

1 See Vedic Index, II, s.v. *ratha*.
2 ŚB. XII.5.1.5.
3 Ibid., III.2.7.8; cf. AB. VIII.10; PB. XVI.1.13.
4 AV. X.8.8; TS. VII.4.20.1; VS. VIII.34; KS. II.6.3; ŚB. V.4.3.17; V.1.4.11; V.2.4.9; IX.4.2.11; PB. XVI.13.12; AĀ. III.1.1.9.
5 TS. VII.3.1.3; AB.IV.9.1; IV.9.4.; VI.27; CHU. IV.2.1; V.13.2.
6 AB. IV.27.
7 AV. III.5.6; KS. XVII.13; MS. II.9.5; TS. IV.5.4.2; VS. XVI.17; XXX.6; TB. I.1.4.8; III.4.2.1; ŚB. XIII.4.2.17.
8 AB. VII.19, *kṣatrasyāyudhāni yadaśvarathaḥ kavaca iṣudhanva.*
9 ŚB. VIII.6.1.18.
10 PB. XIX.1.4; cf. CHI, I, pp. 130, 131.
11 AB. II.25.
12 CHU.V.13.2.
13 Eggeling, SBE., 41, Introduction, XXIV.

The *Nikāyas* and the *Vinaya Piṭaka* affirm the fourfold division of the army,[1] but the chariot does not seem to be so important an instrument of war as it does in the Vedic literature. Elephants and cavalry loom large on the scene. Kings and princes ride in chariots, no doubt; but quite as often they ride on elephants [2] and horseback.[3] The Buddhist canon pictures a period of transition. As new problems clamour for an answer in the arena of unabated conflict, old values are put to the test of experience, and the emphasis shifts from the chariot to the elephant and the horseman. But chariots still cross and recross the fields of battle, and indeed remain part of the army for a long time to come in a country weighed down by the inertia of mass and size.

A king's strength still rests in the four divisions of his army.[4] Warrior kings all train in chariot-riding and fighting.[5] The bow and the sword appear to be the chief weapons of the chariot-warrior.[6] The Kuru king tells Raṭṭhapāla that he has been an expert in handling a chariot and a bow and sword ever since he was a youth of 20 or 25[7]. The *Ambaṭṭha sutta* of the *Dīgha Nikāya* mentions a king standing on the footrug of his chariot.[8] Elsewhere, a king marching with the four divisions of his army, asks his charioteer to drive slowly so that the people may be able to look at him longer.[9] King Pasenadi goes from Sāvatthī to Sāketa in order to attend to some urgent business by means of seven relays of chariots[10]. The king can thus speedily go anywhere in his kingdom to impose discipline on refractory subjects. Speed in war and strategy is a factor to reckon with.

The training of a horse is graphically described in a passage of the *Majjhima Nikāya*.[11] The *Abhaya rājakumāra sutta* refers to an efficient charioteer familiar with the various parts of his vehicle.[12]

---

1 Dīgha, III, 200; Majjhima, III,173, 174,176; Saṁyutta, I, 73,84; Aṅguttara, III,327; Vinaya, I,241,342; II,10, 182; IV,105, 107, 108.
2 See pp. 78, 79.
3 See p. 66.
4 Aṅguttara, III, 151.
5 Ibid., III, 152.
6 Cf. Ibid., III, 327; Vinaya, II,10.
7 Majjhima, II,69.
8 Dīgha, I,103, *rathūpatthara*; cf. Vinaya, I,192, *rathatthara*.
9 Majjhima, III,177.
10 Ibid., I,149.
11 Ibid., I, 446; see pp. 66, 67.
12 Ibid., I, 395.

The *Vinaya* [1] tells us that a war-car has four men; two of them might be armed foot-soldiers looking after each wheel, while the warrior and the driver occupy the chariot.[2] Four men in a vehicle would make free movement impossible. Chariots are arrayed on one side at the massing of the army.[3]

The *Saṁyutta Nikāya* recounts the Buddha's meeting and conversation with a *yodhājīva gāmaṇi*.[4] As we have pointed out elsewhere,[5] the *yodhājīva gāmaṇi* is the head of a village community of mercenary warriors, who presumably fight in chariots. Believing as the *gāmaṇi* does, in the attainment of heaven by his class of people through death on the battlefield, he is castigated by the Buddha for the perversity of his faith.[6] This incipient growth of the professional monopoly in fighting leads logically to the rise of the so-called martial classes of Indian history. As the few keep to themselves the art of fighting and provide the requisite protection, the masses get gradually softened in their fibre and become averse to the profession of arms. This also serves to illustrate one of the many subtle ways through which caste secured its hold on a society which still suffers so much from this blighting imposition of the past.

The Epic story, despite its present form, has an older flavour than the *Nikāyas* and the *Vinaya*. The chariot is still the supreme apparatus of war. The hero in his car invariably carries the day, while vast hordes of warriors toil only to die an unsung death in a heap of promiscuous slaughter. He blasts opposition to dust and ashes, until he is checked and challenged only by one of his own kind. This tradition is indeed earlier than the Buddhist period. Memories of the old bygone days fire the imagination of the poet and painter; time does not efface them, for they are embedded in the thoughts of the people through popular song and story, in the form of the living Epic.

The Epic war-chariot is essentially the same vehicle as that of the Vedic period. A few larger chariots, however, appear on the

---

[1] Vinaya, IV, 105.

[2] The warrior and his driver ride in the chariot according to the commentator, and the remaining two watch the linch-pins. See SBB., XI, ii, p. 375, n. 6.

[3] Vinaya, IV, 107, 108.

[4] Saṁyutta, IV, 308.

[5] See p. 67.

[6] Saṁyutta, IV.309.

scene, to which four horses are yoked,[1] managed by three charioteers.[2] It is almost universally a two-wheeled vehicle, as we can deduce from a number of descriptive passages. Kṛṣṇa's chariot is decked with two wheels resembling the sun and the moon.[3] The axle of Karṇa's chariot runs without noise,[4] which also implies only two wheels in the vehicle. The lightness of the chariot can further be inferred from Karṇa's effort to lift his car out of the morass.[5] The descriptions of the heavy and ornate four-wheelers, wherever they occur, must be attributed to later interpolations.[6] The archaeological evidence is on our side, for the chariots amongst the sculptures of Bharhut and Sānchī, of the 2nd and 1st centuries B.C., have only two wheels.[7] The other important parts of the chariot frequently mentioned are the *rathanīḍa* [8] and the *rathopastha*.[9] The *upastha*, according to Hopkins, denoted the general bottom of the car, while the *nīḍa* meant the little shelf in front, where the charioteer stood.[10] Further, he thinks, that this shelf existed in four-horse chariots only. We should not, however, necessarily suppose that there was any material difference between the two-horse and four-horse chariots; the two terms may signify no more than part and whole of the body. Four or even five horses were yoked to chariots as early as the Ṛgvedic times. *Bandhura*[11] and *talpa*[12] seem to denote, according to Hopkins, seats for the driver and the warrior.[13] Normally, however, the charioteer stands as he manages his horses; while the knight dances, as it were, on his car, facing the enemy in every direction.[14]

---

[1] Mbh. 1.96.37; 1.213.41; 4.52.8, 21; 5.152.10; 5.81.19; 7.47.9; 7.88.22; 7.135.46; 9.24.20. The verse (5.152.10) saying that four horses were yoked to all the chariots is proved wrong by the text elsewhere.

[2] The two *pārṣṇisārathis*, beside the central charioteer, are mentioned in Mbh. 5.152.11; 6.80.22; 7.47.14, 28, 32; 7.48.6; 7.135.46

[3] Ibid., 5.81.15; for two-wheeled vehicles in the *Sūtra* period, see Hopkins, JAOS, 13, p. 237, n.

[4] Mbh. 8.26.56, *akūjanākṣaṁ*; cf. Hopkins, loc. cit., p. 237. It seems that the axle must have been greased or oiled. Cf. AB. IV.7, which says that a cart or chariot, oiled, goes well.

[5] Mbh. 8.66.64.

[6] Cf. Hopkins, loc. cit., p. 250.

[7] See above pp. 29, 30.

[8] Mbh, 6.49.26; 6.67.30, etc.

[9] Ibid., 6.54.16.

[10] Hopkins, loc. cit., p. 238.

[11] Mbh. 3.230.30.

[12] Ibid., 3.231.5.

[13] Hopkins, loc. cit., p. 239, n.

[14] Mbh. 4.57.9.

The word *varūtha*,[1] a guard or protection, must signify the fence, presumably of leather, round the body of the chariot.[2] It might perhaps also rarely denote an overshield.[3] The meaning and purpose of the *triveṇu*[4] or the 'three-fold piece' is not very clear. The chariot-pole held at one end by the yoke was, according to Hopkins, "either regarded as divided at the heavy end into three parts, two of these [the pole the third] being side braces that ran behind the horses and connected at each end with the *kāṣṭha*, axle-wood [box], and this was called the 'threefold piece' (*triveṇu*), literally 'the piece with three sticks'; or this piece was a triangle of bamboo, one side of which was parallel to the axle and the other two ran together to the pole."[5] It seems to have been added to the chariot to lend additional strength and durability to the central pole. The yoke (*yuga*)[6] and the shaft (*īṣā*[7] and *kūbara*[8]) of the chariot are also mentioned, besides various other descriptive terms, the meaning of which is not easily understood. The *jaṅghā* may be the axle-tree;[9] the *pariṣkara* the wheel-guard; the *adhiṣṭhāne* the standing places over the wheels; and the *apaskara* a hind-piece of wood.[10] The chariot sometimes has a *trikośa*, doubtfully explained by Hopkins as three compartments for receiving arms.[11]

The loose piece of wood called *anukarṣa*,[12] suspended to the bottom of the chariot, was, according to one interpretation, meant for quick repair of damages sustained in battle.[13] That, however, is an impossible proposition in the press of battle, and not borne out by our text. Only cord can help repair minor damages and keep broken parts temporarily together. We may, therefore, reasonably suppose that the chariots carried bits of cord to help wherever possible and necessary.[14] Hopkins alternatively suggests that the

---

1 Mbh. 7.42.5, refers to *varūtha* made of iron.

2 Cf. Hopkins, op. cit., p. 240.

3 Ibid.

4 Mbh. 3.231.5.

5 Hopkins, op. cit., pp. 241-242.

6 Mbh. 3.231.5.

7 Ibid., 3.230.29.

8 Ibid., 6.44.5. When the two are distinguished, *īṣā* denotes the lower, and *kūbara* the upper end of the pole.

9 Hopkins, op. cit., p. 249; cf. Mbh. 7.35.32.

10 Hopkins, op. cit., p. 250; cf. Mbh. 7.40.18.

11 Hopkins, op. cit., p. 249.

12 Mbh. 2.49.6; 7.37.6.

13 Hopkins, op. cit., p. 242.

14 Present day carts and *tongas* and *ekkas* in India carry bits of cord to help minor repairs on the way.

anukarṣa was a ballast to guard against the overturning of the light vehicle.[1] But even today in India, carts and other smaller vehicles carry a 'wooden leg' at the back suspended loosely downward, which keeps them level even when the draught animals are unyoked. The use of the *anukarṣa* appears to have been the same. With the use of this, the chariot would not overturn backwards if the horses were loosed free of the yoke in battle; it would be supported at the back by the suspended piece of wood.

Hopkins makes an admirable effort to determine the shape and size of the war-chariot from the Epic text. The poets are not, however, always consistent in their descriptions. Nor are they particularly attentive to the form of the chariot in depicting warriors getting in and out of these vehicles in the heat of battle, which is indeed as it should be. Any conclusions, therefore, must be drawn with caution. Hopkins,[2] for instance, gleans an idea of size from the verse that 'the wheels sank up to the hubs in the blood'. This is a case of gross hyperbole and proves nothing on the point. The vehicles should in fact be fairly high, if they tip over so often and so easily as they seem to do.[3] And, elsewhere, large steeds are yoked to a chariot.[4] The best visual guide, perhaps, will be the sculptures of Bharhut and Sānchī, as being the nearest in point of time to our period.[5] The chariots must have been light vehicles, of course, as they are splintered easily with arrows or even otherwise.[6] Fragments of the broken chariots lie scattered about on the field of battle.[7]

The war-cars are usually adorned with rows of jingling bells.[8] The larger chariots have a covering against the sun called *ātapatra*.[9] The chariots of kings and princes carry an umbrella[10] (*chatra*)

---

[1] Hopkins, op. cit., pp. 242, 243.
[2] Ibid., p. 240.
[3] Ibid., p. 243.
[4] Mbh. 4.53.2.
[5] These are all small two-wheeled vehicles, usually with two or three riders.
[6] Mbh. 3.230.29; 3.231.5; 4.52.21,22; 6.67.30, etc.
[7] Ibid., 7.40.18.
[8] Ibid., 1.212.3; 1.213.41; 2.22.17; 2.54.4. The modern North Indian *rathas* are likewise decorated with rows of little bells, which are also hung round the necks of the draught oxen.
[9] Cf. Mbh. 5.179.13; Hopkins, op.cit., p. 236.
[10] Mbh. 3.230.30; 6.20.9; 7.135.46,etc.

symbolic of their lofty dignity. At the back of the car, presumably in the middle, rises the tall flagstaff [1] (*dhvajayaṣṭi*), surmounted by the hero's ensign in the form of an image or emblem, below which flutters his flag of rich splendour. The *dhvaja* may mean the staff, banner and image all together, and the *ketu* the symbol or the banner alone.[2] Arjuna's chariot bears a large ape on top of the standard,[3] besides numerous flags decked with various other creatures.[4] Bhīṣma's ensign has the tall stately palm bespeaking the might of the grand old warrior.[5] Droṇa has the device of a golden altar decked with a water-pot and the figure of a bow.[6] Karṇa's device is a stout cord for binding elephants.[7] Duryodhana's standard has an elephant;[8] that of Yudhiṣṭhira has two *mṛdaṅgas* or tambourines.[9] Aśvatthāmā boasts a lion's tail;[10] and Kṛṣṇa's chariot, decorated with pennons, carries the *gaḍura* on its flagstaff.[11] The tall ambitious standards with their devices, and the silk-emblazoned flags add an ironic touch of colour to the scene of war. Rallying points of the opposing forces, they impart their name to the whole army, sometimes called *dhvajinī*. The devices are individual and the flags personal, beacons of hope and courage to the soldiers who fight only for their leaders. The idea of a national flag seems not yet to have occurred to any of the kings of the Epic.

The poet's fancy toys much too freely with gold in describing the glory of the chariot. Certain parts of the royal vehicles may have been embossed with gold or silver;[12] the rest must be attributed to poetic exaggeration. When Yudhiṣṭhira stakes his royal chariot in the gambling scene of the *Sabhā parva*, it is described as being covered with tiger skins, and possessed of excellent wheels, a noble flagstaff and strings of little bells. It is drawn by eight horses, with a clatter that vies with the roar of the clouds and the

---

1 Mbh. 1.216.12; *daṇḍaka* in 7.35.31.
2 Hopkins, op.cit., p.244.
3 Mbh. 1.216.8.
4 Ibid., 1.216.14, 15, *nānāpatākābhiḥ śobhitaṁ rathamuttamaṁ*
5 Ibid., 6.17.18.
6 Ibid., 6.17.24.
7 Ibid., 4.50.15.
8 Ibid., 4.50.12.
9 Ibid., 3.254.6.
10 Ibid., 6.17.21.
11 Ibid., 5.81.20. The examples can be easily multiplied from the text. The usual form of *gaḍura* is *garuḍa*.
12 Ibid., 1.212.3,4; 1.213.41. In 5.179.10, Bhīṣma rides in a white chariot of silver to fight Paraśurāma.

ocean.[1] The rattle of the wheels is indeed a matter of approbation, and is often likened to the roar of the kettle-drums.[2]

The footsoldier's burden of arms on the march and the battlefield does not worry the knight in his chariot. His vehicle is provided with every necessity of war, and stored with all kinds of arms and weapons.[3] But fanciful extravagance depicts the chariot as a veritable arsenal, and the passages cited by Hopkins [4] serve only to annoy the student of history. The car-warrior takes good care to superintend the furnishings of his chariot. Thus we find Arjuna instructing Uttara to tie quivers to his chariot.[5] The *Ādi parva* describes his chariot as equipped with every instrument of war.[6] Karṇa elsewhere has sixteen quivers tied to his war-car, and orders a number of excellent bows, shafts, darts and heavy maces, besides his conch.[7] Kṛṣṇa likewise orders his chariot, furnished with his conch, discus, mace, quivers, javelins, and all kinds of weapons.[8] Droṇa's vehicle is likened to a fortified town, a simile of frequent occurrence, fully equipped, with his banner aflutter.[9]

The *Ādi parva* at one place states that Arjuna's chariot would scarcely be able to bear the load of his arrows.[10] It seems that the chariots of these warriors were followed by carts and other vehicles with ready supplies. Thus, Aśvatthāmā shoots as many arrows as are carried on eight carts, each drawn by eight oxen.[11] The figure of eight is a poetic absurdity; but the reference indicates the availability of fresh supplies of arms to the charioted warrior at the front. We know that he cannot carry a limitless load of arms and weapons in his light vehicle. Karṇa desires similarly elsewhere,[12] that carts should carry his arrows, and that chariots, well equipped with horses and arms, should follow him close behind. The supply must have been in practice intended for the whole chariotry in those pitched battles of antiquity, fought on premeditated sites.

---

1 Mbh. 2.54.4-6. The eight horses may be an exaggeration.
2 Ibid., 5.81.21; cf. 1.216.9.
3 Ibid., 1.212.3,4.
4 Hopkins, op. cit., p. 247.
5 Mbh. 4.40.4; cf. 3.18.12.
6 Ibid., 1.216.9.
7 Ibid., 7.2.24.
8 Ibid., 5.81.12.
9 Ibid., 7.6.43.
10 Ibid., 1.215.15.
11 Ibid., 8.15.28.
12 Ibid., 8.22.51.

Two or four horses were usually yoked to these war-chariots. The *Ādi parva* [1] describes the two horses Sainya and Sugrīva yoked to a chariot. Elsewhere, however, the four horses, named Sainya, Sugrīva, Meghapuṣpa and Balāhaka, are yoked to the car of Kṛṣṇa.[2] Horses thus had personal names like elephants. Hopkins [3] assumes that four horses were yoked only to large four-wheeled chariots, and goes on to explain the relative positions of the draught animals: "one bears the right-hand *dhur*, one the left, the 'near' horse; one is attached to the end of the fore-axle (*pārṣṇi*) on the left; another, parallel to this, to the axle-end on the right. Such seems to be the arrangement according to the text, though it would not be impossible to interpret as a double-span, the foremost drawing on the yoke and pole, the hinder pair on the axle". He is not very sure of his own description and says elsewhere[4] that the word *caturyuj* may also possibly signify a double-yoke, one behind the other. It is not necessary to force such a meaning on the word, which simply denotes that four horses are yoked to a chariot, and no more. We must perhaps rule out the possibility of a double-span for our early period. The universal practice attested in Indian sculpture down to the beginning of the Christian era is that of two or four horses yoked abreast to two-wheeled vehicles.[5] Two horses draw on the yoke on either side of the central pole; and if there are four, the outspanners are held by loose straps attached to the ends of the axle on each side, and draw perhaps also on their neighbours' collars. Horses in a double-span would in fact reduce the manoeuvrability of the chariot on the crowded battlefield. Four horses, we repeat, must have drawn only two-wheeled war-chariots during our early period. Any four-wheelers in war, if they existed for the purpose, must have doubtless been few and far between, as tributes to the personal caprice of their owners.

The horses yoked to these chariots were often protected with armour.[6] Droṇa's horses are described as covered with a net of gold.[7] This may imply some form of chain-armour of iron or bronze washed in gold. Leather robes and wooden breastplates are also

---

1. Mbh. 1.212.3.
2. Ibid., 5.81.19.
3. Hopkins, op. cit., p. 241.
4. Ibid., p. 255.
5. See CHI, I, pls. XVI, fig. 43; XXIII, fig. 63; XXIX, fig. 81.
6. Mbh. 3.18.1, *daṅśitairharibhir yuktaṁ;* 4.30.16.
7. Ibid., 7.8.15.

in evidence.[1] The horses are further decked with ornaments.[2] Tail-bands, and plumes, presumably worn on the head as today, are also mentioned.[3] The leather straps, the girth-band, the reins and the bridle and bit are alluded to, among the items of the horse harness.[4]

White horses appear as hot favourites in the Epic story.[5] Both Bhīṣma [6] and Arjuna [7] have teams of white horses, whose colour is likened to silver or fleecy clouds. And Karṇa orders equally white steeds, fleet and powerful, bathed in water and sanctified with *mantras*.[8] But Droṇa's horses of the Sindhu breed [9] are red and far-famed. They bear coolly the blare of conches and the beat of drums, the twang of bows and the showers of arrows. Their very appearance forebodes the defeat of the enemy; above fatigue and pain are those fleet steeds that draw the old *ācārya's* car.

The Epic describes horses of all possible colours.[10] Horses of the *tittiri* and *kalmāṣa* colours are often mentioned, meaning 'partridge-coloured' and 'speckled' respectively.[11] Many of the variegated colours must, however, be attributed to the flights of fancy, and there is little justification for the conjecture that 'quaggas or zebras were imported and called horses'.[12]

The horses of the north and north-west are held in high esteem, as before. The regions of Kāmboja[13] and Sindhu[14] are celebrated for their horses. The *Āraṇyaka parva*[15] furnishes a characteristic picture of horses, lean-fleshed yet strong, possessed of breeding and docility, speed and stamina, wide nostrils and swelling cheeks, and free from all inauspicious marks. The war-horses are specially

---

1 Hopkins, op. cit., p. 257.
2 Mbh. 4.36.3.
3 Hopkins, op. cit., p. 258.
4 Ibid., pp. 257, 258.
5 Mbh. 2.49.5.
6 Ibid., 5.179.10; 6.20.9.
7 Ibid., 1.215.16; 1.216.8; 5.47.46.
8 Ibid., 7.2.26.
9 Ibid., 7.8.15-18; cf. 4.53.2; 6.20.11.
10 Ibid., 2.48.23; cf. Hopkins, op.cit., pp. 256, 257.
11 Mbh. 2.47.4; 2.25.19.
12 Hopkins, op. cit., p. 256. In a passage of the *Udyoga parva* (5.104.26), Viśvāmitra asks his pupil Gālava to present 800 horses, each with one black ear, as his teacher's fee. For white horses with black ears in Vedic literature, see AV.V.17.15
13 Mbh. 2.49.5.
14 Ibid., 7.8.15,16.
15 Ibid., 3.69.11,12.

bred and trained, and never mind the din of battle.[1] Ever obedient to their driver's commands, the sensitive steeds weep for their masters in scenes of grief and agony.[2]

Mules and asses are frequently used as draught animals for long journeys, and even for purposes of war. The *Udyoga parva* refers to Dhṛtarāṣṭra's chariot drawn by mules capable of going as far as 14 *yojanas* in a day.[3] The *Ādi parva* speaks of mules of white colour and black manes, swift as the wind, and well-trained.[4] And large asses of white colour and black necks are described in the *Sabhā parva* as possessed of speed and docility, and famous far and near.[5] In the *Rāmāyaṇa*, Rāvaṇa abducts Sītā in a chariot drawn by asses.[6] The beasts are covered with armour,[7] signifying their use for war.

Victory or defeat in battle depended as much on the sagacity and dexterity of the charioteer, as on the warrior's courage and skill. The knight indeed relied on his driver's experience in order to show his prowess with any effectiveness. The charioteer is known by various names to the Epic, such as *sūta*, *sārathi*, *yantar*, *niyantar*, etc. If a vehicle has three charioteers, those that manage the outer steeds are called *pārṣṇisārathī*.[8] The *Udyoga parva* tells us that each chariot has three drivers, and that the *pārṣṇisārathīs* are also skilled warriors.[9] But numerous other passages prove or imply the presence of a solitary charioteer beside the knight. In the *Āraṇyaka parva*,[10] Pradyumna argues with his charioteer who takes him away from the battlefield; we hear only of one charioteer, and the others seem to be absent. Another passage of the same *parva*[11] mentions Kṛṣṇa's charioteer Dāruka alone, and omits the others. Yet elsewhere,[12] we come across a knight destroying a war-car, lock, stock

---

1 Mbh. 7.22.7, *sarvaśabdakṣamair yudhi*.

2 Hopkins, op. cit., p. 256. Homer also describes horses weeping. Poetry apart, the horse is a very sensitive animal. The Buddha's horse died immediately after his Great Renunciation, according to the traditional story, unable to bear separation from its master. More recent examples are not lacking.

3 Mbh. 5.84.12.

4 Ibid., 1.213.43.

5 Ibid., 2.47.21.

6 Rām. Araṇya, 49.19.

7 Ibid., 51.16.

8 Mbh. 5.152.11; 6.43.16; 7.47.14,28,32; 7.48.6; 7.135.16.

9 Ibid., 5.152.11.

10 Ibid., 3.19.3-12.

11 Ibid., 3.22.5-7.

12 Ibid., 3.230.29,30; 4.52.21,22.

and barrel, including the horses and the charioteer; the completeness of the description ignores the two extra drivers. In the *Virāṭa parva*,[1] Uttara agrees to act as Arjuna's charioteer, which implies only one driver. Bhīma, in the *Bhīṣma parva*,[2] kills the charioteer of Droṇa, who controls his horses and fights on. Similarly, elsewhere, Duḥśāsana both manages his horses and fights, when his charioteer is slain.[3] These references indicate the presence of only one driver. Further, when Kṛṣṇa[4] and Śalya[5] act as charioteers of Arjuna and Karṇa respectively, nothing at all is heard of the side-drivers. The passages cited should suffice to support the conclusion that one charioteer for a team of horses must have been the usual practice in early antiquity, and that most of the passages assigning three drivers to a chariot crept only later into our text.

The charioteer is usually a person of good birth.[6] Bhīṣma's charioteer is described as well-born and brave, versed in horse-lore and careful in battle. He is well trained in his art, and has seen many encounters.[7] Pradyumna's charioteer proudly asks his master to watch his skill in driving horses.[8]

Kings and princes do not consider it below their dignity to act as charioteers for their friends of equal rank. Kṛṣṇa grasps the reins of Arjuna's horses; and Śalya acts as Karṇa's charioteer.[9] Prince Uttara drives the steeds of Arjuna in the *Viraṭā parva*.[10] The car-warriors are all skilled charioteers.[11] Karṇa says that he is Arjuna's superior in the knowledge of horses, while Śalya is better than Kṛṣṇa.[12] Kings and princes in distress serve as stable-masters and charioteers of other rulers. Unexcelled in the knowledge and management of steeds, Nala is appointed as an *aśvādhyakṣa* or superintendent of stables by king Ṛtuparṇa.[13] He also acts as his master's counsellor in matters of moment.[14] Nakula, the Pāṇḍava,

---

1 Mbh. 4.40.1.
2 Ibid., 6.71.30, 31.
3 Ibid., 7.163.5.
4 Ibid., 5.7.35.
5 Ibid., 5.8.29; 8.22. 50ff.
6 Ibid., 5.152.9.
7 Ibid., 5.179.11, 12.
8 Ibid., 3.20.5, *paśya me hayasaṁyāne śikṣāṁ keśavanandana*
9 See footnotes 4 and 5.
10 Mbh. 4.40.1.
11 Ibid., 5.152.11.
12 Ibid., 8.22.52ff.
13 Ibid., 3.64. 2, 6.
14 Ibid., 3.64.3.

desires to become the keeper of king Virāṭa's horses.[1] He knows the temper of horses, and the art of training them; he can correct vicious horses, and treat all their diseases.[2] He pleases Virāṭa by showing him fast and perfectly trained horses that follow him wherever he goes.[3]

Despite the importance of his profession, the *sūta* or charioteer still occupies a position unmistakably lower than that of the chariot-warrior. Bhīṣma calls Karṇa a low-born *sūta*'s son, whereupon the latter protests that he has adopted the duties of a *kṣatriya*.[4] Śalya bursts into rage when Duryodhana requests him to act as Karṇa's charioteer.[5] 'Behold these two massive arms of mine', says the humiliated royal warrior, 'strong as the thunder. Behold also my excellent bow and these arrows that are like snakes of virulent poison. Behold my chariot. . . , and my mace decked with gold and twined with hempen cords. Filled with wrath, I can split the very earth, scatter the mountains, and dry up the oceans. . . . '[6] How can Śalya, a consecrated monarch, stoop to be the charioteer of a parvenu of low extraction? He asks Duryodhana's permission to go home, but is brought round by the latter's praise and adulation. The driver of the chariot, says Duryodhana, should be superior even to the warrior, like Brahmā who acted as the charioteer of Rudra in an hour of peril.[7]

It is the charioteer's prime duty to protect the knight in his car, even as the warrior should do all that he can to guard the life of his driver.[8] The knight, if wounded, unconscious, or otherwise disabled, is hurried out of harm's way by his dutiful charioteer.[9] Unconscious Pradyumna is carried off the field by his charioteer.[10] The warrior is angry when he regains consciousness, but the charioteer insists on his duty to protect him when he is helpless. Pradyumna orders him back and asks him never to leave the field

---

1 Mbh. 4.3.2, 3, *aśvabandha*

2 Ibid., 4.11.7.

3 Ibid., 4.12.30.

4 Ibid., 5.48.28. 29.

5 Ibid., 8.23.1ff.

6 Ibid., 8.23.19ff. Śalya's boast is characteristic of the age; the Epic knights beat their drums and shout their self-praise with unabashed impudence.

7 Ibid., 8.25.1,2.

8 Ibid., 3.19.8.9

9 Ibid., 5.181.15; 6.54.16, 17; 6.79.51, 52; 7.39.12.

10 Ibid., 3.19. 3-16.

while he is alive. Thus, the charioteer is no ordinary menial; he can teach a rash master that discretion is sometimes the better part of valour. The *Rāmāyaṇa* illustrates a similar scene, wherein the afflicted Rāvaṇa is hurried away from the battle by his expert charioteer, only to receive a sharp reprimand from the king when he gets better. Rāvaṇa accuses him of complicity with the enemy.[1] But the servant knows the right reply.[2] He knows that the master is tired, and so are the horses. A good charioteer knows time and place, the auspicious from the inauspicious, and above all, the temperament of his master. He takes his warrior's hints, and knows when he is glad or downcast. He has a measure of his knight's prowess. He knows the battlefield as the palm of his hand, and finds the chinks in the enemy's armour. He knows the moment of attack even as the hour of retreat; and he knows when to surprise the foe's rear. Rāvaṇa, pleased and appeased, orders the chariot back to the scene of action, and rewards the intrepid driver with an ornament from his hand. That the charioteer can occasionally act as a warrior, is demonstrated by an episode of the Bhārata war. When the mighty Bhīṣma bears down the opposition of Arjuna and the Pāṇḍavas, Kṛṣṇa forgets his horses and his post as Arjuna's charioteer, and makes a dash for the grandsire.[3] He is, however, held back by Arjuna.

A less reputable role of the charioteer is indicated by Śalya's behaviour as Karṇa's driver. He promises Yudhiṣṭhira before the war that he will do all to dispirit Karṇa and bring about his downfall.[4] And when the day arrives, Śalya as charioteer enters on a sharp wordy duel with Karṇa with a view to disturbing his equanimity. He may have been accountable for the chariot mishap in the original story; the sin was only partially mitigated by later interpolations.

The true art of the charioteer lies in driving fast and straight, wheeling and turning rapidly about, so that the chariot faces every direction at once. These circles are called *maṇḍala*, and *yamaka* or the double wheel to the left and right.[5] The expert Kṛṣṇa saves the life of Arjuna from Karṇa's sure-aimed shaft by making the horses bend down on their knees.[6]

---

1 Rām. yuddha, 106. 1ff.
2 Ibid., 106. 15ff.
3 Mbh. 6.55.86ff.
4 Ibid., 5.8. 27-31.
5 Ibid., 3.20.8; 4.52.27; 6.48.53.
6 Ibid., 8.66.11.

The charioteer is braver than the brave, whose praises are sung in the Epics. Having no other protection except what is offered by the car-warrior, he goes about his job with supreme nonchalance.[1] One and all, the self-righteous warriors cry fie on the code of morality, declaring the inviolability of the horse and charioteer.[2] Regarded as no better than the horses, the servant invariably falls before his master,[3] unnamed and unknown. But if the knight is opaque to compunction in striking the helpless charioteer, the poet is alike apathetic to his sorry fate; there is not a line in the Epic which could serve as an epitaph for the slaughtered heap of his kind. How much was demanded of him, with death the usual reward of his exertions?

So much for the charioteer on the field of battle. He also acts as a herald or ambassador, and carries messages from one camp to another. Sañjaya is the charioteer and personal friend of the old Dhṛtarāṣṭra, and daily goes from camp to town to report to the king on the progress of the war.[4] Not infrequently in peace, the *sūta* figures as a musician singing the glory of his master.[5]

Kings and princes, commanders of the army, and other warriors of note usually ride in chariots. In the *Sabhā parva*, Yudhiṣṭhira speaks of his chariot-warriors, who receive a thousand coins each as their monthly emoluments, irrespective of peace and war.[6] Thus, the army was organised on a permanent footing, and not merely hastily got together in the hour of need. Dhṛtarāṣṭra also refers to the Kaurava troops, tried and tested in the management of chariots.[7] The *atirathin*, the *mahārathin*, and the *rathin*, make the three grades of charioted warriors in a descending order. Arjuna is an *atirathin*,[8] the highest in estimation. Accoutred in mail and armed with his bow, he rides in a chariot with a tall standard.[9] He also wears a golden garland and a *kirīṭa* diadem.[10] Bhīṣma goes to fight Rāma in white armour and white headgear;

---

1 Cf. Mbh. 3.22.5, 7.

2 Ibid., 6.1.32.

3 Ibid., 1.96.38; 4.32.8; 4.49.12; 4.52. 21; 5.183.6; 6.43.14,16, 24; 6.45 12. 18; 6.49.26; 6.71.30; 6.73.66; 6.80.22, 23; 7.88.22; 7.98.56.

4 Cf. Ibid. 9.1.14ff.

5 Hopkins, op. cit., p.255.

6 Mbh. 2.54.19, 20.

7 Ibid., 6.72.9.

8 Ibid., 1.123.43.

9 Ibid., 1.205.21, *mahābāhur dhanvī varmī rathī dhvajī*

10 Ibid., 3.171.4, 5.

he carries a white bow and sits beneath a white umbrella, fanned by white chowries.[1] The chowrie-bearers must have figured only in the drive-in-state to the battlefield before the beginning of the fight; their presence in battle is not attested in the various descriptive passages. Such effeminate attentions would only serve to obstruct the warrior in shooting his arrows and facing the enemy on every side. The chariot-warriors usually appear in armour, and an oft-repeated formula describes them as armed with swords besides, with their fingers encased in gloves of leather.[2] Karṇa wears ear-rings and his coat of mail;[3] elsewhere, he orders garlands for adorning his person.[4] Bracelets and armlets of gold are also worn by the Epic car-warriors.[5]

Every charioted warrior carries his conch with him. Bhīṣma on the battlefield blows his conch and sets up a roar.[6] Kṛṣṇa, elsewhere, challenges Śālva to a fight by blowing his conch Pāñcajanya.[7] The loud blare of Pāñcajanya, and of Devadatta, the conch of Arjuna, terrifies the animals and warriors.[8] Karṇa speeds up his army's battle-formation with the blasts of his conch.[9]

Famous chariot-warriors occupy positions in the front as well as the rear of an army. In the *Virāṭa parva*, Bhīṣma asks Karṇa to stand in the van of battle, while he would himself protect the rear.[10] In the *Bhīṣma parva*, we have Bhīṣma at the head and Droṇa in the rear.[11] This significantly points to the anticipation of surprises in the rear. Every warrior has his wheel-guards, who are knights of equal rank, though young in years and experience, and who ride in their own chariots. They learn the art of fighting and find their feet under the protective wings of a tried hero. And one knight protects another in his rear. Dhṛtarāṣṭra asks who protected Bhīṣma's right, left and rear.[12] Arjuna's right and left wheels are

[1] Mbh. 5.179. 12-14. Bhīṣma is a lover of the white colour, and again at the head of the Kaurava host, the old warrior has a white turban and a white umbrella, a white bow, conch and flag, and white horses (6.20.9).

[2] Ibid., 1.212.5, *sannaddhaḥ kavacī khaḍgī baddhagodhāṅgulitravān*; cf. 1.216.16; 3.18.3, etc.

[3] Ibid., 8.24.160, *sakuṇḍalaṁ sakavacaṁ* . . . .

[4] Ibid., 7.2.29.

[5] Ibid., 6.17.17.

[6] Ibid., 6.23.12.

[7] Ibid., 3.15.20.

[8] Ibid., 6.1.18.

[9] Ibid., 8.7.13.

[10] Ibid., 4. 47.19.

[11] Ibid., 6.20.9, 11.

[12] Ibid., 6.15.30ff.

protected by Uttamaujas and Yudhāmanyu; and Arjuna himself protects Śikhaṇḍī.[1] Aśvatthāmā is followed by seven bowmen cased in mail in their chariots.[2] The knight in his chariot is, besides, followed by *anugas* and *anucaras*, who represent, according to Hopkins,[3] 'what remains of the clannish corps of an older age'. The foot-soldiers behind are called the *padānugas*, but the Epic knight often stands at the head of a whole army. Arjuna stands in the van of the Pāṇḍava forces, while we find the other chariots on the beak, head and neck, and the joints of the wings in a strategic formation.[4]

Heroes of the Pāṇḍava army are selected to be pitted against rivals of equal might on the opposite side—like Arjuna against Karṇa, and Bhīma against Duryodhana.[5] In actual battle, however, things do not always turn out quite as planned or foreseen. Heroes, no doubt, seek one another in single combat.

The first blows are usually dealt at the flagstaff and the umbrella of the opponent;[6] and their fall is construed as a disgrace to the might of the contending warrior. The knights then try to slay each other's horses and charioteers,[7] and also splinter the chariots with their shafts. A characteristic duel is thus described between Arjuna and Kṛpa:[8] Arjuna pierces the steeds of his adversary; and as they rear, Kṛpa reels from his chariot. Arjuna refrains from shooting until Kṛpa resumes his place; he seldom shows such chivalry in the Bhārata war. He then cuts through the bows of Kṛpa, his leathern fences and coat of mail. He cuts through the javelin hurled at him and reduces Kṛpa's chariot to pieces; he kills his horses and his charioteer. Kṛpa leaps down from the broken vehicle and hurls a mace at his enemy.[9] Such scenes are repeated throughout the Epic with a monotonous regularity. If a warrior loses his vehicle,

---

1 Mbh., 6.16.19.
2 Ibid., 6.17.21, 22.
3 Hopkins, op. cit., p. 260.
4 Mbh. 6.46.41ff. The army is disposed in an array of the shape of a bird.
5 Ibid., 5.161.5-10.
6 Ibid., 3.231.5; 4.52.22; 4.59.6, 7, 8; 6.43.14, 16; 6.67.30; 7.135.46.
7 See above, p. 48.
8 Mbh. 4.52.9-25.
9 The mace is according to the text returned by the shafts of Arjuna. Such feats are frequently narrated in the Epic, and one is reasonably disposed to doubt their veracity. We have, however, seen a football held up in mid-air for five minutes by a ceaseless shower of arrows shot by a professional archer at a public display. But it may be a different story with a heavy mace hurled by force in a particular direction.

he fights his way to a friend's chariot with a sword and shield, to be taken up and away from danger.[1] Deprived of his chariot, a knight sometimes runs away on foot, like Nakula, pursued, teased and spared by Karṇa.[2] Warriors made chariotless by elephants ask to be taken up on others' cars.[3] Chariots break as they collide, and find it impossible to move on the crowded battlefield.[4] Loose horses running around add to the pattern of the Epic confusion.[5]

A curious mode of encounter between two knights is the confrontation of their chariots; the horses are forced right up to the opposing chariot, so that the forequarters of those of the one side enter between those of the other; and then the fight begins.[6] Dhṛṣṭadyumna thus takes up his sword and shield, and climbs upon the shaft of Droṇa's chariot. He balances himself awhile on the yoke and the pole; but Droṇa cuts off his shield and thwarts his bold attack.

When two famous rivals meet, the passage of arms is often preceded by a sharp exchange of words. Challenged by Arjuna to taste the fruit of his wrath, Karṇa tells him that his words verily exceed his deeds, before they actually fight.[7] Elsewhere, they shout their own names in order to frighten each other.[8] Knights, deprived of their chariots, fight each other with their clubs and swords.[9] If a chariot-warrior performs prodigies of valour, he is applauded by his whole army. The Pārthas and their followers shout and beat their musical instruments in honour of the young Abhimanyu.[10]

When the mighty car-warriors exert their prowess, opposition is set at nought, and even lesser charioted knights seek safety only in flight. There are cries of oh and alas, when the redoubtable Karṇa twangs his large bow.[11] Bhīṣma shoots continuous lines of blazing arrows in all directions; he names the Pāṇḍava chariot-warriors as he slays them. The Pāṇḍava army is crushed and routed.[12] Droṇa scatters the Pāṇḍava and Pāñcāla hosts like

1 Mbh. 3.230.29-31; 3.255.15; 7.81.46, etc.
2 Ibid., 8.17.87ff.
3 Ibid., 6.44.43.
4 Ibid., 6.44.5, 6.
5 Ibid., 3.255.25.
6 Ibid., 7.72.21ff.; cf. 4.53.11ff.
7 Ibid., 4.55.5ff.
8 Ibid., 7.120.70.
9 Ibid., 6.80.22-28; cf. 7.13.62-65.
10 Ibid., 7.39.31; cf. 6.73.71, etc.
11 Ibid., 4.54.15.
12 Ibid., 6.45.60ff.; 6.48.9ff.; 6.71.32.

a row of cranes broken by the force of the wind;[1] warriors run away, if he even looks at them.[2] He proclaims aloud his own name in battle, as he shoots his arrows engraved therewith.[3] The chariot-warrior learns to shoot his arrows fast and far; Aśvatthāmā speedily exhausts the arrows carried by as many as eight carts.[4]

We have seen elsewhere [5] that the theoretical divisions of the armed forces are divorced from the actual dispositions of battle, and not worthy of any serious attention. The car-warrior fights other charioted knights as well as the other divisions of the opposing army. He slaughters foot-soldiers with a peculiar delight. The code of morality does not bother him in action, and fulminations of righteous wrath at a dastardly act never seem to impede its execution. So act the arbiters of victory and defeat; the incongruous mass of the armies is only incidental to the poetic picture. The Epic invests the deeds of heroes with supernatural proportions, to the disadvantage of the humble rank and file who shed their blood not in vain in the battles of antiquity. The prize was, however, invariably snatched away by the few, who deserved it little more than the many.

Chariots had serious limitations as instruments of battle. They served well on even ground in ideal conditions, but told a pathetic tale in difficult terrain and adverse weather. The battle of the Hydaspes demonstrated the futility of chariotry in mud and rain. As the rivalries of expansionist kingdoms embraced an ever widening area of struggle, surprise played an increasingly important part in their expeditions, and the sites of battle could no longer be easily chosen. The cumbersome chariot made way for the horseman and the elephant, who found themselves at home in any conditions. The change came with time and experience; and the *Nikāyas* furnish the first evidence of this gradual military transition. Chariots, though, continued to play a secondary and comparatively insignificant role right down to the 7th and 8th century A. D., in the hide-bound Indian army.[6]

---

1 Mbh., 7.6.34.
2 Ibid., 7.148.19.
3 Ibid., 7.101.45.46.
4 Ibid., 8.15.28; cf. 4.54.14. We must make due allowance for exaggerations.
5 See pp. 82, 83.
6 P. C. Chakravarti, The Art of War in Ancient India, p. 26.

CHAPTER THREE

THE HORSE AND CAVALRY

Looking back as we do across the many millennia of past history, in a quest for the origins of warlike techniques and equipment, we have to trace first the story of the horse's domestication, before we set out to demonstrate its use as a machine of war. A few bones of the horse have been found in association with the second phase of the Sialk culture (c. 4th millennium B. C.) in Northern Persia.[1] At Rana Ghundai in the Zhob valley of Baluchistan, teeth of the domesticated horse have been discovered in the deposits of RG I;[2] these people bred, besides horses, asses and cattle which were distinctly Indian.[3] Ross tells us that they 'had little constructional ability, perhaps no knowledge of metal', and to them even 'the potter's wheel was unknown'.[4] The evidence of RG I suggests that they were nomadic horse-riding herdsmen who used the site as a camping ground. Clearly, the horse was ridden first and yoked later in the story of its domestication. It will be interesting in this connection to draw attention to two little known terra-cotta specimens found by Sir Aurel Stein during the course of his explorations in Baluchistan. One of these comes from Periano-ghundai in the Zhob district and represents a horse.[5] It was found in association with ceramic wares characteristic of the chalcolithic age. The second fragment of a coarsely made terra-cotta figurine comes from Zayak

---

1 Stuart Piggott, Prehistoric India, p. 157; Childe, New Light on the Most Ancient East, p. 193. Bones of the horse found at Anau I in Turkestan (cf. Piggott. loc. cit.; Childe, What Happened in History, 1950, pp. 82-83) have been reidentified as those of the onager by Lundholm, Abstammung und Domestikation des Hauspferdes, Zoologiska Bidrag Fran Uppsala 27:1-289 (1949). Engravings of riders on bone objects from Susa (c. 3000 B. C.) do not clearly depict the ridden species. But for more evidence, see Le Grain, L.L., Horseback Riding in Mesopotamia in the Third Millennium B. C., Bulletin of the University Museum 11: (4): 27-32, Philadelphia, University of Pennsylvania Press, 1948.

2 Journal of Near Eastern Studies, V, 1946, p. 316.

3 Ibid., p. 311.

4 Ibid.

5 Stein, An Archaeological Tour in Waziristan and Northern Baluchistan, 1929, p. 38, pl. VII, P. W. 6; cf. Piggott, loc. cit., p. 126.

and 'seems to represent the head of a horse'.[1] The painted pottery points to the occupation going as far back as the chalcolithic times.[2]

Again, among the potsherds of painted ware on Gushanak hill, Stein found a small fragment showing a horse with rider, a subject not otherwise known to him from chalcolithic or later ware.[3]

Bones of the domesticated horse were unearthed at Mohenjodaro, a foot and ten inches deep beneath the surface.[4] We have already noted the occurrence of horse's bones in the earliest pre-Harappan layer at Rana Ghundai, and it is more than likely that the people of the Indus also bred horses.[5] Bones of the domestic ass, too, were found at Harappā, at varying depths.[6]

Further light on the subject is thrown by the discovery at Lothal in Kathiawar of three terra-cotta horses, doubtless representing the domesticated animal.[7] The horse may also be seen in a small terra-cotta fragment [8] and in a stylised painting [9] on pottery from Rangpur.

Przyluski has argued that names like Satvant, Sātvata and Nāsatya have a non-Aryan radical *sata* which appears in the modern Muṇḍa languages in the form of *sadam*, meaning 'horse'.[10] Of the two radicals meaning 'horse', *sat* is non-Aryan, *aśva* is Aryan. Some breed of the horse or pony (*sāda* as in Skt. *sādin* = rider) must have been known to the Austric speaking pre-Aryan peoples of India.[11]

---

[1] Stein, MASI, No. 43, An Archaeological Tour in Gedrosia, p. 34, pl. I, Z.W. 5.

[2] Ibid., p. 33.

[3] Ibid., p. 118; pl. XXII, Gush. 4.

[4] Marshall, Mohenjodaro and the Indus Civilization, 1931, vol. II, p. 653; pl. CLXII, fig. 9.

[5] Stuart Piggott, op. cit., p. 157; Wheeler, The Indus Civilization, 2nd. ed., 1960, p. 65; The Dawn of Civilization (ed. Piggott), p. 231.

[6] B. Prasad, MASI, 51, Animal Remains from Harappa, p. 28; cf. Piggott, op. cit., p. 157.

[7] Indian Archaeology, 1959-60—A Review, p.18, pl. XVE.

[8] Cf. H. D. Sankalia, Prehistory and Protohistory in India and Pakistan, Bombay, 1962-63, p. 169 and f.n. 51; M. G. Dikshit, BDCRI, vol. XI, 1950, p. 51, pl. XVII.

[9] Sankalia, loc. cit., f.n. 52; Dikshit, loc. cit., pl. XII, I, p. 41. The design depicts a horse's head with mane according to Professor Mallowan quoted by Sankalia, even though it has also been erroneously described as a palm 'frond'.

[10] Przyluski, 'Hippokoura et Satakarni', JRAS, 1929, p. 273 ff.; Satvant, Sātvata and Nāsatya, IHQ., IX, 1933, pp. 88-91.

[11] S. K. Chatterji in The Vedic Age, p. 150; cf. also, Polyglottism in Indo Aryan, Seventh Oriental Conference, pp. 183-185.

Whatever the original centre of the horse's domestication and the exact routes of its diffusion eastward and westward, if we deny the possibility of independent achievements, it has to be conceded in the light of archaeology and philology that the tame horse was certainly known to the inhabitants of India even before the advent of the Ṛgvedic Aryans and their galloping beasts that brooked no opposition in their sweeping onslaught. There is no evidence to prove the use of the horse in warfare in pre-Aryan India. There might have been some stray and sporadic experiments in this period; but the heyday of the war-horse dawned with the age of the *Ṛgveda*.

All earlier scholars believed that the horse was seldom ridden in peace, and never in war, during the Vedic times. There are a number of passages, however, interspersed through the Vedic literature, which prove the contrary to be true in both cases. The horse was perhaps first domesticated to round up and drive home grazing herds of cattle. Man rode him first; the invention of the wheeled vehicle came later. Before, however, we come to the analysis of literary data, we should cast a glance across the borders of India, and not study the problem in isolation.

The Hittites made use of messengers on horseback in war.[1] Four tablets from Boghaz Köy reveal that they had in their employ a horse-trainer of the land of the Mitanni, who worshipped Aryan gods under Indian Vedic names.[2] Wolfram von Soden and H. Kronasser have pointed out that Indian horse-terms are present in the Akkadian text of the Nuzi documents.[3] Vittore Pisani thinks that in some adjectives for the horse,—*babrunnu/paprunnu, b/pinkarannu* and *zirramannu/zirrannu*,— Sanskrit words such as *babhru, piṅgala* and *jīra* are recognisable.[4] This constitutes an important evidence of Aryan associations with Akkad.

The word *lú šušanu*, signifying a horse-trainer in the Assyrian records, has also been traced to an Indo-European etymology.[5]

---

[1] O.R. Gurney, The Hittites, p. 106.

[2] See above, p. 26.

[3] Cf. Wiener Zeitschrift für die Kunde des Morgenlandes, vol. LIII, 1957, p. 181ff.

[4] ABORI, vol. 39, 1958, pp. 133-134.

[5] E. Ebeling, Bruchstücke einer mittelassyrischen Vorschriftensammlung für die Akklimatisierung und Trainierung von Wagenpferden, Berlin, 1951, p. 11. Scholars like F.W. Thomas, D. R. Bhandarkar, N. G. Majumdar, and R. N. Dandekar have suggested the derivation of the Vedic Asura from *assur*, which is not inherently improbable, and may point to the re-

The Assyrians had a different word for the horse in general, *sisu*, including the chariot or draught horse, as distinct from the cavalry horse called *pitḫallu*. The Assyrians had cavalry from an early date. In the period between the middle of the second millennium B. C., and the end of the New Assyrian empire, cavalry, largely though not entirely, took the place of chariots.[1] Ethiopean cavalry is also mentioned in the records of the Assyrian campaigns.[2] And there is a reference to an Urarṭian king running away from the battlefield on a mare. Indeed, the organisation of a superb Urarṭian cavalry is adumbrated in the record of Sargon's VIIIth campaign: "[As to] the people who live in that area in the land of Urarṭu, everyone there is, their like does not exist for skill with cavalry horses. The foals, young steeds born in his [the king's] spacious land, which they rear for his royal contingents and catch yearly, until they are taken to the land of Subi [the area which the people of Urarṭu call 'Mannai-land'] and their quality (?) becomes apparent, will never have had anyone straddling their backs; yet in advancing, wheeling, retreating, or battle disposition, they are never seen to break ranks".[3] The description is full and vivid, fully supported by the discovery of a bronze quiver and helmet adorned with friezes of chariots and horsemen, at Karmir-Blur in the Urarṭian territory.[4] The horsemen are armed to the teeth, with helmets, long lances and shields, while the spirited small beasts gaily prance forward with erect manes and upraised tails.[5] The beginning of the earlier period at the site may be dated to the late 9th or 8th century B. C., while its destruction probably took place in about 625 B. C.[6]

But let us return to Vedic India. The association of the chariot with royalty and the high and mighty, its shattering force and

---

miniscences of contacts outside India. Cf. JRAS, 1916, pp. 363-64; Bhandarkar's Aśoka, Third Ed., pp. 194, 195, 196ff.; JDL., XI, 1924, pp. 178-179; ABORI, vol. 31, p. 41.

1 Armas Salonen, Hippologica Accadica, pp. 15-16, Helsinki 1956.

2 J. B. Pritchard, Ancient Near Eastern Texts Relating to the Old Testament, Princeton University Press, 1950, p. 287.

3 F. Thureau-Dangin, Une relation de la huitième campagne de Sargon, lines 170-173; translation by Dr. H. W. F. Saggs, S.O.A.S., London.

4 R. D. Barnett and W. Watson, Iraq, vol. 14, Russian Excavations in Armenia, pp. 139 ff.

5 Iraq, 14, p. 140, fig. 15. The horse is of an extinct small species; cf. Ibid., p. 144.

6 Ibid., p. 134.

great projectile efficacy against the ranks of the enemy put in the shade the cavalry, which is nevertheless mentioned now and then in the whole range of the Vedic literature. Addressed to the Maruts, RV. V.61 proves beyond doubt the use of cavalry in war:

1. 'O heroes lordliest of all, who are ye that have singly come Forth from a region most remote?
2. Where are your horses, where the reins? How came ye? how had ye the power?
   Rein was on nose and seat on back.
3. The whip is laid upon the flank. The heroes stretch their thighs apart,
   Like women when the babe is born'.[1]

The evidence suggests that the Maruts, representing the fighting people, must have largely ridden horses, though some of them did make use of chariots. Passages like RV. VII.56.1, referring to 'Rudra's young heroes borne by noble steeds' with swords and lances for their weapons, reinforce the idea. Another verse describes them as so crowded in their onward sweep that those in front feel the quick breath of those behind.[2] The *Sāma Veda* also thus describes the Maruts: 'the strong youths have come forth to view, to show their strength, God Savitar's quickening energy: ye warrior horsemen, win the heavens'.[3] The *Sāma* speaks again of the 'banded Maruts in the forefront of the heavenly hosts that conquer and demolish'.[4] And the *Atharva Veda* refers to the sharp and formidable front of the Maruts.[5] Of these Maruts, indeed, many rode horses. The *Taittirīya Saṁhitā* mentions the seven troops of the Maruts,[6] which must have been seven bodies of cavalry and chariotry.

[1] RV. V. 61.1, *ke ṣṭhā naraḥ śreṣṭhatamā ya ekaeka āyaya. paramasyāḥ parāvataḥ* 2 *kva vo 'śvāḥ kvā bhīśavaḥ kathaṁ śeka kathā yaya. pṛṣṭhe sado nasoryamaḥ* 3 *jaghane coda eṣāṁ vi sakthāni naro yamuḥ. putrakṛthe na janayaḥ.*

[2] Ibid., VII.56.3. Also see Griffith's note on p. 54 of his 'The Hymns of the Rigveda', Second Ed., vol. II.

[3] SV. I.V.I.5.9, *avirmaryā ā vājaṁ vājino agmaṁ devasya savituḥ savaṁ. svargāṁ arvanto jayata.*

[4] Ibid., II. IX. 3.3.2.

[5] AV. IV.27.7.

[6] TS. V.4.7, also designates the Maruts as 'the people'. RV. VIII.85.8, refers to sixty-three Maruts—according to Sāyaṇa, nine companies of seven each. ŚB. II.5.1.13, speaks of the Maruts as distributed in troops of seven each; cf. also IX.3.1.25.

In many of the passages where the Maruts are described as riding, no specific mention of chariots occurs, and it is simpler and more natural to interpret them as referring to riding on horseback. The Maruts are in fact the most numerous among the gods,[1] and are apparently thought of on the analogy of the commoners in the army of a king and his nobles. More of this, however, later.

The *Ṛgveda* refers to heroes well-mounted and eager for battle,[2] and to 'fighting hand to hand and on horseback'.[3] We must not forcibly bring in the chariot where it is not mentioned. Horsemen are again mentioned in an unmistakable military context in a Ṛgvedic hymn,[4] which is also repeated in the later *Saṁhitās*:[5]

> 'the war drum speaks aloud as battle's signal.
> Our heroes, winged with horses,[6] come together. Let our car warriors, Indra, be triumphant'.

Here is a distinction, clear and deliberate, between the cavalry and the chariots who have gathered together on the field of battle to court the goddess of victory. 'Loud neighed the steed in frays for kine', says another Ṛgvedic hymn.[7] Light cavalry must have played an indispensable part in cattle raids and border depredations, as horsemen would be very useful in surprises and rounding up cattle and driving them home. That much of the warfare consisted of mere cattle raids, is proved by the very word *gaviṣṭi* used in the *Ṛgveda* to denote a fight.

Riding in peace and war is suggested by a number of other Ṛgvedic verses. RV. I.163.2, clearly refers to Indra mounting a horse,[8] while verse 9 points out that he was the first of all to do so. This seems to indicate the antiquity of riding; Indra, ever impatient

---

1 PB. XXI.14.3.

2 RV. IV.42.5, *māṁ naraḥ svaśvā vājayanto māṁ vṛtāḥ samaraṇe havante* .... See Wilson's translation.

3 RV. I.8.2, *ni yena muṣṭihatyayā ni vṛtrā ruṇadhāmahai. tvotāso nyarvatā.* The word *arvatā* meaning literally 'with a horse', is explained by Sāyaṇa as fighting on horseback. Wilson follows him. It is curious that in the Vedic literature, the horse as *arvan* is often associated with the Asuras. Cf. TS. VII.5.25.2; ŚB. X. 6.4.1. *Arvantaṁ* definitely refers to a ridden horse in RV. I.163.9; VS. XXIX.20; TS. IV.6.7.4.

4 RV. VI.47.31, ... *ketumad dundubhirvāvadīti. samaśvaparṇāścaranti no naro 'smākamindra rathino jayantu*

5 AV. VI.126.3; TS. IV.6.6.7; VS. XXIX.57.

6 'mounted on their steeds' according to Wilson.

7 RV. I.36.8, *krandadaśvo gaviṣṭiṣu.*

8 Ibid., I.163.2, *adhyatiṣṭhat ... aśvaṁ*; cf. TS. IV.6.7.1.

of peace, must have pressed heels into his horse in the arena of war.

RV. I.162.17, thus addresses the sacrificial horse: 'If one, when-seated-in-the-saddle (*sāde*), has by excessive urging with heel or whip distressed thee'.[1] There is nothing to preclude the possibility that the horse had been ridden on the field of battle before it was chosen for the honour of sacrifice.

Akra, in several passages of the *Ṛgveda*, means according to Roth a riding horse.[2] A simile in RV. IX.100.4, mentions a victorious warrior's horse. From the fact that a single horse is referred to and the chariot, normally drawn by two or four horses, is not mentioned, it appears that the horse in question must have been ridden.

Ghate points out that the Aśvins are identified or connected with the Greek Dioskouroi, the sons of Zeus, Castor and Pollux.[3] Aśvin means one having a horse, and Przyluski has shown that the Aśvins were Horse-Gods before they became horsemen.[4] The connection with horses comes out singularly in the case of the Dioskouroi, who are renowned tamers and riders of horses as well as charioteers.[5]

The use of the term *sāda* or *sadas* in RV. I.162.17 and V.61.2, makes it clear that *sādinaḥ* in AV. XI.10.24 must mean, in accordance with the commentary, *aśvārūḍhāḥ*, i.e. 'mounted on horses'.[6] Whitney translates: 'Who have chariots, who have no chariots, those without seats and they who have seats. . . . . ' The commentator explains the *asādas* by foot-soldiers.[7] The reference is more likely to enemies 'whether in chariots, on horseback, or on foot,' than to enemies 'possessed of chariots, or seated [in chariots] or on foot,' which is meaningless and tautologous. We have also noted

---

1 See A. K. Coomaraswamy, Horse-riding in the Ṛgveda and Atharvaveda, JAOS, vol. 62, 1942, pp. 139:140; cf. TS. IV.6.9.2.

2 Cf. RV. I.143.7; I.189.7; III.1.12; IV.6.3; X.77.2; ZDMG, 48,118; Vedische Studien, I,168,169. The word *aśvīva* in RV. II.27.16, also means a horseman.

3 Ghate's Lectures on the Rigveda, Second Ed., 1926, p. 151.

4 J. Przyluski, Indian Culture, vol. 3, 1936-37, 'Asses, Horses and Gandharvas', p. 617.

5 Ghate, loc. cit., p. 151.

6 AV. XI.10.24, *ye rathino ye arathā asādā ye ca sādinaḥ*; cf. Vedic Index, II, p. 444.

7 *aśvādiyānarahitāḥ padātayaḥ*

earlier the derivation of the Sanskrit *sādin* from the pre-Āryan Austric languages of India.[1]

Coomaraswamy[2] points out in connection with RV. IV.40.4 as cited in TS. I.7.8.3 that "Dadhikrā, the Sun, is not here a chariot horse". "In our text the *kratu* 'after which' (*anu*) the horse is effective is the rider's, i.e. that of the Person in the Sun, he 'whom not all men see with the mind', rather than that of the Sun himself 'whom all men see with the eye'." He illustrates his point by referring to the Buddhist sculptures of the *Abhinikkhamana* where the presence of the Bodhisattva on the back of the saddled and riderless horse is felt but not seen.

AV. XIX.53.1 refers to 'Time' as 'a horse that drives with seven reins ... him the vibrant poets mount.'[3] The same verse says further that 'his wheels are all the worlds'.[4] The 'wheels', according to Whitney, show that the mounting 'is not on the back of the horse, but on the chariot drawn by him'.[5] Coomaraswamy remarks that 'the words mean what they say, i.e. that Time is a horse, and this horse rides in a seven wheeled chariot drawn by seven horses ....' ; Time is the 'source and principle of the Sun... the chariot is essentially identical with the solar chariot as described elsewhere, while the Sun is explicitly a steed in RV. VII.77.3, as is Prajāpati elsewhere. The Sun is thought of as a wheel, and also thought of as riding in a chariot having one or more, often seven, wheels. It is perfectly possible to combine these images, and to think of the God as a horse in a horse-drawn chariot, or as a wheel in a wheeled vehicle'.[6] Coomaraswamy refers to the illustration in Forrer of an Indian saddled sun-horse borne on a four-wheeled car,[7] and also to that of a horse and rider borne on a four-wheeled chariot.[8] Bulls as solar symbols are also represented on chariots.[9] A horse with wheels in place of feet is also illustrated.[10] A man with wheels instead of

---

[1] See above, p. 54.

[2] JAOS., 62, p. 139.

[3] AV. XIX.53.1, *kāla aśvo vahati saptaraśmiḥ . . . taṁ ā rohanti kavayo vipaścitaḥ.*

[4] *tasya cakrā bhuvanāni viśvā.*

[5] Whitney, H.O.S., vol. 8, 1905, p. 987.

[6] Coomaraswamy, op. cit., pp. 139-140.

[7] Forrer, Les chars cultuels préhistoriques et leurs survivances aux epoques historiques, fig. 33.3 (Paris, 1932).

[8] Ibid., fig.20.4; cf. pl. IV.

[9] Ibid., figs. 11 and 30.1.

[10] Ibid., fig. 20.5.

feet is found amongst the signs of the Harappan culture.[1] Buddha, likewise, identifies himself with the *Dhamma* and speaks of both as charioteers, and bears the marks of the wheels on his hands and feet.[2] A Sun-wheel drawn by a single horse standing on a six-wheeled chariot from Trundholm, making up a total of seven wheels, is another illustration in point. The imagery of the Atharvavedic hymn is presumably of the same kind.

The *Atharva Veda* refers to the tramp of the 'dust-raising horseman' [3] in a context that seems to point to a cattle-raid. Another passage mentions the body of the horse carrying another body; the commentator very plausibly takes *tanvaṁ* to refer to the rider.[4] And elsewhere, the same *Veda* talks about 'a horseman's day's journey'.[5] The *Vājasaneyi Saṁhitā* refers to the horse-rider,[6] the horse-keeper,[7] and the stable-master.[8] The rider of the horse represented a vocation, presumably that of the mercenary warrior. The same *Saṁhitā* calls the earth 'Manu's mare',[9] which thus metaphorically carries the representative man on its back.

The ass, and perhaps also the horse, were even used as beasts of burden.[10]The pride of place in this category was, of course, given to the ass which is called in the *Taittirīya Saṁhitā* the best burden-gatherer of animals.[11] The *Taittirīya Saṁhitā* speaks of the *śūdra* and the horse being born of the feet of Prajāpati.[12]One would normally expect the horse to be associated with the *kṣatriya* warriors, which, however, is not done; and one suspects that the *śūdras*, who included large parts of the conquered native population, may

1 Hunter, The Script of Harappa and Mohenjodaro, London, 1934, pl. XXXII,f.

2 Coomaraswamy, op. cit., p. 140.

3 AV. IV.21.4, *na tā arvā reṇukakāṭo 'śnute* . . . ; cf. Whitney, H.O.S., vol. 7, p. 187.

4 AV. VI.92.3, *tanūṣṭe vājintanvaṁ nayanti*. . . ; the commentator explains: *ārūḍhasya sādinaḥ śarīraṁ*.

5 AV. VI.131.3. *yaddhāvasi triyojanaṁ pañcayojanamāśvinaṁ*. *Cf.* Whitney, loc. cit., p. 380.

6 VS. XXX.13, *aśvasādin*

7 Ibid., XXX.11, *aśvapa*; TB. III.4.9.1. VS. XVI.24 and KS. XVII.13 mention *aśvapati*.

8 VS. XXX.6, *sūta*.

9 Ibid., XXXVII.12, *manoraśvāsi*; ŚB. XIV.1.3.25.

10 TS. IV.1.4.2, *sthiro bhava vīḍvaṅga āśurbhava vājyarvan. pṛthurbhava suṣadastvamagneḥ purīṣavāhanaḥ*; V.5.10.7; VS. XI.44; ŚB. VI.4.4.3; AB. III.47.

11 TS. V.1.5.5, *gardabhaḥ paśūnāṁ bhārabhāritamo*.

12 Ibid., VII.1.1.4-6.

have known and ridden the horse even before the advent of the Aryan. That such indeed was the case, we have already seen, and riding rather than charioteering would have been their usual practice, for the latter is, within the Indian context, characteristically Aryan.

The *Śatapatha Brāhmaṇa* refers to 'the animal which people mount by the [middle] body', which 'carries them forward and does not hurt them'.[1] Another passage in the same *Brāhmaṇa* refers to the horses of mail-clad men,[2] pointing in all probability to cavalry. The *Aitareya Āraṇyaka* speaks of people mounting a horse sideways;[3] the *Pañcaviṁśa Brāhmaṇa* talks of a journey on horseback;[4] the *Taittirīya Brāhmaṇa* clearly mentions riding;[5] and Āśvalāyana distinguishes between a *sādya*, 'riding horse', and a *vāhya*, 'draught animal'.[6] The *Chāndogya Upaniṣad* refers to the *aśvanāya*,[7] who seems to have been the leader of a body of cavalry. The same *Upaniṣad* contains another allusion to the Kurus being saved by a mare, pointing thus perhaps to the prowess of cavalry.[8] We possess the clear testimony of the *Nikāyas* and the Epics to conclude that cavalry must have by now become an established and time-honoured branch of the armed forces. The word *caturaṅga* occurs as early as the *Ṛgveda*[9] in the sense of 'four-limbed' with reference to the human body; in the later literature it is regularly used to denote a fourfold army. The *Sāma Vidhāna Brāhmaṇa* mentions clearly the fourfold classification of the army with elephants, horses, chariots and infantry.[10]

To credit the Ṛgvedic Aryans with the organisation of a disciplined cavalry will no doubt be forcing the evidence beyond its warrant; but to deny the existence of warriors fighting on horseback will also amount to a baseless rejection of the affirmative

---

1 ŚB. VII.3.2.17.

2 Ibid., XIII.5.4.16. The St. Petersb. Dic. construes *trayastriṁśāḥ* along with *ṣaṭ sahasrāṇi* = 6033 horses of mail-clad men.

3 AĀ. I.2.4.5.

4 PB. XXI. 1.9; cf. Caland, Pañcaviṁśa Brāhmaṇa, p. 548.

5 TB. III.4.7.1.

6 Sūtra, IX.9.14.

7 CHU. VI.8.3 and 5.

8 Cf. CHI., I, p. 120.

9 RV. X.92.11; cf. ŚB. XII.3.2.2. The word *caturaṅga* in the sense of the army occurs in the *Atharva Veda Pariśiṣṭas* but these are supposed to be later in point of time.

10 SVB., III.6.11, *hastyaśvarathapadātayaḥ*.

data we have drawn from the text of the *Ṛgveda* and the rest of the Vedic literature that follows it. The onus of proving the contrary lies on him who cannot find a textual basis to vindicate the validity of his preconceptions. Macdonell and Keith, indeed, admit that riding was known in the Ṛgvedic period,[1] but at the same time hold that it was unsuited to Vedic ideas and never practised in battle. The warrior depended on his bow and arrow, which could not be effectively used from horseback in the absence of stirrups and a proper saddle.[2] The fallacy of this sweeping argument is amply demonstrated by the spirited sculptures of Assyria in the British Museum, which depict kings and nobles riding on horseback, galloping at full speed, without proper saddles or any kind of stirrups, shooting arrows and hunting lions. Such feats are indeed no child's play, and indicate the sureness of aim that could be combined with speed on a careering horse. As far as we know, no stirrups were known to the *Nikāyas* and the Epics;[3] they do not appear even in the days of Alexander, who was himself a splendid horseman, and had an efficient cavalry and a body of mounted archers in his army. Indeed, stirrups are not known anywhere else in the world until we find them first in India, among the sculptures of Sānchī, Bhāja, Pītalkhorā and Mathurā.[4] The lack of stir-

[1] Vedic Index, II, p. 444; cf. Macdonell in JRAS, 1893, p. 437, n.6; Zimmer, AL., p. 296.

[2] Vedic Index, II, p. 416; cf. Whitney, JAOS, 3, p. 312; CHI., I, p. 98; Rau, Staat und Gesellschaft im alten Indien, p. 101. Indian historians and writers on military affairs only repeat the earlier authorities, with but slight reservations. See, Date, The Art of War in Ancient India, 1929, p. 44; P. C. Chakravarti, The Art of War in Ancient India, p. 33; V.R.R. Dikshitar, War in Ancient India, 1948, p. 174; B.K. Majumdar, Military System in Ancient India, 1960, p. 16.

[3] Hopkins, JAOS, 13, pp. 264, 265 and note.

[4] Marshall, Guide to Sanchi, p. 138, n. 3; Piggott, Prehistoric India, p. 266; Bachhofer, Early Indian Sculpture, vol. II, pl. 72, lower left; Ancient India, no. 15, The Rock-cut Caves of Pitalkhora in the Deccan, pl. LV facing p. 77, fig. B. Also see Basham, The Wonder That Was India, p. 374, fig. xxiii. This stirrup was perhaps no more than a loose rope loop. The true metal stirrup in India before the 9th century A.D. remains to be demonstrated. (Coomaraswamy, JAOS, 52, 1932, p. 85). The robust sculpture of the horseman from Amarkantak illustrated in MASI., no. 23, 1931, pl. LI, (b), p. 108, shows his foot in a true stirrup, long before India resounded with the hoofs of the Mughal horses. 'Stirrups cannot be traced in China before, nor does the character for stirrups with radical denoting metal, come into use until after, the Han period. . . . ' (Coomaraswamy, loc. cit.). In India, riding was commonplace early enough, as well as popular, as evidenced by the sculptures of even women riding at Bharhut (Cunningham,

rups or the saddle, therefore, as we know them today, never bothered the ancients who developed their cavalry to suit the needs of their day. The evidence in our possession suggests, moreover, that the Vedic cavalrymen made use of the lance and the sword as their chief weapons of offence.[1]

The chariot, as we have said before, was the symbol of royalty and ridden in war by the kings and their nobles. The less fortunate among the *kṣatriyas* probably, and a section of the people certainly, fought on horseback, as the various references to the Maruts and warriors cited above seem to indicate. The Maruts are identified with the people,[2] and must have had their counterparts in the army of the mortals. We may lend support to our contention with an apt analogy. Some strata of population amongst the people of ancient Mesopotamia (c. 1850 B. C.) considered it undignified for their king to ride on horseback. 'My lord should not ride on a horse. Let my lord ride on a chariot or indeed on a mule, and let him do honour to his royal status'.[3] It proves that though the king seldom rode a horse, but usually a chariot or even a mule in conformity with his dignity, the practice must have been widespread amongst other parts of the population. It further proves that even the king could at times ride a horse, forgetting the while his august status. Certainly in Assyria in the first millennium he did so, as the British Museum sculptures show. The Urarṭian king, likewise, rode his royal chariot, but had a splendid cavalry, and could himself ride on horseback, if necessity so dictated. Says Sargon of him: 'With my single chariot and the cavalry that goes at my side, [namely] the body-guard(?) commanded (?) by Sin-ah-uṣur, like a furious arrow I fell upon his centre and smote him. . . . To save his life he abandoned his chariot and rode on a mare, and fled in front of his troops'[4].

Stupa of Bharhut, pl. XXXII, 6) and Sanchi (Maisey, Sanchi and its Remains, pl. XXX, 6). Also see Bachhofer, Early Indian Sculpture, vol. I, pl. 22, right, female flag-bearer on horseback at Bharhut.

1 The Maruts invariably make use of these weapons; see, for example, RV. I. 31.1; 37.2; 64.11; 85.4; 88.1, 3; 166.4; 168.3; V.54.11; 57.2, 6; VIII. 20.11.

2 TS. V.4.7.7; ŚB. II.5.2.27, 34, 36; IV.3.3.6.

3 Archives Royales De Mari, vol.VI, no. 76, Rev. 22 to 25; H. W. F Saggs, The Greatness that was Babylon, p. 195. For a brief discussion of the meaning of this text, see I. J. Gelb, J. C. S., XV, 1961, p. 37, n. 31 p. 41, n. 45.

4 F. Thureau-Dangin, Une relation de la huitième campagne de Sargon lines 132-133 and 140; translation by Dr. H. W. F. Saggs.

In Assyria and the land of the Urarṭu, therefore, the people not infrequently rode horses in war as in peace, while the kings rode in their chariots. So also, presumably, did the Vedic people and their kings and nobility. The intimate Aryan knowledge of the horse and love for the animal presupposes a riding tradition of long duration.

The question has never before been examined from a practical and economic point of view. Did all the Aryans, or indeed most of them, the noble and the plebeian, ride across the passes of Khyber on chariots— as they poured into India in their thousands—their wheels with only four or six spokes rumbling along the tortuous paths of the rocky, bumpy and difficult terrain? Was it possible? Did most of the Aryans who came to India, possess chariots? Did every Aryan who owned a horse, necessarily own a chariot as well? How many among them owned two or more horses that they could yoke to their chariots? A horse with the old strangling harness would not be able to pull the chariot along the steep paths, let alone the passengers as well. The primitive chariot, held together by belts of ox-hide and cords, would fall to bits and pieces on such a rugged highway. The Aryan chariots imported into India must have been dismantled and loaded on horseback through the Khyber and the difficult mountainous roads. Most of our travellers must have ridden their horses or wended their way on foot up and down the hilly tracts. The chariot in those ancient times was as complicated and costly a machine as the car is today, and certainly not everyone could afford the luxury.[1] Keeping a single horse, again, is different from keeping two or four at a time. Hymns are not lacking in the *Ṛgveda*, depicting transparently, indeed pathetically, the want and nakedness, poverty and misery of the average Aryan. Thus,

> 'The ribs that compass me give pain and trouble me like rival wives.
> Indigence, nakedness, exhaustion, press me sore: my mind is fluttering like a bird's.
> As rats eat weaver's threads, cares are consuming me, ...'[2]

Herein lies the economic interpretation of the Aryan influx into

[1] Cf. W. R. Arnold, Solomon's Horse-trade, JAOS, 26, First Half, 1905, p. 104, furnishes an idea of the cost of a horse and chariot in the ancient world. They were the essentials of aristocratic life.

[2] RV. X. 33.2, 3.

India; the explanation of unceasing wars, prayers for heroes, wealth, horses and kine. There are a number of passages in the *Ṛgveda* and the rest of the Vedic literature where single horses are mentioned without being specifically associated with the chariot; the inference that many of them must have been ridden is quite justifiable. Though chariots with only one horse were not unknown, they formed exceptions rather than the rule on the field of battle. The chariot was doubtless the most telling instrument of war; victory or defeat depended largely on the courage and skill of the charioteers. The Vedic cavalry must only have been a light irregular force, excellent for skirmishing, harassing and terrifying by their shouts and gallop, and rounding up the booty of cattle and driving them home. Horses must have operated where chariots could not, in the rough and rugged hilly terrain, where fighting is indicated in the hymns of the *Ṛgveda* and the later Vedic literature.

The *Nikāyas* [1] and the *Vinaya* [2] presuppose the existence of the four divisions of the army at an early period. The cavalry is an integral part of the armed forces. It does not appear as a new growth, but as an institution sanctified by time and usage. Riding in ordinary life is too commonplace to surprise us; the Buddha himself leaves home on horseback to wander forth into homelessness. Kings [3] ride on horses as well as commoners. In *Raṭṭhapāla sutta* of the *Majjhima Nikāya*,[4] the Kuru king is asked whether he was at the age of 20 or 25 expert in handling a horse and in war. The king says that he assuredly was.

The horses of the north are prized in the *Vinaya* as in the Epics. Horse-dealers of Uttarāpatha are mentioned as arriving with 500 horses.[5] The *Majjhima Nikāya* refers to the taming and training of the horse.[6] Horse-trainers are repeatedly mentioned.[7] The *Bhaddāli sutta* [8] vividly describes the training of the horse in the matter of wearing the bit and the harness, going straight along, running in

---

1 Dīgha, III, 200; Majjhima, III, 173, 174, 176; Saṁyutta, I, 73, *hatthikāyo, assakāyo, rathakāyo, pattikāyo*, 84; Aṅguttara, III, 151 has: *balavā kho pana hoti caturaṅginiyā senāya samannāgato assavāya ovādapaṭikarāya*; III, 157-158, 161-162, 397, etc.

2 Vinaya, I, 241, 342; II, 182; IV, 105.

3 Dīgha, I, 103-104.

4 Majjhima, II, 69.

5 Vinaya, III, 5.

6 Majjhima, II, 129.

7 Ibid., I, 446; III, 222.

8 Ibid., I, 446.

a circle, the art of the special tread,[1] galloping and neighing to command, the 'royal trick', the 'royal acrobatic feat', matchless speed and manners. The horse thus becomes 'worthy of a king, a royal treasure, ... an attribute of royalty'.

The *Saṁyutta Nikāya* [2] mentions the *assāroho gāmaṇi* together with the *assadamaka*, the horse-trainer. The former typifies the head of a village community, presumably of mercenary cavalrymen. The context helps us grasp the real meaning of the *assāroho gāmaṇi*. The Buddha receives visits from the *yodhājīvo-gāmaṇi*,[3] the *hatthāroho-gāmaṇi*,[4] the *assāroho-gāmaṇi*, and the *asibandhakaputta*.[5] The four seem to represent the four divisions of the army. They live in their respective villages with their professions governed by heredity. It is interesting to observe how social stratification grows apace with the specialisation of functions handed down to posterity.

The *Saṁyutta Nikāya* describes a war between Ajātasattu and Pasenadi. All the four divisions of the army are brought into action, and Pasenadi, the ultimate victor, confiscates the elephants, horses, chariots and infantry of his adversary.[6] That the cavalry fought in a body and not merely scattered at random over the field, is indicated by the *Vinaya Piṭaka* [7] which explains the massing of the army: 'Let elephants be on this side, let horses be on this side, let chariots be on this side, let foot-soldiers be on this side'.

The Epics teem with references to the four divisions of the army; almost every *parva* of the *Mahābhārata* mentions the cavalry as an immemorial and inseparable arm of the fighting forces.[8] The poets cannot conceive of an army without the cavalry, and not the slightest iota of evidence could be adduced from the text to show that the idea was comparatively new to the age. Riding and fighting on horseback formed an obligatory part of a prince's mi-

---

[1] *Khurakāya.*'The horse is trained to go along on the tips of its hoofs so that no sound is heard, MA. iii. 159.' (Horner, PTS. Trn. Series, no. 30, *p.* 118, n. 4).

[2] Saṁyutta, IV, 310. Woodward renders *assāroha* as 'jockey', which is misleading.

[3] Ibid., IV, 308.

[3] Ibid., IV, 310.

[5] Ibid., IV, 312, 314. Woodward is quite wrong when he takes the *asibandhaka-putta* to mean a snake-charmer, cf. PTS. Trn. Series, no. 14, p. 218, n. 5. Also see above, p. 16.

[6] Saṁyutta, I, 83-84.

[7] Vinaya, IV. 107-108.

[8] Mbh. 1.105.9; 2.25.20; 3.16.11; 3.17.2; 3.268.6; 4.30.28; 5.19.11; 5.149.61; 5.161.2; 6.43.83; 12.100.9, etc.

litary training. Thus the education of Dhṛtarāṣṭra, Pāṇḍu and Vidura includes the inevitable course in horsemanship.[1] Rāma is an expert rider and tamer of horses.[2] Droṇa teaches Arjuna the art of fighting on horseback.[3] The *Ādi parva* describes a tournament organised by Droṇa to test the skill of his pupils after the completion of their education.[4] The princes ride their horses with commendable skill, and hit the targets while in full career with shafts incised with their respective names.[5] That archery and horsemanship were not mutually incompatible, is again demonstrated by our evidence.

The *Virāṭa parva* refers to the cavalry of the Kurus.[6] And the *Udyoga parva* admires the well trained and obedient steeds of brave warriors accoutred in mail, decked with ornaments and furnished with flags.[7] Dhṛtarāṣṭra dwells on the virtues of his troops tested many a time in the management of horses.[8]

Hopkins wrote that 'in the Epic age we have, indeed, cavalry, but unorganised. The mounted soldiers are recognised as a body (*kulaṁ*) apart from others, of course, but do not act together. They appear as concomitants of the war-cars, dependent groups; but separate horsemen appear everywhere. Their employment was much influenced by that of the elephants. A body of horsemen is routed by an elephant. They were therefore detailed in small numbers to guard the war-cars and keep on the flanks of their own elephants. To the latter, indeed, they are formally assigned, but seem generally to be circling about the chariots'.[9] His argument follows from the supposition that the cavalry was an arm of relatively late growth, yet in its infancy. He has, therefore, restricted himself only to such passages as support him, and turned a blind eye to others that militate against his hypothesis. That the employment of the horses was influenced by that of the elephants is very true; but so it was by the use of the whole army. That the horses were routed by an elephant, may be right; but so were the chariots.[10]

1 Mbh. 1.102.17.
2 Rām. Ayodhyā, 1.28, *ārohe vinaye caiva yukto vāraṇavājinām*.
3 Mbh. 1.123.7.
3 Ibid., 1.124.
5 Ibid., 1.124.24.
6 Ibid., 4.51.2.
7 Ibid., 5.152.16.
8 Ibid., 6.72.9.
9 Hopkins, JAOS, 13, pp. 262, 263.
10 Mbh. 6.44.24ff.

That a number of horses were assigned to each war-car, may not be disputed;[1] but that the horsemen never acted in concert as a body of cavalry, is totally unacceptable.

The *Bhīṣma parva* provides a vivid spectacle of the feats of cavalry. Horsemen on chargers of speed and mettle rush against one another and send their 'bearded darts' whistling through the air.[2] They sweep across the field of battle creating confusion and slaughter with their lances.[3] Their horses fall down as they dash against those of the enemy.[4] Leaping high on their spirited steeds, some brave horsemen cut off the heads of the charioted warriors.[5] Kaurava warriors on their horses of precious breeds surround the army of the Pāṇḍavas.[6] The king of Gāndhāra alone has a dreaded force of ten thousand horsemen who fight with lances.[7] Even a monarch could in distress, like the Urarṭian example discussed earlier, ride on horseback. Duryodhana, deprived of chariot, horses and driver, rides on a horse to join Śakuni.[8]

The references cited above suffice to show that the Epic cavalry also acted in a body by itself, besides adding to the strength of chariots and elephants in a subsidiary capacity. No doubt, single horsemen are described here and there; but the Epic invariably pictures a pandemonium as soon as the battle starts, and all the order is blown to the four winds. Conclusions from poetic descriptions of this confusion are hard to draw, and generalisations are seldom valid. The Epic is poetry and at times must not be taken too literally, while elsewhere it is dismissed with a shrug and without apology.

The cavalry in the Epic does not make any significant contribution to victory or defeat. Fortunes fluctuate with the rise and

---

[1] Mbh. 6.20.16 assigns a hundred horsemen to every chariot of the Kuru army; did they not then form a body virtually in their own right? Everyone admits that the Epic gives an unreal picture of the army units. Most of such passages are later interpolations made by poets and theorists who had little knowledge of the usages of battle. See pp. 17, 82, 83.

[2] Ibid., 6.44.20,21.

[3] Ibid., 6.86.31 (see f.n. 31 on p. 484 of the Bhīṣma P., Cr. Ed.); 6.86.52 describes Rākṣasas riding on horseback with *śūlas* and *paṭṭiśas*.

[4] Ibid., 6.89.29; 6.86.17. Poetic exaggeration, as both man and horse try to avoid a head-on collision.

[5] Ibid., 6.44.22.

[6] Ibid., 6.86.1-4; verse 5 speaks of the Pāṇḍava cavalry meeting the challenge.

[7] Ibid., 9.22.29, *prāsayodhinām*

[8] Ibid., 9.24.20-22.

fall of the charioteering heroes. The poet is far too much engrossed with these supermen to do justice to any other arm of the forces. The cavalrymen, says Hopkins, 'are mainly conspicuous through falling off their horses, quite often from fear alone'.[1] But who in the Epic is impervious to fear except the chosen few; exaggerated verses describing the terror which the heroes strike in the enemy are unworthy of quotation as serious historical documents. And yet it must be true that sometimes the horsemen slipped from their mounts. We must remember that the Epic horseman sat on no proper saddle;[2] nor did he have stirrups. He wore his armour and carried his javelin, lance and sword, besides a whip[3] tied to his wrist to manage his horse. How long could he keep his horse and seat in a real close fight?

We must also look beyond India to understand why the ancient cavalry was so ineffective. Polybius gives us a vivid account of the battle of Cannae where Hannibal exterminated a Roman army twice as big as his own. The Romans leapt from their horses when they had scarcely become engaged, and each seized his adversary.[4] This indicates that the Roman cavalry did not usually fight hand to hand like the foot-soldiers. They threw themselves in a gallop on the enemy cavalry. When within javelin range, they slackened their gait if the enemy had not turned their backs, and threw some javelins. They then took to the rear again and prepared to repeat the charge. The other side did the same, until one of the two thought that the enemy was really going to attack, turned in flight and was pursued to the limit. At Cannae, however, the opposing cavalries engaged, and man fought man. For riders mounted on simple saddle-cloths and without stirrups, encumbered with a lance, sword and shield, to fight man to man is to fall together and fight on foot. And that is what invariably happened whenever two ancient cavalry organisations really had to fight.[5] Examples taken from Caesar indicate that the ancient cavalryman could achieve little against formed infantry, or even against the isolated infantryman possessing coolness.[6]

---

1 Hopkins, op. cit., p. 263. 2 Ibid., p. 264. 3 Ibid.

4 Cf. Polybius, The Histories, vol. II, Loeb Edn., Book III, 115.

5 In a fight against the Hernici the Roman horsemen, according to Livy, asked the consul for permission to fight on foot. The Gauls, Germans, Parthanians also dismounted whenever they had really to fight. See Ardant Du Picq, Battle Studies, p. 78.

6 Ibid., p. 64.

Back in India, the Epic horsemen did comparatively little to affect the issues of the combat precisely for the same reasons. The charioteer, the *mahārathin*, was in command.[1]

Fighting apart, knights on horseback attend on the monarch in the Epic and act like aides-de-camp.[2] The *Bhīṣma parva* refers to messengers on horseback sent by the Pāṇḍavas to make their troops desist from further fight.[3] The Epic, in short, knows every use of the horse in war.

---

[1] Cavalrymen fled from fear of Arjuna, leaving their horses behind (Mbh. 6.51.25). The horse enabled man to charge with speed, but it also provided the means of an equally rapid escape. The chariot-warrior shot down a number of horsemen whenever he got them within his range (Mbh. 6.44.23).

[2] Hopkins, op. cit., p. 263.

[3] Mbh. 6.115.26. The Hittites also made use of messengers mounted on horseback; see above, p. 55.

CHAPTER FOUR

ELEPHANTS

The association of man and elephant dates back to a period of remote antiquity. The bones of the animal unearthed at Mohenjodaro, the realistic figurines and the familiar representations on the seals of the Indus sites point to the beginnings of this fateful friendship;[1] the docility, intelligence and easy obedience of the elephant must have quickly led to its domestication, once it was known and captured. That the civilization of the Indus, in the plenitude of its prosperity, made use of the elephant for riding and other purposes, appears almost certain;[2] 'the representations on the seals show the two breeds recognised today in India, the Kamooria Dhundia with its flat back, square head, and stout legs, and the

---

[1] Marshall, Mohenjodaro and the Indus Civilization, II, p. 653; Mackay, Further Excavations at Mohenjodaro, II, pls. ixxix, 7, 8, 13; lxxxiv, 57; lxxxvi, 171, depict docile elephants with a thorough familiarity. Marshall, loc. cit., vol. III, pl. CXII, 369 shows an elephant with a manger in front. The animals are shown with a line extending from the top of the back to just behind the foreleg. As no such fold is shown by the natural conformation of the elephant's skin at this place, the line seems to indicate the forward edge of a saddle or drapery. At Kalibangan, a newly excavated Harappan site in northern Rajasthan, lumps of clay with clear seal impressions of the image of a horned elephant have been found; the animal looks like being caparisoned, with something like a cloth flung across its back. See, The Illustrated London News, March 24, 1962, p, 454, fig. 1; Indian Archaeology, 1960-61 – A Review, pl. XLVIII, B.

[2] Marshall, op. cit.; Piggott, Prehistoric India, p. 157; Childe, New Light on the Most Ancient East, 1952, p. 176; Wheeler, The Indus Civilization, 1960, p. 65, seems to accept the use of the elephant, with a slight reservation inevitable in the study of so much archaeological material. In an article entitled 'The Prehistoric Climate of Baluchistan and the Indus Valley' published in the American Anthropologist, vol. 63, no. 2, Part 1, April 1961, pp. 265 ff., R. L. Raikes and R.H. Dyson, Jr., argue that the climatic conditions of that region are not materially different today from those of the past, and that the elephant (p. 276) 'has never been reported west of the Central Provinces in India, although the possibility of a more western extension in earlier times cannot be ruled out. At the same time the extent of the Indus Civilization makes the importation of these animals from its periphery a perfectly reasonable possibility.' The question of the climate is problematical, but the domestication of the elephant does not seem to be disputed.

Cf. Sarva Daman Singh, *The Elephant and The Aryans*, JRAS 1963, Parts 1 and 2, pp. 1ff.

inferior Meergha, less heavily built and with a sloping back.'[1] The proto-Australoids were perhaps the first people to domesticate and train the elephant; the words *gaja* and *mātaṅga* have been traced to the pre-Aryan peoples of India speaking Austric languages.[2]

The elephant was known and tamed not in India alone, but also in other parts of the world at a comparatively early date. A clay plaque from Southern Mesopotamia, dated late 3rd or very early 2nd millennium B. C., clearly depicts an Indian elephant ridden by a man.[3] Definite evidence of the elephant in Western Asia is found in the Egyptian monuments, specially those of the 18th Dynasty. Thothmes II received elephants from his Syrian tributaries, which indicates that the animal existed in Western Asia and, more important, that it was already being tamed.[4] Thothmes III slew no less than 120 elephants in a great hunt in the land of Nii, in northern Syria. Indeed, elephants must have abounded in that region.[5] The Assyrian records, too, tell much the same story. Tiglath Pileser I (c. 1100 B. C.) killed ten elephants and took four alive in the Haran region, in the middle Euphrates, not very far from the scene of the hunt of Thothmes III.[6] Elephants were kept in the menagerie of Ashur-nasir-pal at Kalhu in the first half of the 9th century B.C.[7] The Black Obelisk of Shalmaneser II, dating from about the middle of the 9th century B. C., mentions both ivory and elephant skins among the articles of tribute from Yakin and Adini near the head of the Persian Gulf. [8] If not a native of these parts, the elephant may possibly have been imported from India, where it was already serving man in various ways. Another statement on the same monument includes living elephants among the items of tribute from the land of Musri. As these elephants must have been domesticated, scholars believed that they were somehow obtained from India.[9] And if elephants once abounded around the southern

---

[1] Piggott, op. cit., p. 157.

[2] S. K. Chatterji in 'The Vedic Age', 1951, p. 150.

[3] James F. Downs, The Origin and Spread of Riding in the Near East and Central Asia, American Anthropologist, vol. 63, no. 6, Dec. 1961, p. 1197.

[4] J. H. Breasted, A History of Egypt, II Ed., London, 1951, p. 271.

[5] Ibid., p. 304.

[6] E. A. W. Budge and L. W. King, Annals of the Kings of Assyria, pp. 85, 86.

[7] A. T. Olmstead, JAOS, 38, p. 250.

[8] C. W. Bishop, The Elephant and its ivory in Ancient China, JAOS, 41, p. 291.

[9] Ibid., p. 292.

shores of the Caspian, the Aryans— at least some of them—might have seen and known the animal even before they came to India. The elephant disappeared from Western Asia perhaps owing to the destruction of its environment by man, and also his insatiable appetite for ivory.[1]

The elephant was once widely distributed in China.[2] The Yu-Kung, dating from a time fairly early in the first millennium B. C., speaks of the 'country of docile elephants',[3] in present Southern Honan. The name indicates not the mere presence of the elephant in Central China, but even its domestication.[4] The state of Ch'u undoubtedly kept domesticated elephants.[5] Elephants were certainly used in battle between the states of Wu and Ch'u in the later part of the sixth century B. C.[6] Elephants, however, could not find a permanent place in Chinese warfare, as they were rapidly becoming scarce; indeed, their extinction was complete in the Yangtse valley—their last habitat in China— before the close of the fourth century B. C.[7]

The Cambridge History of India [8] says that the elephant appears in the *Ṛgveda* as a wild beast, *mṛga*, with a hand, *hastin*, while the later texts call it *hastin* only, 'a sign that the novelty of the animal had worn away'. When the authors of the Cambridge History wrote, little was known about the older Indus Civilization, the later

---

[1] Arrian, Anabasis, Bk. 3, ch. 8, records the presence of an Indian contingent with fifteen elephants at Gaugamela in 331 B. C. The disappearance of the animal is attested by the march of Alexander through Western Asia, where he did not come across any wild elephants.

[2] A. A. Macdonell, The Origin and Early History of Chess, JRAS, 1898, p. 131, n.1.

[3] C. W. Bishop, op. cit., p. 299.

[4] Ibid.

[5] Ibid.

[6] P. Albert Tschèpe, Histoire du Royaume de Tch'ou, Changhai, 1903, p. 263 and n. 5; JRAS, 1898, p. 131, n.1; JAOS, 41, p. 302.

[7] Ibid., p. 303.

[8] CHI., I, p. 81; cf. Whitney, JAOS, III, p. 312; Vedic Index, II, p. 501, says that 'there is no trace of its use in war'. Is it reasonable to ask whether the inhabitants of the Indus drove an elephant here and there to scare away an enemy? Though direct evidence is lacking, it is not utterly improbable. Recent writers on early Indian warfare have failed to take note of the elephant's domestication in the Indus Civilization. Thus for the Vedic period, P. C. Chakravarti, The Art of War in Ancient India, p. 47, and B. K. Majumdar, The Military System in Ancient India, p. 16, repeat only the earlier authorities. Dikshitar, War in Ancient India, p. 167, admits the use of elephants in war in the Ṛgvedic period, though he does not cite any textual evidence.

discovery of which necessitated the rewriting of our ancient history and fresh explanations for various so-called Vedic and Hindu practices. If the Aryans were the people responsible for the destruction of the Indus cities,[1] they must have learned much indeed in the process. And if the earliest Aryans in India were struck by the novelty of the elephant, it was but natural. Even Nadir Shah, in comparatively modern times, was equally impressed and refused to ride an elephant when invited to do so by the Mughal emperor. The elephant is a novelty even today in India as well as abroad. Its use was always confined to the kings and their nobility. But the novelty of the animal would not have deterred the Aryans from making use of it, if they were at all sensitive to previous example and precept. Even the word *mṛga* may not necessarily imply 'wild'; a mere assumption of Roth [2] became axiomatic for later writers, who refused to look around themselves, inside and outside India. Various other explanations can equally plausibly be given for the word. It may simply mean an 'animal'; it may imply a distinction between the wild and domesticated elephants; it may be no more than a poetic term. *Parvatagiri* used for a mountain in the *Ṛgveda*, does not mean that mountains were unknown to the Aryans.[3] The word *mṛga* also means 'an elephant characterised by particular marks' in Sanskrit literature.[4] We do not, however, dispute the inevitable increase of familiarity in the later Vedic period.

The elephant is mentioned in the *Ṛgveda* as *mṛga*, *hastin*, *ibha* and *vāraṇa*.[5] RV. X.40.4 describes hunters following wild elephants, possibly to capture them. And RV. IV.4.1 thus addresses Agni: '. . . proceed like a king attended by his followers on his elephant (*ibha*): thou art the scatterer [of thy foes]: following the swift-moving host consume the Rākṣasas with thy fiercest flames'.[6] Sāyaṇa, Wilson and Geldner rightly take *ibha* to signify an elephant, which

---

[1] Wheeler, Ancient India, no. 3, 1947, p. 82; Early India and Pakistan, 1959, pp. 113-115; The Indus Civilization, 1960, pp. 96-99; Piggott, op.cit., pp. 261ff. Cf. also, G. R. Sharma, The Excavations at Kauśāmbī (1957-59), 1960, pp. 6-10.

[2] Vedic Index, II, pp. 171-172.

[3] The Vedic Age, p. 217.

[4] 'One of the three classes of elephants', Monier Williams, Sanskrit Dictionary.

[5] RV. I.64.7; IV.16.14; IV.4.1; VIII.33.8.

[6] Ibid., IV.4.1, *yāhi rājevāmavāṁ ibhena*, etc.; cf. U. N. Ghoshal, Kingship in the Ṛgveda, IHQ., 20, 1944, p. 37.

is its usual meaning in Sanskrit literature. The passage is significant as presaging the shape of things to come; the elephant makes its debut as a royal mount in the Vedic literature; and if the context proves anything, the venue is the field of battle.

RV. IX.57.3 compares Soma to a well disciplined and obedient king of the elephants.[1] The reference clearly points to the taming and training of the elephant. A very obscure passage of the *Ṛgveda*[2] seems to speak of 'two mad elephants bending their fore-quarters and smiting the foe'. If Wilson's translation of this enigmatic passage be correct, here is another explicit proof of the use of elephants in war.

We must not be misunderstood. We are aware that the Aryan speciality was their chariotry, which indeed swept away all opposition like an avalanche. Nevertheless, we suggest that the use of the elephant was not impossible in the Ṛgvedic period as hitherto assumed, contrary to evidence, both literary and archaeological. It would be difficult to explain the supposed Aryan indifference towards the elephant throughout the five hundred years or more of Ṛgvedic composition, specially if we recall its domestication by the people of the Indus valley. The animal was caught at some hazard, but tamed without much difficulty; it must have been occasionally used in some engagements—not in large numbers, of course—though its efficacy on the field of battle was yet far from established. If there are no more references to prove the point, we must remember the nature of our literature, the non-Aryan associations of the animal, and also that negative evidence is at best only hypothetical, at worst utterly misleading. The word *caturaṅga*[3] occurs in RV. X.92.11, with reference to the human body; the epithet was later applied to the fourfold army.

A certain hymn of the *Atharva Veda*[4] was entitled by Weber 'Taming of a wild elephant'. The splendour of the animal and his superior position are described; verse 6 tells us that the elephant

---

[1] RV. IX.57.3, *ibho rājeva suvrataḥ*; Geldner, HOS., vol. 35, p. 40, inaccurately renders it as 'folgsamer Königselefant'. Cf. P. S. Sastri, The Imagery of the Ṛgveda, ABORI, vol. 29, p. 168.

[2] RV. X.106, 6, *sṛṇyeva jarbharī turpharītū naitośeva turpharī parpharīkā*, etc.; cf. Dikshitar, op.cit., p. 167. Another Ṛgvedic passage, VIII.45.5, may probably refer to the use of the elephant in war, if the word *apsaḥ*, as explained by Sāyaṇa, is taken to mean a *darṣanīyo gajaḥ*. That, however, is doubtful.

[3] Its occurrence in the late tenth book may be significant.

[4] AV. III.22.

has become chief of all the pleasant beasts to ride.[1] The elephant starts as a wild beast before it is caught and trained, and is rarely, if ever, bred in captivity. If, therefore, the early Aryans described it even as a wild beast—such as it remains today—it by no means follows that they had not tamed or trained it. In modern India, it is a sign of ill omen for the owner if a tame she-elephant gives birth to a calf. In the *Atharva Veda*, we are on more familiar ground. One passage tells us how flies anger an elephant;[2] and another describes how 'the elephant strains foot with foot of the she-elephant',[3] thus possibly referring to the capture of males with the help of female elephants. AV. IX.3.17 speaks of a hall or house, presumably raised on posts, standing on the earth with feet like those of a female elephant. The simile was obviously inspired by the usual sight of the tireless elephant standing not far from the poet's residence. All these references are evidence of a thorough familiarity and association with the animal; it was captured, tamed, used and studied. A question that one might ask here pertinently is whether or not the *Atharva Veda* records many traditions even older than the Aryans.

The *Yajur Veda Saṁhitās* refer to the elephant-keeper, *hastipa*,[4] as the representative of a regular profession. The *Vājasaneyi Saṁhitā* even mentions the sacrifice of elephants.[5] The *Aitareya Brāhmaṇa*[6] describes the conquest and horse-sacrifice of Aṅga who gave away ten thousand elephants and ten thousand female slaves to the brāhmaṇas. It again speaks of Bharata Dauḥṣanti as going round conquering and performing the *aśvamedha*, in which he gave away 'beasts black with white tusks, covered with golden trappings'.[7] These elephants were most probably used in war and seized, together with the female slaves, from the worsted enemy. The *Aitareya Brāhmaṇa* also gives us an idea of the animal's exemplary obedience; the elephant comes by itself, when bidden by

---

[1] AV. III.22.6, *hastī mṛgāṇāṁ suṣadāmatiṣṭhāvānbabhūva hi*. Cf. Griffith, The Hymns of the Atharva Veda, vol. I, Sec. Ed., 1916, p. 116.

[2] AV. IV.36.9, . . . *hastinaṁ maśakā iva*.

[3] Ibid., VI.70.2, *yathā hastī hastinyāḥ padena padamudyuje*.

[4] VS. XXX.11; TB. III.4.9.1; cf. CHI., vol.I, p. 137.

[5] VS. XXIV. 29. The elephant is also mentioned in TS. V.5.11.1; MS. III.14.8; PB. VI.8.8; XXIII.13.2; AB. VI.27.2; ŚB. III. 1.3.4; JUB. III.22.1.

[6] AB. VIII.22.

[7] Ibid., VIII.23.

the voice.[1] The *Sāma Vidhāna Brāhmaṇa* mentions elephants among the four divisions of the army.[2]

The *Chāndogya Upaniṣad* [3] talks of cows and horses, elephants and gold, slaves, wives, fields and houses, in terms of which wealth and status were reckoned.

The elephant was already used in warfare in the time of Ktesias.[4] The *Nikāyas* and the Epics likewise point to the early use of elephants in war. The Buddhist and the Epic tradition of the fighting elephant must have owed something to earlier antiquity; the absence of direct and more explicit references to the use of elephants in war in the later Vedic literature is doubtless due to the character of that literature; there was not much room in the *Brāhmaṇas* or the *Upaniṣads* for discussing the arms of the army or the dispositions of battle.

The numerous references in the *Nikāyas* [5] and the *Vinaya* [6] to elephants as an indispensable part of the army are all redolent of an unageing tradition. A symbol of regal grandeur, the elephant is at home alike in scenes of war and of peace. Thus the *Ambaṭṭha sutta* of the *Dīgha Nikāya* mentions a king seated on the neck of his elephant;[7] the *Sāmaññaphala sutta* describes the riding-elephants of king Ajātasattu;[8] and elsewhere, king Pasenadi sets forth from Śrāvastī on his elephant Ekapuṇḍarīka.[9] The *Raṭṭhapāla sutta* of the *Majjhima Nikāya* refers to the proficiency of the Kuru king in the matter of handling an elephant and in war, ever since he was a youth of 20 or 25.[10] Elsewhere, the Buddha asks prince Bodhi if he is skilled in elephant-riding and also in the art of hand-

---

1 AB., IV.1.

2 SVB. III.6.11, *hastyaśvarathapadātayaḥ*. The *Adbhuta Brāhmaṇa* uses the word *gaja* for the elephant; see Vedic Index, s.v.

3 CHU. VII.24.2; cf. Kaṭha Up. I.1.23, *bahūn paśūn hastihiraṇyamaśvān*.

4 Vedic Index, II, p. 501.

5 Dīgha, III, 200; Majjima, III, 173, 174,176; Saṁyutta, I, 73, 84; Aṅguttara, III, 151, 157-158, 159, 160, 162, 397, etc.

6 Vinaya, I, 241, 342; II, 182; IV, 105.

7 Dīgha, I, 103.

8 Ibid., I, 49.

9 Majjhima, II, 112. Aṅguttara, III, 345, mentions Seta, an elephant of Pasenadi. The practice of naming elephants is in evidence also in the Epics. We know of the elephant Aśvatthāmā whose fate precipitated the fall of Droṇa in the *Mahābhārata*; in the *Rāmāyaṇa, Ayodhyā*, 32.10, Rāma gives away his elephant called Śatruñjaya. Kings and princes in the Epics, however, usually ride in chariots.

10 Majjhima, II, 69.

ling a goad.[1] No doubt, the elephant was a favourite royal mount in the sixth and fifth centuries B. C.

The *Cūlahatthipadopama sutta* of the *Majjhima Nikāya* describes in graphic detail how a skilled elephant tracker acts with an intimate knowledge of elephants, their habits and their forests.[2] The *Dantabhūmi sutta* tells us how the elephant-hunter mounts the king's elephant, goes into the forest, ties the wild elephant to the neck of the king's elephant, and brings it out into the open. The elephant trainer then comes forward and ties the beast to a post. He addresses him gently and offers him grass, food and water. He teaches his charge to take up and put down, advance and retreat, get up and sit down, and to stand his ground. He ties a shield to his trunk; a man holding a lance sits on the elephant's neck, while others holding lances stand on all sides. The elephant-tamer stands in front, holding a stout lance. The animal refuses to budge while standing his ground. The king's elephant endures blows of sword and axe, arrow and hatchet, and the deafening din of drum and kettle-drum, conch and tom-tom. He is like burnished gold purged of all its dross, 'fit for a king, a royal possession, and reckoned as a kingly attribute'.[3] The *Aṅguttara Nikāya*[4] likewise enumerates the qualities of a king's elephant, who should be able to endure frightening sights, sounds, smells, tastes and touches. He is a 'hearer, destroyer, warder, endurer and goer',[5] in as much as he is obedient to the command of his tamer, and in fight destroys elephants, horses, chariots and infantry,[6] protects and bears blows and goes wherever asked. The Buddha elsewhere describes a king's bull-elephant with tusks as long as a plough-pole, whose home is the field of battle. He fights with his fore-legs and his hind-legs, his head and his ears, his tusks and his tail, and even his trunk.[7]

Kings as well as commoners ride on these beasts of war. An elephant is said to have twelve men in the *Vinaya Piṭaka*, ex-

---

[1] Majjhima, II, 94.

[2] Ibid., I, 175-178.

[3] Ibid., III, 132, 133. Cf. Saṁyutta, I, 141, also mentions a tame elephant with vices purged. The *Mahābhārata*, too, speaks of trained elephants not afraid of the din of war.

[4] Aṅguttara, III, 157-162.

[5] Ibid., III, 161, *nāgo sotā ca hoti hantā ca rakkhitā ca khantā ca gantā ca.*

[6] There is no indication in the *Nikāyas* or the *Vinaya* of the Epic rule that the elephant should fight only an elephant.

[7] Majjhima, I, 414-415.

plained by Buddhaghoṣa to mean four men on the back of the elephant, and two looking after each foot.[1] The *Saṁyutta Nikāya* mentions a *hatthāroho gāmaṇi*'s visit to the Buddha.[2] He is the head of a village community bound together by an identity of profession —mercenary soldiers of the elephant corps.[3] Their compact settlement presupposes the heredity of their calling, which is also independently attested by other references.[4] Elephant-lore and the art of fighting from elephants' backs must have come to these men naturally with the memories of their fathers' deeds stretching far back in time from the 6th century B. C.

Elephants carried rugs on their backs, called *hatthatthara*;[5] the huge elephant-saddle of a later day was not yet in evidence. That they were employed in battle in a block or a line, is indicated by the 'massing of the army' as known to the *Vinaya Piṭaka*, which has: 'Let elephants be on this side. . . . '[6]

The Epics,[7] like the *Nikāyas* and the *Vinaya*, assign the elephants their proper place in the army organisation. The battle-scenes in the *Mahābhārata* bristle with elephants and their stampedes; they form an essential part of the royal and military paraphernalia. King Duḥṣanta is said to be a skilled rider of elephants;[8] Dhṛtarāṣṭra, Pāṇḍu and Vidura learn how to manage an elephant during the course of their military training;[9] and Droṇa likewise teaches Arjuna how to fight from the back of an elephant.[10] Duryodhana rides a magnificent elephant on the field of battle,[11] the rallying point of a teeming host. King Bhagadatta charges on his elephant Supratīka, raining arrows on the enemy;[12] and so does king Śaibya take his seat on a princely elephant with a proud banner on its

---

1 Vinaya, IV, 105; See SBB., vol. XI, p. 375, n. 4.

2 Saṁyutta, IV, 310.

3 Also see above, p. 67.

4 Cf. Majjhima, I, 340, refers to Pessa, the son of an elephant-trainer, who can make an elephant under training display all kinds of deceit and trickery.

5 Ibid., II, 112; Vinaya, I. 192.

6 Ibid., IV, 107, 108.

7 Mbh. 1.1.138; 1.63.3; 1.105.9; 3.17.1, 2, 5; 3.268.6; 4.30.8; 5.161.2, etc.; Rām. Bāla, 6.23.

8 Mbh. 1.62.12.

9 Ibid., 1.102.17, *gajaśikṣā*.

10 Ibid., 1.123.7; cf. Rām. Ayodhyā, 1.28, Rāma is a celebrated rider of elephants.

11 Mbh. 6.20.7.

12 Ibid.. 6.91.23, 33; cf. 5.164.38; 6.17.36.

back.[1] Elsewhere, prince Vikarṇa rushes against Arjuna on an elephant supported by four chariots.[2] Even Bhīmasena leaves his chariot for a while and fights seated on the neck of a huge elephant.[3] These references to kings riding elephants show clearly that the beasts were often employed independently, and not as mere concomitants of the war-chariots. Kings and princes, however, principally ride on their chariots, and seldom on the backs of elephants. The titanic *mahārathins* rise above horses and elephants to dictate their terms on the field of battle; their successes and their reverses provide the patterns of the Epic tapestry. This is significant as revealing the antiquity of the Epic tradition harking back to the Vedic days of rattling chariots; but we cannot subscribe to the view of Hopkins [4] that passages describing kings and princes riding on elephants were later additions to the Epic story. The *Nikāyas* prove that the practice of riding on elephants in peace and war was well known among Aryan and non-Aryan, prince and commoner, in the sixth and fifth centuries B. C. Indeed, as we have seen earlier, the practice is so old as to be beyond the ken of proper history.

Various breeds of elephants are known to the Epics.[5] In the *Sabhāparva* [6] Yudhiṣthira describes his huge elephants with fine white tusks, decked with golden girdles, ornaments and garlands, capable of carrying kings on their backs and bearing every kind of noise on the battlefield.[7] They can indeed batter down the walls of enemy strongholds.[8] Sixty-year-old elephants are always prized as being at the most suitable age for battle service, and gifts of elephants of this age are looked on as particularly generous.[9]

---

1 Mbh. 6.17.20.

2 Ibid., 4.60.7, *rathaiścaturbhirgajapādarakṣaiḥ*.

3 Ibid., 8.8.21.

4 Hopkins, JAOS, 13, pp. 266-267.

5 Rām. Bāla, 6.23-25, Ayodhyā has huge elephants of the Airāvata, Mahāpadma, Añjana and Vāmana families, of the *Bhadra*, *Mandra* and *Mṛga* breeds. Ayodhyā, 100.50 speaks of the elephant-forest as deserving of the king's care. Mbh. 12.137.35 refers to the catching of wild elephants with the help of tame she-elephants.

6 Mbh. 2.54. 8-10.

7 *sarvaśabdakṣamāyudhi*. The *Nikāyas* also stress this quality. See above, p. 79.

8 *sarve ca purabhettāro*.

9 Ibid., 2.49.7; 4.12.20; 4.30.26. But in India today, an elephant is considered to be at the height of his powers between the age of 25 and 40. Elephants, though, as old as 80, are sometimes used for tiger-hunt, for they are more disciplined and experienced.

The elephants of war [1] are provided with armour, girths, blankets, neckropes and bells, hooks and quivers, banners and standards, *yantras* (stone-or-arrow-hurling contrivances?) and lances. On the back of each beast seven warriors take their seats.[2] Two among them carry hooks; two are excellent archers; there are two swordsmen, and last but not the least, a man with a lance and banner.[3] In the *Bhīṣma parva* Dhṛtarāṣṭra speaks of the Kaurava troops, adepts in mounting and descending from the backs of elephants, in moving forward and stepping back.[4]

The Epic evidence indicates that the elephants were used either in a block or in a line, or even often individually in war. Thus the elephants make the body of the Kaurava array;[5] and Yudhiṣṭhira marches in the centre of his huge army surrounded by elephants.[6] Elsewhere, the elephants are placed on the joints and extremities of the wings.[7] We notice that they are stationed so as to give stability to the army, to support and cover its flanks, and to maintain links between the centre and the wings. At the head they push on and contain the counter-attack; on the defensive they furnish a wall of stiff opposition; while individual beasts pulverize the ranks of the enemy. A study of the various battle dispositions reveals that verses assigning a hundred chariots to each elephant, or ten or even 50 elephants to each chariot, are all later interpolations divorced from truth and practice—mutually contradictory concoctions of theorists for their own delectation.[8] The Matsya army in the *Virāṭa parva* has, for example, 8,000 chariots, 1,000 elephants, and 60,000 horses.[9] Elsewhere, a division of the Pāṇḍava army under Bhīma's command has 10,000 horses and 2,000 elephants, 10,000 foot-soldiers and 500 chariots.[10] The figures fail to

[1] Mbh. 2.48.20, *kuñjarān kavacāvṛtān*; 5.149.82, *gajāḥ kaṅkaṭasannāha lohavarmottaracchadāḥ*; 6.19.30; 7.35.34, 35; 6.92.67-69, the *paristara* may be a padded covering on the backs of elephants. Cf. Hopkins, op. cit., p. 268, n.

[2] Mbh. 5.152.13.

[3] Ibid., 5.152.14. Sometimes they also carry pots of oil, stones, etc. Cf. Hopkins, op. cit., p. 265.

[4] Mbh. 6.72. 8-9; cf. 4.30.27 speaks of trained and skilled warriors on elephants, *yuddhakuśalaiḥ śikṣitairhastisādibhiḥ*.

[5] Ibid. 6.17.38.

[6] Ibid., 6.19.24.

[7] Ibid., 6.46.53.

[8] Ibid., 6.20.16; 5.152.19, 20, etc.

[9] Ibid., 4.30.28.

[10] Ibid., 5.197.13-14.

correspond to the formal ratios of the interpolating theorist in either of the cases.

The covenant,[1] similarly, laying down the code of ethics and chivalry, and prohibiting all but those equally circumstanced from mutual combat, is duly honoured in its regular breach. The idea is noble but impracticable. Elephants rush against elephants,[2] of course, but they spare none else—horse, chariot or foot-soldier. Vikarṇa, on an elephant fights Arjuna on a chariot;[3] and so does Bhagadatta.[4] Their bells ringing,[5] the elephants rush around in utter confusion, crushing steeds and chariots.[6] King Bhagadatta shoots arrows of *black* iron [7] and hurls spears from the neck of his elephant;[8] the beast drenches the horses of Bhīma with water from his trunk,[9] and kills horses and charioteers.[10] Other combatants get down on the tusks of their elephants and despatch horses and men. The *Bhīṣma parva*[11] also describes the foot-soldiers that protect the elephants, armed with pikes, bows, battle-axes, maces, clubs, *bhiṇḍipālas*,[12] lances, iron-mounted bludgeons and bright swords, running to and fro, seeking their enemies' lives.

Thus we see that the elephant slaughters and destroys, but is not able to oụtdo the knight in his chariot. Riders, leaving their elephants, run away from fear of Arjuna.[13] Bhīṣma kills an elephant with a single arrow.[14] Hopkins[15] doubts this, but it is perfectly possible. The verse, however, saying that Arjuna never shot two arrows at an elephant[16]—only one was invariably fatal—is a plain case of poetic exaggeration. Arjuna kills Vikarṇa's elephant with an iron arrow shot from his bow drawn up to the very

---

1 Mbh. 6.1.26ff.
2 Ibid., 6.43.79.
3 Ibid., 4.60.7.
4 Ibid., 7.27.24ff. Cf.6.53.14ff.; 6.89.21, 22.
5 Ibid., 6.43.5.
6 Ibid., 6.44.24ff.; 6.99.24.
7 Ibid., 7.28.4.
8 Ibid., 7.28.7.
9 Ibid., 7.25.43. The water may have been carried originally in a leather bucket on the back of the elephant.
10 Ibid., 7.25.49.
11 Ibid., 6.44.13-15. The Vinaya, cited above, p. 134, also refers to them.
12 See below, p. 109.
13 Mbh. 6.51.25.
14 Ibid., 6.55.29.
15 Hopkins, op. cit., p. 266.
16 Mbh. 7.29.39.

ear.[1] Elsewhere, many elephants with their colours fall at Arjuna's hands.[2] With his keen-edged weapons, Abhimanyu cuts into pieces elephants and their riders, their hooks and standards and banners, quivers and coats of mail, girths and neck-ropes, blankets and bells, and also those foot-soldiers who protect them from behind.[3] Needless to say, these prodigies of valour are much exaggerated; but they reveal the temper of the Epic tradition, cognizant of the use of the elephant in war though sceptical of its value. This feeling must be associated with the Aryans soon after their arrival in India, to which the Epic seems to point. Elephants were already regarded as the chief arm of the fighting forces in the fifth century B. C. Indeed, Alexander encountered them everywhere in the succeeding century, during his brief sojourn in India.

The elephant served the old armies in various ways. He cleared the way for their marches and forded the rivers that lay in their paths; he guarded their front, flanks and rear, and battered down the walls of the enemy. No doubt, he frequently became ungovernable when wounded, and caused more damage than good. Yet he was a force to reckon with, until the invention of gun-powder reduced his efficacy. And that was the beginning of the end of an immemorial role chequered by glory and obloquy.

In the Epics, however, the elephant is finding his feet on the field of battle, and is even used to proclaim a king's victory in his capital. In the *Virāṭa parva*, the ruler of the Matsyas asks a bellman to ride on an elephant through the city and announce his victory at the crossroads.[4]

---

[1] Mbh. 4.60.8, *ākarṇapūrṇena dṛḍhāyasena bāṇena*; 9 ,10; cf. 7.28.37ff.

[2] Ibid., 3.255.29, *sapatākāśca mātaṅgāḥ.*

[3] Ibid., 7.35.34,35. Elephants are killed with *nārācas*, cf. 6.67.35. Bhīma despatches elephants with mace and sword, cf. 3.255.7; 6.50.34ff. Elsewhere, 3.40.38, Arjuna says that an elephant is killed with a stake (of iron ?)—*śūlāgreṇeva kuñjaraṁ.*

[4] Ibid., 4.63.25.

CHAPTER FIVE

ARMS AND ARMOUR

As civilization advanced apace with the technical ability of man, effective weapons of offence and defence facilitated the conquest of the surrounding environment as well as the diffusion of populations over wider areas. Even the vast extent of the Indus Civilization was, as Sir Mortimer Wheeler remarks, 'initially the product of something more forcible than peaceful penetration . . . it must be remembered that at present we know almost nothing of the earliest phase of the civilization'.[1] The weapons found in the cities may suffer by comparison with those of the outside world, but their efficacy in a given territory at a given time is undeniable.

That the bow was a favourite weapon is proved by the discovery of numerous arrow-heads of copper or bronze at the Indus sites.[2] Thin flat pieces of copper with long narrow barbs and no tang, these arrow-heads must have been in some way provided with a mid-rib by the shafts in which they were set. The arrow-heads found at Mohenjodaro average 1.9 inches in length, 0.64 in. in breadth, and 0.07 in. in thickness.[3] They remind us of the swallow-tailed flint arrow-heads of Egypt and Northern Iran.[4] However, no stone arrow-heads were found in the area, except for a solitary leaf-shaped chert specimen from Harappā [5] and another from Periano-ghundai in Northern Baluchistan.[6] Recently, more chert arrow-heads have been unearthed at Kot-Diji in association with pre-Harappan levels.[7]

---

[1] Wheeler, The Indus Civilization, 1960, p. 57.

[2] Mackay, Further Excavations at Mohenjodaro, I, p. 461; II, pls. CXXI, 1-5; CXXV, 42-7; CXXVII, 7-11; CXXXI, 18; CXXXII, 28-30; Vats, Excavations at Harappa, I, p. 391; II, pl. CXXV, 13 and 14; Wheeler, loc. cit., p. 58, fig. 10, 11. Copper arrow-heads have been unearthed at Lothal; cf. Indian Archaeology, 1954-55, p. 12; ibid., 1957-58, p. 13, pl. XXI A.

[3] Mackay, loc. cit.

[4] Ibid., Wheeler, loc. cit., pp. 58, 60.

[5] Vats, loc. cit., I, p. 360; II, no. 63 in pl. CXVIII.

[6] A. Stein, An Archaeological Tour in Waziristan and Northern Baluchistan, MASI, 37, 1929, p. 40.

[7] Wheeler, loc. cit., pp. 15, 60.

Most of the spear-heads found are tanged, thin, flat and leaf-shaped blades that must have been reinforced by being set back between the split ends of the shaft, which would thus serve as a kind of mid-rib.[1] Occasionally, two holes near the base of the blade suggest the binding for such a device.[2] The clear illustration of a barbed spear on a Mohenjodaro seal has not yet been supported by the discovery of any actual specimen.[3]

There are four or five blades with a mid-rib, tang, and rivets to hold a handle; they are up to 18½ inches long, double-edged, well made and heavy for their size.[4] Best described as short swords or dirks,[5] they all come from late levels, and have parallels of c. 2200-1750 B. C. in Syria and Palestine.[6] Foreign as they are to the common Harappā tradition, Piggott thinks that they may have been 'brought by invaders from somewhere outside the western frontiers of the Harappa kingdom'.[7]

Daggers or knives have also been found.[8] They have long tangs and slightly sinuous recurved points,[9] and are edged only on the convex side. Some of them taper along both edges; the cutting-edge is sharp and the back-edge blunt. Vats records the discovery of a double-edged dagger-tip with a mid-rib at Harappā;[10] Mackay

[1] Mackay, op. cit., I, p. 459; Marshall, Mohenjodaro and the Indus Civilization, II, p. 497; III, pls. CXXXV and CXXXVI; Vats, op. cit., I, pp. 87, 386.

[2] Wheeler, op. cit., p. 58.

[3] Mackay, op. cit., I, p. 336, cites a barbed spear-head from Ur; II, pl. LXXXVIII, seal no. 279.

[4] Ibid., I, pp. 466, 467; II, pls. CXIII, 3; CXVIII, 9; CXX, 17; CXXVIII, 5; CXXXI, 19; CXIX, 9.

[5] Wheeler, The Indus Civilization, p. 58; Piggott, Prehistoric India, pp. 228, 229; Childe, New Light on the Most Ancient East, p. 177.

[6] D. H. Gordon, The Early use of Metals in India and Pakistan, JRAI., LXXX, 1952, p. 57; Piggott, loc. cit.

[7] Piggott, loc. cit., p. 229. Childe, loc. cit., regards them as 'technically very Indian'. Recently, the excavators at Navdatoli in District Nimar, M. P., found a copper fragmentary sword or dagger with mid-rib raised; see Indian Archaeology, 1958-59, pp. 30-31, fig. 14. There is nothing like it, according to them, in the Indus civilization, while there are parallels in Iran and elsewhere. Carbon-14 datings of samples from the site range from 1631 B. C. to 1169 B. C.

[8] Vats, op. cit., I, pp. 86, 87.

[9] Wheeler, loc. cit. It is a characteristic of the Harappan specimens; only one example is reported from Hissar III in north-eastern Iran. A hafted knife is depicted on an Indus pot-sherd in Wheeler, loc. cit., pl. XXIVc.

[10] Vats, op. cit., p. 89. He compares it with Fatehpur daggers, specially no. 3 in pl. III of IA., vol. 34.

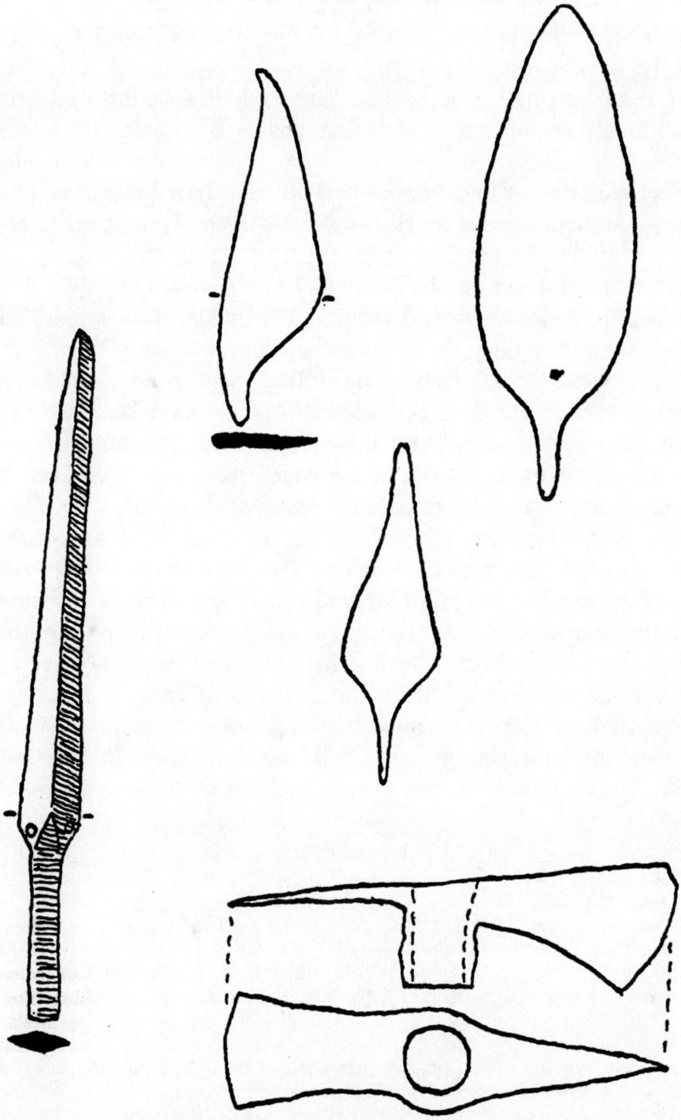

Fig II

Weapons, Mohenjodaro.
(Reproduced from Wheeler, The Indus Civilization, p. 59) Scale 1:4

found double-edged knife-cum-dagger blades at Mohenjodaro, useful both for thrusting and cutting.[1] Some, it seems, were used exclusively as daggers; for their concave sides suggest thrusting rather than cutting.[2] Two bronze daggers had a definite mid-rib, unlike the others unearthed at Mohenjodaro. Both came from later levels.[3]

Flat axes of copper and bronze, without the shaft-hole, have been found at Mohenjodaro and Harappā, and recently at Lothal and Rangpur in south western India.[4] Either long and narrow, or short and broad, these axe-blades must have been laid in a split handle at right angles to it and secured by thongs of raw hide. The shorter axes with a deep and circular edge suggest weapons of war.[5] Several axe-blades at Mohenjodaro bear signs and inscriptions incised on them.[6] The inscribed axe-blades must have been designed for something more important than mere wood-chopping. In view of the time-honoured practice of inscribing weapons, it will not be unreasonable to assume that they were weapons of war. There is evidence to indicate the arrival of the shaft-hole axe during the last days of the Indus civilization. Two pottery models of shaft-hole axes have come to light at Mohenjodaro,[7] and a bronze specimen at Chanhudaro, in a late Harappan or Jhukar layer.[8] Another example from Shahi Tump in South Baluchistan probably belongs to the same period.[9] A fine copper axe-adze from a late level at Mohenjodaro itself 'is a completely exotic object among the metal types of the Harappa culture'.[10] It has analogies in Northern Persia, North Caucasia, Assur and Sialk, and dates presumably

---

[1] Mackay, op. cit., I, p. 465; II, pls. CXIX, 4; CXX, 15.21; CXXVII, 3; CXXIX, 1; CXXXIII, 32.

[2] Ibid., I, p. 465; II, pls. CXXIX,4; CXXXIII, 23,29, 30.

[3] Ibid., I, p. 466; II, pls. CXX, 18, 19; CXXIII, 6, 7.

[4] Marshall, op. cit., II, pp. 494, 495; pls. CXXXVIII and CXXXIX; Mackay, op. cit., I, pp. 453, 454; Vats, op. cit., I, p. 86. For Lothal, see Indian Archaeology 1957-58, p. 13, pl. XXIA; for Rangpur, ibid., 1953-54, p. 7.

[5] Vats, op. cit., I, p. 86.

[6] Mackay, op. cit., I, p. 454. We are reminded of the later-day inscribed swords and arrows. The Epics mention inscribed arrows.

[7] Ibid., I, 458-459; II, pl. CXII,1; Wheeler, op. cit., p. 60.

[8] Mackay, Chanhudaro, p. 188.

[9] A. Stein, An Archaeological Tour in Gedrosia, Pl. XIII, Sh. T. VII, 135; Wheeler, op. cit., p. 60.

[10] Piggott, op. cit., p. 228, fig. 28; Mackay, Further Excavations at Mohenjodaro, II, pls. CXX, 27; CXXII, 12.

from the 2nd millennium B. C.[1] A weapon of war, it is perhaps an intimation of trouble from the western quarter to the somnolent people of the Indus valley.[2]

The use of the mace is attested by the discovery of many mace-heads, generally made of a very close-grained limestone, grey

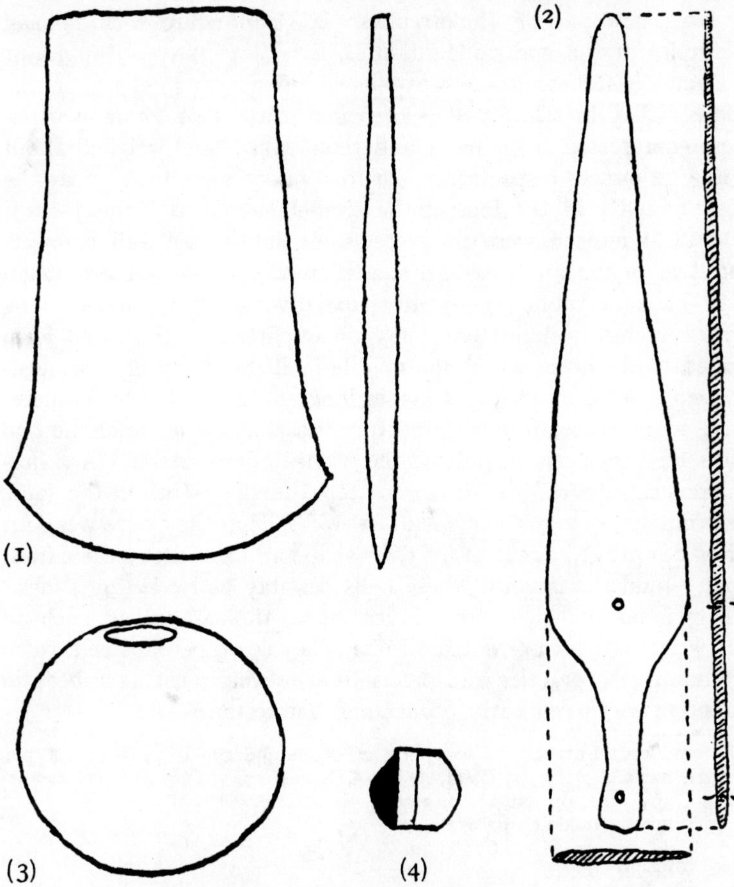

Fig III

Weapons, Mohenjodaro and Harappā.
(After Marshall, Mackay and Vats) Scale: 1-2, 1:2; 4, 1:4.

---

[1] Piggott, op. cit.; Wheeler, op. cit.
[2] Cf. Childe, New Light on the Most Ancient East, pp. 178, 187-8.

sandstone, alabaster or marble, and rarely of metal.[1] The normal shape is lentoid, but there are also round and pear-shaped specimens. This type was common also in Egypt, Susa, the Caucasus and prehistoric Europe.[2] Vats reports the find of a round metal mace-head with a cylindrical hole through the centre at Harappā.[3] And Sir Mortimer Wheeler compares a bronze or copper mace-head of late Harappan or Jhukar phase at Chanhudaro with Persian examples of the 2nd millennium B. C.[4]

Commonest among the weapons of offence and defence in the Indus valley are sling pellets of baked clay. Two common types were compressed in the hand and then baked, and weighed about 6 and 12 ounces respectively.[5] In 1950 many were found near the great granary at the foot of the citadel mound at Mohenjodaro, and 98 six-ouncers were discovered along the parapet walk connecting two of the south eastern citadel towers.[6] More rare are baked clay balls of round or ovoid shape, averaging 2.5 inches long by 1.6 inches in diameter.[7] The spin imparted by the ovoid form added to the accuracy of the missile in flight. Fifty or more egg-shaped objects averaging 4 inches long and 2.5 inches in diameter were found stored in a large pottery vessel in the lesser of the two halls on the southern half of the Mohenjodaro citadel.[8] And numerous large pottery balls lay scattered further south in the same area outside 'a very thick enclosure wall'.[9] That they were weapons of war is proved as much by their shape and size as by their find-spot. Could the larger of these balls possibly be hurled by slings? There is no evidence of the invention of the catapult at such an early date either in or outside India. They could perhaps be thrown by hand with practice and precision. The sling must have been in common use, as in early Sumer and Turkestan.[10]

[1] Mackay, Further Excavations at Mohenjodaro, I, p. 397; II, pls. LXXI, 22; CIV, 1, 2, 4; CVII, 37,38; CIX, 24, 27, 28, 35, 44; CX, 21, 22, 28, 29, 36; Vats, op. cit., I, p. 367.

[2] Wheeler, op. cit., p. 61.

[3] Vats, op. cit., I, p. 87; II, pl. CXXI, 9.

[4] Wheeler, op. cit., p. 61.

[5] Ibid.

[6] Ibid., pp.30, 61.

[7] Marshall, op. cit., II, p. 466.

[8] Ibid.; Wheeler, op. cit., pp. 36, 61.

[9] Marshall, op. cit.

[10] Ibid., pp. 466-7. Round and ovoid sling pellets have been dug up in early Sumer and Turkestan. Ovoid sling pellets have been unearthed at the neolithic sites on the Iranian tableland. In later times, the sling was used in Palestine and Syria. It was introduced in Egypt at a still later date.

No material evidence exists to prove the use of body-armour, helmets and shields by the people of the Indus valley.[1] It has been suggested, however, that domed pieces of copper, each pierced by two holes, were stitched on to a piece of cloth and used as a coat of mail.[2] And a few pictographs of the Indus script may represent men holding shields.[3]

Other weapons of copper, and sometimes of bronze, used by the hunters and warriors of the prehistoric age in the Ganges valley and beyond, included barbed spears and harpoons, and swords, found in hoards at places such as Fatehgarh in the upper Ganges valley, and Kallur in Hyderabad, Deccan.[4] Heine-Geldern assigned the copper antennae swords from the Ganges plain to the Vedic period. But the Kallur swords in the south, similar in shape and design, present an insuperable difficulty, associated as they are with an early prehistoric site.[5] Aryans could have had little to do with the south at such an early date. In fact, B. B. Lal points out that Childe, Piggott, Wheeler and Haimendorf agree with him that the hoards need no longer be associated with the Aryans.[6]

---

1 Marshall, op. cit., II, p. 506; Mackay, op. cit., I, p. 224.

2 Marshall, op. cit., II, p. 533; III, pl. CXLIII; Mackay, op. cit., I, p. 546; II, pl. CXL, 54 and 66.

3 Marshall, op. cit., III, pl. CXXIX, nos. ccclxxxix and cccxc.

4 See V. A. Smith, The Copper Age and Prehistoric Bronze Implements of India, IA., 1905, vol. 34, pp. 230 ff.; Piggott, op. cit., pp. 236-8; Wheeler, Early India and Pakistan, pp. 123-127, figs. 26 and 28. The harpoons represent a local development in river-side areas for purposes of fish-spearing. The metal types provide an evolutionary series, originally inspired by prototypes of bone and horn. The earliest of them have a rough blade with bilateral barbs, a slight mid-rib and a tang, with one or more holes below the lowest barbs. In the later harpoons the barbs are placed below the blade; and in its most developed form the blade is leaf-shaped, the barbs curved, and twice as big as the other examples. Harpoons were used also for hunting animals even as big as the rhinoceros. See Wheeler, loc. cit., p. 126; B. B. Lal, Further Copper Hoards from the Gangetic Basin and a Review of the Problem, Ancient India, no. 7, 1951, p. 20ff.

5 Cf. A. V. Naik, A note on the copper swords from Kallur, BDCRI., vol. IV, no. 4, 1943, pp. 376-378.

6 Lal, Protohistoric Investigation, Ancient India, no. 9, p. 93. In 1961 a seven inch dagger or spearhead of copper with a faint mid-rib and flat antennae was found at Chandoli in Poona District in association with Jorwe-Navasa pottery of about 1000 B. C. Cf. Indian Archaeology 1960-61 — A Review, p. 27, pl. XXXIV, 2. The fragmentary sword or dagger from Navdatoli has already been referred to (p. 86, f.n. 7). Recently another hoard from Khurdi in District Nagaur (Rajasthan) has been brought to light; see Sankalia, Prehistory and Protohistory in India and Pakistan, p. 223. Most of these copper finds are however confined to the Ganges valley

The flat copper and bronze axes present in the Ganges basin and at Gungeria, are 'similar in general terms to the flat axes of the Harrappa culture'.[1] Professor Piggott thinks that the 'bar-celt' among these finds is derived from the very narrow and elongated axes unearthed at Chanhudaro, and draws attention to a small version of the 'bar-celt' among the copper tools from Nal in Baluchistan.[2] But Sir Mortimer Wheeler holds that 'the barbed harpoons, the spearheads with basal projection, the 'bar-celts', the so-called anthropomorphs, the shouldered axes—are not Indus types', and also points to the absence of the distinctive Indus blade with curved end from the copper hoards.[3] It seems that there was an initial diffusion of metallurgical techniques eastwards from the Indus valley, even though most of the Gangetic tools and weapons owed their origin to local inventiveness. The finds of these weapons may be contemporary with the last days of Harappā or the period immediately following its fall.

Of all the Aryan weapons mentioned in the Vedic literature, the bow and arrow are the most applauded. The famous battle-hymn of the *Ṛgveda* describes the warrior on his chariot, armed with his bow and arrow, and dressed in armour, with a hand-guard called *hastaghna* on the left arm to avoid the friction of the bow-string.[4] The horse-chariot, bow and arrow, and corslet constitute the warlike equipment of a *kṣatriya*.[5] The oft-repeated word for the bow is *dhanus*.[6] The best beloved of a warrior's possessions, it was removed from the right hand of a dead man in the last act of the funeral rite.[7] Piggott discusses the character of bows,[8] which are

---

and trans-Vindhyan India. At Bisauli and Rajpur Parsu, two of the copper-hoard sites, an ill-fired thick ochre-washed pottery was discovered, though not together with any copper objects. Since such pottery also occurs in the lowest layer at Hastinapur below the Painted Grey Ware, Dr. Sankalia (cited above) suggests that the copper hoards might belong to the pre-Aryan people who made the earlier ochre-washed pottery. The bronze sword from Rajanpur in the Punjab is unexampled elsewhere in India; its hilt is typical of swords from the Luristan graves of Iran, and from the Caucasus, dating from about 1400-1200 B. C. Cf. Piggott, op.cit., p. 236.

[1] Piggott, op. cit., p. 237.

[2] Ibid.

[3] Wheeler, Early India and Pakistan, pp. 125, 127. He places the hoards before the 8th century B. C.

[4] RV. VI.75.

[5] AB. VII.19.2, *aśvaratha, iṣu-dhanva* and *kavaca*.

[6] RV. VIII.72.4; VIII.77.11; IX.99.1; X.125.6; AV.IV.4.6; IV.6.6; V.18.8; VII.50.9; VS.XVI.10; PB. VII.5.6; AB. VII. 14; ŚB. I.5.4.6; V. 3.1.11, etc.

[7] RV. X.18.9.

[8] Piggott, op. cit., p. 282.

generally classified into two main types. Simple bows of wood perhaps originated in and spread out from Africa. But composite bows of horn and sinew, shorter and stiffer, are known from the steppes and Siberia, Turkey, Persia and India, and also among the North American Eskimo. A Danish example dates back to the mesolithic period. The adoption of the composite horn-bow by the Minoans in Crete seems more or less to have synchronised with their use of the war-chariot. A composite bow from Egypt dates from the days of the 19th Dynasty, when there were wars with Syria and the chariot was adopted as an instrument of battle. Another, coming from the 6th or 7th century B. C., is in all probability of Scythian origin. Assyrian sculptures of the first millennium B. C., show chariot warriors using composite bows. Its size must have made it easier to handle by a charioteering hero. Composite bows of horn and sinew were presumably invented in the Asian Steppe, and may have formed part of the Aryan armoury in India, as elsewhere.

The curved shape of the bow is described as *vakra* in the *Atharva Veda*.[1] The bow-string (*jyā*)[2] was made of a thong of cow-hide. The bow was usually kept relaxed, and strung up only when needed for shooting.[3] The stringing of the bow (*ā-tan*), the placing of the arrow(*pratidhā*), the bending of the bow (*ā-yam*), and the shooting (*as*) of the shaft, are all mentioned in the *Vājasaneyi Saṁhitā*.[4] The string was drawn back to the ear, unlike the Homeric method of drawing it to the breast; discharged from the ear, the arrow was called *karṇayoni*,[5] having the ear as its point of origin. The twang of the bowstring sounded sweet to the ear of the warrior.

> 'Close to his ear, as fain to speak, she presses, holding her well loved friend in her embraces.
> Strained on the bow she whispers like a woman, this bowstring that preserves us in the combat'.[6]

The manufacture of bows was a regular profession, as evidenced

---

[1] AV. IV. 6. 4.

[2] RV. IV.27.3; VI.75.3; X.51.6, etc. AV.I.1.3; V.13.6; VI.42.1; VS. XVI.9; XXIX, 51.

[3] RV. X.166.3; AV. VI.42.1.

[4] VS. XVI.22.

[5] RV. II.24.8. Compare Homer, Iliad, IV.123.

[6] RV. VI.75.3. AV. V.21.9 refers to the sound of the bowstring—*jyāghoṣa*. Homer likens the sound of the bowstring to the voice of a swallow.

by the mention of the *dhanuṣ-kāra* [1] and *dhanuṣ-kṛt*.[2] Others specialised in the craft of making strings for bows.[3]

The commonest word denoting an arrow is *iṣu*,[4] the other synonyms of which are *śarya*, *śārī* and *bāṇa*. The *Ṛgveda* refers to arrows with poisoned heads of horn,[5] as distinct from other metal-headed arrows.[6] The *Atharva Veda*, too, speaks of poisoned arrows,[7] and indicates vegetation as the source of poison.[8] The arrows were feathered in order to balance them in their flight.[9] The *Atharva Veda* specifies the parts of the arrow as the shaft (*śalya*), feather-socket (*praṇadhi*), the point (*śṛṅga*),the neck of the point to which the shaft is fixed (*kulmala*), and the *apaskaṁbha* and *apāṣṭha* of dubious meaning.[10] The *Aitareya Brāhmaṇa* mentions an arrow's point (*anīka*), *śalya*, *tejana*, and feathers (*parṇāni*).[11] *Śalya* and *tejana* here stand for the upper and lower parts of the shaft. The *Śatapatha Brāhmaṇa* gives the length of an arrow as five spans or three feet,[12] which suggests a composite bow. Arrow-making had become a distinct profession early in the Vedic period.[13]

The quiver was called *iṣudhi*.[14] The *Ṛgveda* shows how it was slung on the back, though the later practice of carrying two quivers is nowhere in evidence.

> 'With many a son, father of many daughters, he clangs and clashes as he goes to battle.
> Slung on the back, pouring his brood, the quiver vanquishes all opposing bands and armies'.[15]

That spears and lances were used by the Vedic Aryans, there can be no doubt whatsoever. That these weapons were used in India both before and after the arrival of the Aryans, is borne out

---

1 VS. XXX.7.
2 Ibid., XVI.46.
3 Ibid., XXX.7, *jyākāra*.
4 e.g. RV. II.24.8; VIII.7.4; AV. I.13.4; VS. XVI.3; Nirukta, IX.18.
5 RV. VI.75.15, *ālākta*, *ruru-śīrṣṇī*.
6 Ibid., *ayomukhaṁ*.
7 AV. IV.6; V.18.8, 15, *iṣuriva digdhā*; V.31.4.
8 Ibid., IV.6.7, 8.
9 RV. VI.75.11; X.18.14; AV. V.25.1.
10 AV. IV.6; cf. III.25.2; MS. III.8.1,2.
11 AB. I.25.
12 ŚB. VI.5.2.10.
13 *Iṣukṛt* in VS. XVI.46; cf. RV. I.184.3; *iṣu-kāra* in VS. XXX.7; TB. III.4.3.1.
14 RV. I.33.3; VI.75.5; X.95.3; AV. II.33.2; IV.10.6; Nirukta, IX.13.
15 RV. VI.75.5.

by the discoveries of archaeology.[1] Of frequent occurrence in the *Ṛgveda*, the word *ṛṣṭi* denotes a weapon held in the Maruts' hands, the equivalent of the spear in mundane warfare.[2] Macdonell and Keith believe that it means simply lightning;[3] but *ṛṣṭi* certainly signifies a spear in later Sanskrit, and its metaphorical use presupposes the popularity of the weapon among the Ṛgvedic Aryans. In regions widely apart, the spear was likened to thunder and lightning, like the trident and the axe.[4] In a Ṛgvedic passage, we find a *raṁbhiṇī* on the shoulders of the Maruts, doubtless denoting a spear.[5] In the Battle of the Ten Kings too, spears can be recognised in the word *srakti*.[6] And *sṛka* is used in a couple of Ṛgvedic passages to designate a weapon of Indra, a lance.[7] *Sṛkāyin* and *sṛkā-hasta*, meaning 'one bearing a lance in his hand', occur in the *Vājasaneyi Saṁhitā*.[8]

The sword was definitely known to the Aryans. The more ancient swords have been discussed earlier in the chapter. The short sword-blades encountered in the late levels of Mohenjodaro seem to betoken the intrusion of a foreign people.[9] The fragmentary sword from Navdatoli may have had something to do with the Aryan migration from the north-west. And the Rajanpur sword, solitary though it may be, points again to these foreigners and their friends as the bearers of the type. The word *asi*, found in the Ṛgveda and later, denotes a sacrificial sword or knife, as well as a weapon of war.[10] The word *niṣaṅgin* in the *Vājasaneyi Saṁhitā* means, according to Mahīdhara, one 'having a sword', which is equally true of many other passages where it is found.[11] The *Kāṭhaka Sāṁhitā*

---

1 See above, pp. 86, 91.

2 RV. I.31.1; I.37.1,2; I.64.4, 8, 11; I.85.4; I.88.1; I.166.4; V.52.6; V.54.11; V.57.2, 6; VIII.20.11. Cf. Zimmer, AL., p. 301. Indra carries a *ṛṣṭi* in RV. I.169.3; cf. IV.37.8; Macdonell, Vedic Mythology, p. 79.

3 Vedic Index, I, p. 118.

4 See N. G. Majumdar, Notes on Vajra, pp. 173-200, in the Journal of the Department of Letters, vol. XI, 1924.

5 RV. I.168.3.

6 Ibid., VII.18.7; Hopkins, JAOS, 15, p. 264, n.

7 RV. I.32.12; X.180.2; cf. Vedic Index, s.v.

8 VS. XVI. 21.61.

9 See above p. 86.

10 RV. I.162.20; X.79.6; X.86.18; AV. XI.9.1. It is surprising that Piggott does not credit the Ṛgvedic Aryans with the knowledge and use of the sword (Prehistoric India, p. 279) and ignores his own earlier conclusions from archaeological data.

11 VS. XVI.20; KS. XVII.12; XXXVII. 11; MS. II.9.3; TS. IV.5.3.1; SV. II.1199; ŚB. XIII.4.2.5.

mentions a sheath (*vavrī*), to which a belt (*vāla*) was attached;[1] while the *Vājasaneyi Saṁhitā* speaks of a female scabbard-maker.[2]

From the word *kṛti* used in the *Ṛgveda* to describe a weapon of the Maruts, Zimmer concludes that daggers were used in war.[3]

The axe, called *paraśu*[4] or *kuliśa*,[5] served both as a wood-cutting implement and a weapon of war. The Aryans in all probability knew the shaft-hole axe, which also contributed to the ruin of Mohenjodaro's glory.

The club is one of the earliest of human weapons, and we have proof that the Aryans used it.[6] *Vajra* in the *Ṛgveda* can be generally taken to signify a club or hammer.[7] The *Ṛgveda* has the word *vidyut* for the thunderbolt, which alone is associated with Parjanya, the real rain-god of the Veda. Indra is called *vajrahasta*, but never *vidyut-hasta*. In a passage of the *Ṛgveda*, *vajra* is described as whirling about in different directions under the lofty light of the sun.[8] In fact the thunderbolt and the sun do not easily coexist, and *vajra* here probably refers to a weapon. *Vajra* is a fatal weapon,[9] made of *ayas* or metal.[10] It is forged and fashioned by Tvaṣṭṛ, the smith-god.[11] It is said to have been ground, whetted or polished.[12] It has a notched surface and has a hundred or a thousand joints, edges or spikes.[13] Not transient like a bolt of thunder, it is a regular companion of Indra.[14] Indra holds the *vajra* in his two arms or hands,[15] but sometimes only in one.[16] The *vajra* of metal clings to Indra's

---

[1] KS. XV.4; MS. II.6.5. *Asi-dhārā* in JUB. III.139, also denotes a sheath.

[2] VS. XXX.14, *kośakārīṁ*.

[3] RV. I.168.3; Zimmer, AL., p. 301; cf. Schrader, Prehistoric Antiquities, p. 221.

[4] RV. I.127.3; VII.104.21; X.28.8; X.53.9, etc.

[5] RV. III.2.1; I.32.5.

[6] Macdonell and Keith seem to believe that the Aryans used no weapon except the bow and arrow. They categorically deny the use of the club in Vedic Index, I, p. 61.

[7] See V. M. Apte, Vajra in the *Ṛgveda*, ABORI, vol. XXXVII, 1956, pp. 292-295.

[8] RV. X.27.21.

[9] Ibid., I.32.5; I.55.5.

[10] Ibid., I.52.8; I.80.12; I.81.4; VIII.96.3; X.48.3; X.96.3; X.113.5.

[11] Ibid., I.32.2; I.52.7; I.61.6; V.31.4; X.48.3.

[12] Ibid., I.55.1; I.57.2; I.130.4; VIII.15.7; VIII.76.9; X.153.4.

[13] Ibid., I.80.6; VIII.6.6; 76.2; 89.3; I.80.12; VI.17.10.

[14] Ibid., I.33.10; 131.10; VI.21.7.

[15] Ibid., I.51.7; 52.8; 63.2; II.11.4; 6; 17.6; 20.8; III.44.4; IV.22.3; VI.23.1; VIII.61.18, etc.; I.24.4; I.81.4.

[16] Ibid., VI.20.9; VII.28.2; VI.18.9; 22.9.

person.[1] It is firmly held in his locked hands.[2] It is described as *sthavira* [3] or stable, *dharṇasi* [4] or durable. It is indeed a weapon, presumably a club.

Vighana in the *Taittirīya Saṁhitā* signifies a club.[5] The *Atharva Veda* has *drughaṇa*,[6] with the same meaning. Another AV. passage mentions *pināka*, also denoting a club.[7]

Slings were known and used. Zimmer thinks that *adri* [8] and *aśani* [9] meaning 'rock' or 'stone' in the *Ṛgveda*, signified sling stones.

The use of protective armour is evidenced in the *Ṛgveda* as well as the later texts. The common word denoting a coat of mail in the *Ṛgveda* is *varman*.[10] There are references to the sewing of the armour,[11] though the material of which it was made has not been specified. It may have been in the form of a linen or leather corslet reinforced with metal. A passage of the *Ṛgveda* speaks of mailed warriors falling before the arrows like bursting vessels.[12] Whatever it was made of, leather or metal or both, the armour of the early Aryan must have afforded ample protection against the weapons of the day. A later passage mentions corslets of *ayas*, *loha*, or *rajata*.[13]

We find the word *kavaca* in the *Atharva Veda* and the later texts used for a 'corslet' or 'breastplate'.[14] The same *Veda* also mentions a *kavaca-pāśa* or 'corslet strap' which must have kept it in place.[15]

There is some evidence for the use of the helmet. In a few passages the word *śiprā* seems to signify a helmet;[16] and presumably in

---

1 RV. VIII.96.3, *indrasya vajraḥ āyaso nimiślaḥ*. . . .
2 Ibid., I.81.4.
3 Ibid., IV.20.6.
4 Ibid., VIII.6.14.
5 TS. III.2.4.1.
6 AV. VII. 28.1.
7 Ibid., I.27.2.
8 RV. I.51.3.
9 Ibid., VI.6.5; cf. I.121.9; Zimmer, AL., p. 301; Schrader, op. cit., p. 221.
10 RV. I.31.15, *varmeva syūtaṁ pari pāsi viśvataḥ*; I.140.10; VI.27.6; VI.75.1, 8,18,19; VIII.47.8; X.107.7; cf. AV. VIII.5.7 et. seq.; IX.5.26; XVII.1.27.
11 RV. I.31.15; X.101.8.
12 RV. VI.27.6.
13 JUB. IV.1.3; cf. Zimmer, op. cit., p. 298; Schrader, op. cit., p. 222.
14 AV.XI.10.22; VS. XVI. 45, *kavacin*; AB. III.48; VII.19.2; ŚB. XIII. 1.6.3; 2.2.7; 4.1.5; Nirukta, V.25.
15 AV. XI.10.22.
16 RV. V.54.11; VIII.7.25. Geldner accepts *śiprā* here as a helmet

ayaḥ-śipra,[1] *hiraṇya-śipra*,[2] *hari-śipra*[3] and *hiri-śipra*,[4] we have reference to helmets of metal.

The discovery of iron, one of the commonest elements in the earth's crust, much reduced the cost of producing tools and weapons of metal, which had been hitherto very high owing to the comparative scarcity of copper and tin. A few implements of wrought iron had been used both in Egypt and Mesopotamia even in the third millennium B.C.[5] But a suitable process of producing bulk iron of good quality was the achievement of a barbarian tribe living in Kizawadana in the Armenian mountains.[6] However, the high temperatures required for melting iron cannot be obtained without a mechanical blast, which in ancient times could not be produced. The metal when heated left a spongy mass which was compacted into a 'bloom' by prolonged hammering. As it could not be cast like copper and bronze, it was forged or wrought by means of hammering. The Aryan rulers of the Mitanni guarded the secret of iron production and controlled its output. The Hittites also persevered with the policy of secrecy, with the result that iron was a precious metal throughout the second millennium. The earliest reference to it is to be found in the inscription of the Hittite king Anittas, who records that he received an iron sceptre and an iron throne as tribute from the city of Puruskhanda.[7] The passage from a letter of the Hittite king Hattusilis III probably to the king of Assyria is well known. In this document of the 13th century B.C. the Hittite king politely turns down a request for the supply of iron, but sends as a present an iron dagger blade, with promises for the future.[8] But iron weapons were supplied to the Hittite army, and the barbarian mercenaries learned and spread the art of their manufacture.[9]

The archaeologist in India had viewed the evidence of the Vedic literature with cold scepticism, until at last his spade stumbled on finds that lent a character of reality to the literary testimony.

---

1 RV. IV.37.4. 2 Ibid., II.34.3. 3 Ibid., X.96.4.

4 Ibid., II.2.3; VI.25.9; *śiprin* in RV. I.29.2; 81.4; VI.44.14, would denote 'one wearing a helmet'. Cf. Max Müller, SBE., 32, p. 301; Geldner, Vedische Studien, 2, p. 39, n.2.

5 Gordon Childe, What Happened in History, 1950, p. 182; R.J. Forbes, Metallurgy in Antiquity, Leiden, 1950, pp. 416ff.

6 Childe, loc.cit.

7 O. R. Gurney, The Hittites, 1952, p. 83. This evidence is somewhat dubious in character.

8 Ibid. 9 Childe, loc. cit. p. 183.

'Small fragments and shapeless bits' of iron occur at Kauśāmbī as early as SP. I.3, along with the first defences,[1] before the arrival of the Painted Grey and the Northern Black Polished Wares in the Central Gangā valley.[2] The sequence of finds is more important than the dating of the archaeologist, which is sometimes called in question. The corrosive nature of the metal may account for the scarcity of iron objects in proper shape in Pd.I; also perhaps the fact that the earliest smiths must have found it easier to deal with damaged or outmoded articles than to smelt the metal from fresh ore. Smiths were always collecting scrap and melting it down in their furnaces. Objects of distinctive shapes were found in SP. II.5 and indeed throughout the Cultural Period II at Kauśāmbī.[3] They increased a great deal in number with the beginning of the Cultural Period III, characterised by the N.B.P. Ware.[4] At Hastināpura, iron slag and ore were found in the uppermost layers of Period II in association with the Painted Grey Ware.[5] This P. G. Ware occupation began at the site early in the 11th century B.C., and ended owing to floods in the beginning of the 8th century B.C.[6] And the excavations at Ālamgīrpur similarly confirmed the association of iron with the P.G. Ware; iron objects together with those of copper were found throughout the Period II.[7] Further, the ancient city of Śrāvastī also yielded iron in association with the P. G. Ware.[8] And at Atranjikherā in District Etāh, too, arrow-and-spear-heads of iron have recently been found together with the P.G. Ware.[9] This ware cannot now be linked up with the Bronze Age alone; it has been attributed to the Vedic Aryans, spread over the Punjab, U.P., and the Sarasvatī valley.[10]

---

[1] G. R. Sharma, The Excavations at Kauśāmbī (1957-59), Allahabad, 1960, p. 45.

[2] Ibid., p. 13. [3] Ibid., p. 45. [4] Ibid.

[5] B. B. Lal, Ancient India, Nos. 10 and 11, p. 13; No. 9, Protohistoric Investigation, p. 95.

[6] Ancient.India, no. 9, p. 96; nos. 10 and 11, p. 23.

[7] Indian Archaeology 1958-59 - A Review, p. 54. [8] Ibid., p. 2.

[9] Indian Archaeology 1962 - 63 — A Review, p. I-12, cyclostyled copy (to be published).

[10] Ancient India, 10 and 11, pp. 1-3, and 138ff. Cf. Sankalia, Prehistory and Protohistory in India and Pakistan, p. 270, f.n. 333. The radio-carbon dating of a charcoal sample excavated at Atranjikherā has proved that the Aryan settlements in the region date back to a period before 1000 B.C. (Reported in *The Hindustan Times*, August 19, 1964; *The National Herald*, August 21, 1964). At Noha near Bharatpur, too, iron has recently been found in association with the P. G. Ware, and the radio-carbon dating confirms the evidence from Atranjikherā.

The earliest levels of Period III at Rūpar, beginning circa 600 B.C., yielded implements of copper as well as iron.[1] At Purānā Qilā, Delhi, copper had been supplemented by iron by the 6th century B.C.[2] At Jajmau, in Kanpur district of U.P., iron implements were found together with sherds of Grey Ware as well as the N. B. P. Ware.[3]

Excavations at Garh Kālikā mound on the outskirts of Ujjain revealed that iron was known to its ancient dwellers from the earliest period. Iron weapons, such as spears, arrow-heads and knives, have been unearthed from the strata of Period I, assigned to c. 700-500 B.C.[4] And a few interesting objects of iron, including the curved blade of a spade, were dug up from the rampart.[5] A flourishing iron industry is evidenced by the large quantities of iron ore and slag and finished iron objects found in the deposits of Period III. Iron ore was available to the people in the form of limonite from the local trap bed-rock; and calcite was used as a flux.[6] A blacksmith's furnace was excavated; it belonged to the second phase of the site's life.[7]

At Nāgdā on the bank of the Chambal south-west of Ujjain, iron was used before the 5th century B.C., and indeed preceded the appearance of the N.B.P. Ware.[8] Some of the iron implements excavated at Maheshwar and Navdatoli go at least as far back as c. 500 B.C.[9]

The use of iron had spread very widely at a comparatively early date, as we learn from the excavations at places such as Bahal in District Khandesh of the South Western Circle, and Prabhās Patan in District Sorath, Bombay. The layers of Period II at Bahal yielded iron and Black-and-red Ware, assigned to c. 600-300 B.C.[10] At Tekwāḍā, across the river from Bahal, weapons of iron such as spear-heads, arrow-heads, knives and sickles were found in associa-

---

1 Y. D. Sharma, Exploration of Historical Sites, Ancient India, no. 9, p. 123.

2 Indian Archaeology, 1954-55, p. 14.

3 Ibid., 1957-58, p. 49.

4 Ibid., 1957-58, p. 34.

5 Ibid.

6 Ibid., p. 36.

7 Ibid.

8 Wheeler, Early India and Pakistan, pp. 138-9. At Sonepur near Gaya, too, iron occurs earlier than the N. B. P. Ware. Cf. Sankalia, op. cit., p. 171.

9 Wheeler, loc. cit., pp. 140-42.

10 Indian Archaeology, 1956-57, p. 18.

tion with the second phase of the site's life. Here too, as at Nāgdā, the use of the metal precedes the arrival of the N.B.P. Ware, the earliest sherd of which occurs some ten feet higher than the objects or iron.[1] And at Prabhās Patan, iron was found together with Black-and-red Ware in the context of Period III, the second sub-phase of which yielded the N.B.P. Ware.[2] Indeed, vigorous iron-using settlements flourished even as far south as Amarāvatī in the 5th or 4th century B.C.[3]

To sum up, then, the evidence of archaeology, more of which may be forthcoming in future, Kauśāmbī has recorded the finds of iron even earlier than the Painted Grey Ware; and Hastināpura, Ālamgīrpur, Atranjikherā, Noha and Śrāvastī attest the association of iron with this ware. The knowledge of iron must have come to India presumably around 1000 B.C. Itinerant smiths must have travelled from Asia Minor during the 300 years or so that intervened between our date and the original discovery of iron smelting in Anatolia, and thus spread the technique in India. However jealously guarded a secret may be, it tends to leak out as the years pass.

We may not unreasonably conclude that, though *ayas* in the *Ṛgveda* usually means copper or bronze, it may not invariably do so, specially in the later books. There can be no mistaking the meaning of *śyāma ayas* or 'black metal' in the *Atharva Veda*;[4] it cannot but be iron. Another AV. passage has: 'Cut along this skin with a dark [metal], O slaughterer, joint by joint with the knife (*asi*)'.[5] The *Vājasaneyi Saṁhitā*[6] mentions the metals *hiraṇya, ayas, śyāma, loha, sīsa* and *trapu*. While *śyāma* and *loha* must mean iron and copper respectively, it is suggested that *ayas* may here signify bronze.[7]

---

[1] Wheeler, Early India and Pakistan, p. 146.

[2] Indian Archaeology, 1956-57, p. 17.

[3] Wheeler, loc. cit., pp. 148-9.

[4] AV. XI.3.1, 7. Forbes, op. cit., p. 436, rightly concluded on the basis of literary evidence alone that iron smelting was introduced in India around 1000 B. C. But, if *ayas* in the *Ṛgveda* is taken to signify iron, the date will have to be pushed further back, which is not warranted by the available archaeological evidence. M. N. Banerjee's interpretations in the Indian Historical Quarterly, III, pp. 121; 793; V, pp. 432-440; VIII, pp. 364-366, remain largely speculative, and in the absence of earlier iron finds, it would be safer to suggest that *ayas* in the *Ṛgveda* normally denotes copper or bronze, though it may occasionally mean iron in the later books of that Veda.

[5] AV. IX.5.4, *anuchya śyāmena tvacametām*, etc.

[6] VS. XVIII. 13.

[7] Vedic Index, I, p. 31.

Ayas is divided into two species, *śyāma* and *lohita* in the later *Saṁhitās* and texts;[1] the first must mean iron, and the second copper or bronze. The *Śatapatha Brāhmaṇa* draws a distinction between *ayas* and *lohāyasa*,[2] between iron and copper according to Eggeling,[3] who seems to be right. *Ayas* alone thus signifies iron in a number of places. The sense of iron in AV. V.28.1, is certain according to Macdonell and Keith.[4] There are numerous references to the smelting of metal in the Vedic literature; the word *dhmā*[5] seems to have been derived from the sound of the bellows. The *Maitrī Upaniṣad*[6] mentions a lump of iron 'overcome by fire and beaten by workmen', passing into a different form. The *Chāndogya Upaniṣad* speaks of *kārṣṇāyas* and also *kṛṣṇāyasa*,[7] which certainly mean iron. And so also the *Aitareya Āraṇyaka*[8] and the *Maitrāyaṇa Brāhmaṇa Upaniṣad*[9] refer to iron.

The famous crucible steel (Wootz) had its origin in India. The Chera steel was renowned for its quality. Indian iron smiths must have invented the 'wootz' process in the 6th or early 5th century B.C. Ktesias saw two wonderful swords of Indian steel at the court of Artaxerxes Mnemon.[10] Herodotus speaks of the arrows of Indian soldiers tipped with iron,[11] while Curtius refers to a hundred talents of Indian steel presented to Alexander.[12]

The archaeological discoveries and the literary evidence seem to be mutually corroborative, and 1000 B.C. may be suggested as the provisional date for the introduction of iron smelting into India. The switch over from the old metals to the new, hard to work, yet much more useful, must have doubtless taken some length of time. But the suggestion that iron came into India with the Achaemenids towards the end of the 6th century B.C. and the

---

1 AV. XI.3.1.7; MS. IV.2.9.

2 ŚB. V.4.1.2.

3 SBE., 41, p. 90.

4 Vedic Index, I, p. 32.

5 RV. X. 72.2, *karmāra ivādhamat*; X. 81.3; ŚB. VI.1.3.5; VI.i.i.13; XII.7.1.7. VS. XXX.14 has *ayastāpaṁ*; cf. TB. III.4.10.1.

6 Maitrī Up. III.3.

7 CHU. IV.17.7; VI.1.5; JUB. III.17.3; cf. *kārṣṇāyasa* also in Mbh. 4.49.15; 7.102.55; 7.154.37, Cr. Ed.

8 AĀ, II.5.1.14.

9 MBU. VI.27.

10 D. H. Gordon, The Prehistoric Background of Indian Culture, p. 162.

11 W. H. Schoff, The Eastern Iron Trade of the Roman Empire, JAOS, 35, p. 231; Herodotus, vii.65.

12 Curtius, IX, viii. 1.

beginning of the 5th,[1] is outweighed by the evidence reviewed in the foregoing pages.

The supreme weapon in the Epics, as in the Vedic literature, is the bow and arrow. Every knight of note is a distinguished archer, and the best bowmen invariably decide the fate of an armed engagement. The Epics teem with references to the weapon held so highly in honour, called variously *dhanus*, *cāpa*, *śarāsana*, *kārmuka* and *śārṅga*. The last two names derive from the materials of which bows are made, wood and horn respectively.[2] The bows of horn were presumably composite weapons, smaller than the specimens of wood and bamboo which existed side by side, and which seem to be meant when bows are described as *tālamātrāṇi*, i.e. a 'palm' long.[3] This signifies a length of 6 cubits according to Hopkins, who compares it with the numerical qualification employed in such terms as *ṣaḍaratni*.[4]

The bows of the rich and the powerful were frequently inlaid with figures of golden elephants, little insects, dots and other such decorations.[5] Arjuna's bow is described as backed with gold.[6] Favourite bows were given names, like the Gāṇḍīva of Arjuna, and Vijaya of Karṇa.

The bowstring was made of the *mūrva*, a type of hemp,[7] or of cowhide as in the earlier period. The bow was usually unstrung when not in use. In the Epic, there are cries of "Oh" and "Alas", when a hero twangs his bowstring.[8] Indeed, the sound of the bowstring flapping against the hand-guard of leather calls for poetic notice. The bow is held perpendicularly while the string is pulled back to the ear to discharge the arrow. Arjuna alone among the host of warriors is left-handed or ambidextrous (*savyasācin*), and uses either hand as he pleases to draw the bowstring.

Quivers full of arrows were usually fastened to the backs of warriors, or carried on elephants and chariots. The frequent use of

---

1 Wheeler, Ancient India, The Civilization of a Subcontinent, in the Dawn of Civilization edited by Piggott, London 1961, pp. 230, 241, 251; Early India and Pakistan, p. 132.

2 Kṛṣṇa's bow is made of horn. Bows of ram's horn are mentioned in the *Jātakas*. Cf. *Khaṇḍahāla Jātaka*, No. 68; *Sarabhaṅga Jātaka*, No. 522.

3 Mbh. 7.46.6.

4 Hopkins, JAOS, 13, p. 270.

5 Mbh. 4.38.20ft.

6 Ibid., 4.56.4, *suvarṇapṛṣṭhaṁ*.

7 *jyā maurvī*.

8 Mbh. 4.54.15.

iṣudhi, the commonest word denoting a quiver, in the dual number, suggests that two quivers were tied together on a man's back to ensure an adequate supply of arrows. The fact that the god Varuṇa presents a couple of quivers to Arjuna, appears to bear out our inference.[1] There are other words used for the quiver such as *tūṇīra*,[2] or *upāsaṅga*.[3] From the context it appears that the latter usually connotes a larger quiver fastened to a war-chariot or an elephant.

The Epics describe numerous varieties of arrows. The words *iṣu*, *śara* (reed), and *śalya* usually denote an arrow, the last meaning more specifically the point only, and the whole by inference. Many more names are, however, met with, such as *bāṇa*, *bhalla*, *nārāca*, *nālīka* and *pradara*,[4] *vipāṭha* and *vaitastika*.

Most of the arrows were made of reed or cane, as we learn from the term *vaiṇava*.[5] The normal length of the arrow was equal to that of the chariot axle.[6] Arjuna's arrows are described as made of reed and metal, well-tempered, tied with sinew, and engraved with his name.[7] Droṇa's arrows, too, are said to be incised with his name.[8]

The arrows called *vaitastika* [9] were very small in size and used to great advantage at close quarters. Their length of one span only argues for their use in a small composite bow, or even suggests the possibility of some form of cross-bow. Though we have no other evidence of the use of this in India in our other sources, it is known to certain quite primitive peoples of South East Asia, and it is possible that the Aryans adopted some such weapon from the indigenous inhabitants.

Iron arrows are usually meant where the term *nārāca* is used;[10] but we also come across the *ardha* (half)-*nārāca*.[11] Arrows made of

---

1 Mbh. 1.216.7.
2 Ibid., 5.152.3.
3 Ibid., 4.40.4; 5.152.3.
4 *Pradara* means 'to split apart'.
5 Ibid., 7.74.8.
6 Hopkins, op. cit., p. 276.
7 Ibid,. 7.74. 7-8.
8 Ibid., 7.101.46. The old practice of engraving arrows with owners' names continued right down to the modern times. See the article on 'The Old Tanjore Armoury' by M. J. Walhouse in IA., vol. 7, p. 195. Cf. Rām yuddha, 44.23.
9 Mbh. 7.98.50, 51.
10 Ibid., 3.170.17; 7.37.22; 8.14.29.
11 Ibid., 7.37.22.

black iron are specifically mentioned in the *Droṇa parva*.[1] The *Virāṭa parva* speaks of large shafts (*vipāṭha*), flighted with vultures' feathers, whetted on stone and sharp pointed, wholly made of metal.[2] The term *nālīka* may also denote a hollow metal arrow, if not a shaft of reed.[3] Elephants were often resisted with arrows of iron. Arjuna kills an elephant with a stout iron arrow which penetrates the animal's body right up to the feathers.[4] The *Karṇa parva* refers to *nārācas* steeped in oil.[5] They may have been lubricated to pierce surely and smoothly.

The Epics as well as the later texts tell us of iron arrows, but none have been found during the course of widespread archaeological excavations extending over a long period of time. May we ask if these shafts of metal existed in fact or in the poet's imagination? It would not be easy to shoot an iron arrow to a worthwhile distance. Even if a singularly strong man could make use of one with a singularly strong bow at short range, its efficacy would be as dubious as its accuracy. These arrows may nevertheless have existed, and discoveries of a few old specimens would indeed be welcome.

Arrow-heads of different types figure in the Epics. The *kṣurapra* [6] is a knife-shaped arrow with a blade-head, and even cuts a head from the body, if the Epic is to be believed. A favourite arrow-head is the *ardhacandra*,[7] or crescent-shaped, frequently described as very sharp and cutting off people's heads. It is a very old type, and was known even in ancient Rome, where it was used in circus games.[8] Another variety is the *vatsadanta*,[9] often alluded to, said to be of the shape of a calf's tooth and exceedingly sharp. The *Āraṇyaka parva* speaks of *bhallas*, or sharpened arrows with flattened tips.[10] These sharp but broad-headed varieties must have been

---

[1] Ibid., 7.28.4, *kārṣṇāyasairbāṇaiḥ*.

[2] Ibid., 4.38.26, *sarvāyasāḥ śarāḥ*

[3] Ibid., 3.170.17; 5.51.3 has *karṇinālīkān*. *Karṇi* seems to mean eared or barbed.

[4] Ibid., 4.60.8-10, *dṛḍhāyasena bāṇena*.

[5] Ibid., 8.14.29, *tailadhautāñśca nārācān*.

[6] Mbh. 3.230.13; 3.255.24; 7.37.22.

[7] Ibid., 3.255.13; 7.28.40; 7.101.59, etc.

[8] IA., vol.7, p. 195; also see figures of old Hindu arrowheads, esp. nos.1 and 7, facing p. 194.

[9] Mbh. 7.37.22.

[10] Mbh. 3.116.24, *niṣitairbhallaiḥ*. The *añjalika* is also one to the common arrowhead types, broad and sharp (Mbh. 7.37.22). At Kauśāmbī, arrowheads of iron and bone have been found from SP. II.5 onwards. Iron arrowheads

useful in cutting bows and bowstrings as well as the limbs of the human body.

Sometimes we find mention of a serpent-headed arrow, which must be dismissed as a poetic fancy.[1] The assumption of Hopkins [2] that this term may have signified arrows with poisoned tips, does not appear justified, as there is no description of the poison's work on its victim; there are in fact other words found in our literature to denote a poisoned arrow-head, such as *ālākta*, *digdha* and *lipta*.

Arrows are not infrequently described as steeped in oil;[3] they may have been incendiary arrows. We hear of blazing and flaming arrows,[4] and the so-called divine *āgneya* or 'fire-weapon,'[5] looms large in the Epic story. It must have been a flaming arrow, which was definitely used in the earlier Vedic period.

Hopkins [6] holds that the standard of archery is relatively low in the Epics; the heroes strive to excel only in lightness of hand, in the matter of shooting as many arrows as fast as possible, without much care for the accuracy of their aim. Whenever two knights fight, the others witness spellbound; the sky becomes dark with the downpour of their arrows. He also thinks that the arrows were not very effective even if they hit their object, for we find the heroes spending so many arrows to kill one another. The few legends of accurate aiming are accretions of a later day, out of harmony with the tone of the Epic archery. But is Hopkins right?

The great heroes of the story could in fact achieve the impossible with their bows and arrows. The rapid discharge of many arrows did not go in vain on the field of battle. They took toll of untold numbers in every scene of war. Bhīṣma alone accounted for 10,000 lives a day.[7] And others like Arjuna and Karṇa, Droṇa and Bhīma,

---

of eleven types occur; one of them has a knife-blade and lozenge cross section. Some bone arrowheads bear black stains due either to poisoning or blood. See G. R. Sharma, op. cit., pp. 45-47.

[1] Cf. Mbh. 5.61.10.

[2] Hopkins, op.cit., p. 278. He too says, however, that it may perhaps be 'better understood of the sharp bite, the whizzing sound, and the darting motion'.

[3] Cf. Mbh. 5.19.4, *tailadhautaiḥ*.

[4] Ibid., 4.55.23, *bāṇena jvalitena*. This may be metaphorical, though one would assume that the metaphor is derived from actual practice.

[5] Cf. Ibid., 3.234.7, etc.

[6] Hopkins, op. cit., pp. 272-3.

[7] cf. Mbh. 5.153.16ff.; 5.194.14ff.; also 5.170.20.; 3.255.8, 9; 1.1.158, etc.

and many more, were not far behind; they exterminated two gigantic armies, if one is to argue from the impossible figures of the Epic. Almost every battle scene presents a net-work of arrows crossing and cutting one another in mid air. Bows are rent asunder and bowstrings are cut in twain; charioteers are slain, and the chariots are destroyed together with their horses. The archer strikes wherever he likes with an impeccable accuracy of aim. An arrow is often enough to fell a huge elephant. Yet if many arrows do not kill a hero despite the fact that they rip across his body, we must remember the superhuman prowess of these Epic characters. They are no ordinary men, but would hold their own even against the gods if challenged. How would they succumb to ordinary blows? How would the story go on if they did so? The text on which Hopkins based his arguments, cannot support them.

We must also judge the question from a practical point of view. How many arrows could a warrior possibly shoot in a given time? How many arrows could he carry in his two quivers, which would have contained no more than 20 or 25 arrows at the most? His chariot indeed must have carried more. But how many more? All the rains of arrows from a hero's bow darkening the earth and sky must be treated as no better than gross exaggerations. Yet the greatly exaggerated accounts of the archer's prowess in the Epics must have had some basis in the actual human skill of the warrior of the period.

We have some fine descriptions of delicate archery. To cite only two or three, Ekalavya shoots seven arrows into a barking dog's mouth before he can shut it; the dog is not seriously hurt, but barks no more.[1] Arjuna shoots 21 arrows into a cow's hollow horn swinging on a rope.[2] The feat is repeated by Karṇa [3] who never aims an arrow twice.[4]

Spears and javelins vie in popularity with bows and arrows, and are indeed inseparable from any scene of war. The commonest word denoting a spear or javelin is *śakti*,[5] made of iron and often oiled for smoothness. Not many *śaktis* can have been enriched with gold and beryl, as the poet would have us believe; for, once hurled

---

[1] Mbh. 1.123.19ff.
[2] Ibid., 1.125.24.
[3] Ibid., 1.126.12.
[4] Ibid., 8.66.8. For feats of display archers in modern India, see appendix.
[5] Ibid., 1.26.44; 1.63.2; 3.21.32; 3.170.17; 3.255.6; 4.31.9; 5.19.3; 5.152.3.

in battle, they would normally be lost. Sometimes we hear of a *mahāśakti*, a large and powerful weapon adorned with a hundred bells.[1] Such a weapon seems rather unpractical, and may have been reserved for ceremonial occasions; but it is possible that the bells were fastened to the butt of the shaft, and served to balance the spear in flight. Frequently flung at their opponents by the knights in their chariots, spears are fitly called *rathaśaktis*. They were effective weapons, as implied by their constant use, even though we are told how flying *śaktis* are cut to pieces by a shower of arrows.

Various other words in the *Mahābhārata* generally describe weapons of this class. It appears that these names may have been used synonymously quite as often as to distinguish one variety from the other. The *ṛṣṭi* [2] seems to be one of the weapons of the ordinary soldier, and probably signifies a javelin. The *tomara* [3] is conspicuous for its sharp point, and may be, as explained by the commentator, a kind of javelin. The *prāsa* [4] has a broad and sharp head and must be a spear or javelin. Occasionally, a *prāsa* is described as having a barb or handle;[5] and in the *Bhīṣma parva* we hear of *mahāprāsas* hurled by horsemen on the field of battle.[6] The *Śalya parva* speaks of the cavalry of *Gāndhāra*, 10,000 strong, who fight with *prāsas*, lances or spears.[7] The *kampana*,[8] literally 'trembler', appears to mean a dart or javelin, which quivers when it strikes its target, and is often mentioned along with *prāsa* and *tomara*. The *śūla* [9] presumably represents a sharp iron spike used as a piking spear. The *triśūla*[10] or trident also figures in the list of weapons used. The *paṭṭiśa*[11] appears to denote a spear; the *Bhīṣma parva* refers to Rākṣasas riding on horseback with *śūlas* and *paṭ-*

---

[1] Mbh. 3.270.3, *śataghaṇṭām*.

[2] Ibid., 5.19.3; Hopkins, op. cit., p. 289.

[3] Ibid., 1.17.11, *sutīkṣṇāgra*; 1.63.2; 1.123.8; 3.152.16; 3.170.17; 3.255.6; 5.152.3.

[4] Ibid., 1.17.11, *suvipulāstīkṣṇā*; 3.21.32; 4.31.9; 5.19.3.

[5] Ibid., 3.255.26 has *talayukta*. *Tala*, 'surface', 'lower part', may also imply the broad barbed part of the spearhead.

[6] Ibid., 6.44.20, 21, *mahāprāsāḥ*. . . *āśugā vimalāstīkṣṇāḥ*.

[7] Ibid., 9.22.29, *prāsayodhinām*.

[8] Ibid., 6.72.6; 7.35.24.

[9] Ibid., 1.28.12; 3.21.32; 3.22.2 has *dīptāñśca śūlān*, which may mean blazing, or more probably, bright spears.

[10] Ibid., 1.26.43.

[11] Ibid., 3.152.16; 1.28.12.

ṭiśas.[1] *Kunta*[2] and *kaṇapa*[3] likewise signify projectile weapons of the same order, made of iron, thrust or flung at the enemy. And the *bhiṇḍipāla*[4] is probably a short javelin thrown by the hand. In many of the passages cited, quite a few of these names occur together, pointing to some difference in their shapes and sizes, not otherwise determinable.

The sword has an honoured place in the armoury of the Epic warrior. Its efficacy has increased since the Vedic period, as attested by its prominence in the Epics as well as the *Nikāyas*. Bhīṣma tells Nakula that the sword is the foremost of weapons, next, of course, in order to the bow.[5] It is an essential part of knightly equipment; a warrior of rank almost invariably wears a sword, besides his coat of mail and bow and arrows.[6] The words employed to denote a sword are *asi*,[7] *khaḍga*,[8] *nistriṁśa*[9] and *karavāla*.[10] The *asi* is sometimes called *mahāsi* or *dīrghāsi*, just as the *khaḍga* is called *mahākhaḍga*. A long sword may be meant where the word *asi* is used; a broad-sword where we have *khaḍga*, and a short sword where *nistriṁśa* occurs. It is not possible to be definite about the distinctions connoted by these names; they may also have been sometimes loosely used to mean swords in general. The word *sāyaka* has also been used to signify a sword, described as adorned with bells.[11] Sheaths of tiger-skin,[12] cow-skin,[13] and goat-skin[14] are referred to. Swords forged in the country of the Niṣādhas are specially mentioned.[15]

---

1 Mbh. 6.86.52, *śūlapaṭṭiśapāṇibhiḥ*. *Paṭṭiśa* can sometimes perhaps be explained as an axe.

2 Ibid., 7.35.25.

3 Ibid., 1.218.24 has *ayaḥ-kaṇapa*.

4 Ibid., 5.19.3. Cf. Monier Williams Dictionary, s.v. Kauṭilya, *Arthaśāstra*, Bk. II, ch. 18, mentions and defines it, like the *śakti*, *prāsa* and *tomara*, as a weapon with edges like a ploughshare. Later writers sometimes used it in the sense of a sling.

5 Mbh. 12.160. 81-84.

6 *sannaddhaḥ kavacī khaḍgī*, etc.; cf. Ibid., 1.216.16; 3.18.3.

7 Ibid., 1.17.12; 1.123.8; 3.230.31; 4.7.1; 4.31.9.

8 Ibid., 2.66.14; 5.19.4; 7.13.60 has *mahākhaḍga*.

9 Ibid., 4.38.34. *Nistriṁśa* or *niśtriṁśa*, meaning more than 30 *aṅgulas*, may also be an indication of the weapon's size. If so, the *nistriṁśa* will not be a particularly short sword.

10 Ibid., 1.26.44; 5.19.3.

11 Ibid., 4.38.31.

12 Ibid., 4.38.30.

13 Ibid., 4.38.32.

14 Ibid., 4.38.33.

15 Ibid., 4.38.32.

Swords are hurled as often as they are held in the hand to fight with. Nakula is described as a great swordsman.[1] When a warrior's bow and arrows failed him, when his charioteer, horses and chariot were destroyed, his sword and shield came to his rescue. In the *Āraṇyaka parva*, Nakula jumps down, sword and shield in hand, from his chariot attacked by an elephant, and lops off the trunk and the tusks of the infuriate beast.[2] We repeatedly hear of knights jumping out of their wrecked chariots and hacking their way (*asipatha*) to safety through the ranks of their enemies.[3] The sword must have been worn by the chariot warrior at all times.

Occasionally, we find two distinguished warriors engaged in a sword duel. Cekitāna and Kṛpa fight with swords and strike each other until both fall unconscious.[4] In the *Rāmāyaṇa* Lakṣmaṇa says that he would encounter with his sword the enemies of Rāma.[5] *Maṇḍalas* or manoeuvres of the sword-fight are elaborately described in the *Droṇa parva*, where as many as 21 standard movements are specified.[6] The old Indian passion for classification is here in evidence, for the so-called technical terms do not mean anything more than 'swinging the sword about, or over the foe, guarding by a false movement, approaching, touching, forcing the foe's guard, twisting to one side or the other, retreating, clashing, assault from above, below on an exposed part, flashing quick passes',[7] and sheathing.

Daggers and knives [8] also figure in the Epic as projectile and hand weapons used for thrusting at close quarters. But they are used only by common soldiers, and are part of the equipment of the elephantry.

The battle-axe, designated as *paraśu*,[9] *paraśvadha*,[10] or *kuṭhāra*,[11] is fairly common. It is not infrequently described as a missile used by the nobility. The *kuṭhāra* was a favourite weapon of Paraśurāma.

---

1 Mbh. 3.254.15. Hopkins, op. cit., p. 281, is wrong when he says that none holds to the sword as a favourite weapon.

2 Ibid., 3.255.18ff.

3 See above, p. 51; Mbh. 3.230.31.

4 Ibid., 6.80.27ff.; cf. 6.70.27.

5 Rāmāyaṇa, Ayodhyā, 23.35.

6 Mbh. 7.192.37ff., *mārgān. . . ekaviṁśatiṁ*, Cal. Ed.

7 Hopkins, op. cit., p. 286, n.

8 *vāśī* and *kṣura*.

9 Mbh. 5.19.3.

10 Ibid., 3.21.32; 1.26.43.

11 Ibid., 5.152.7.

The discus or quoit (*cakra*) is indeed a very ancient weapon, harking back to the *Ṛgveda*, where it is mentioned as a weapon of Indra.[1] In the *Mahābhārata* it is the principal weapon of Kṛṣṇa, whose *cakra* has a name, Sudarṣana. It is described as made of iron, sharp-edged and revolving.[2] Kṛṣṇa cuts off the head of Śiśupāla with a fling of his discus.[3]

Dating back as it does to prehistoric times, the popularity of the club or mace is symbolic of the antiquity of the Epic tradition. For, it is a celebrated weapon in the great Epic, wielded by knights of rank and distinction. The words commonly used to denote a club or mace are *gadā*,[4] *musala*,[5] and *parigha*.[6] The *Āraṇyaka parva* speaks of *mahāgadās*[7] or large maces, and all three varieties are now and then described as made of iron.[8] They must have been in fact made of wood as well as metal.[9] Bhīma's ponderous mace is said to be plated with gold.[10] The weapon must have usually had the shape of a sharp-cornered and heavy tapering post, girded with iron spikes and sometimes adorned with gold. In the *Karṇa parva* Śalya speaks of his mighty mace decked with gold.[11] In one place, a mace is said to be hexagonal in shape and four cubits in length.[12] Favourite maces have specific names, like Modakī and Śikharī, given by Viśvāmitra to Rāma.[13]

The mace was used by well-born and commoners alike, provided that they had the requisite strength and stamina to wield it. Its heavy size must have militated against its popularity with the average fighter. Only the strongest could use it to purpose and advantage. The mace-fight was a highly developed art with royal exponents like Balarāma, Śalya, Duryodhana and Bhīma. The *Ādi parva* refers to four modes of fighting with a club or mace,[14]

---

1 RV. VIII.96.9.

2 *paribhramantaṁ, tīkṣṇadhāraṁ* and *ayasmayaṁ*; Mbh. 1.33.2ff. Cal. Ed.

3 Mbh. 2.42.21.

4 Ibid., 1.26.44; 1.63.2; 1.123.8.

5 Ibid., 3.22.2; 1.63.2.

6 Ibid., 1.17.16; 1.26.43; 1.28.12; Rām. Araṇya, 26.10,11, speaks of a *parigha* with iron prickles.

7 Mbh. 3.22.2.

8 Ibid., 3.234.21 has *gadāṁ sarvāyasīṁ*; 6.66.18 has *āyasaiḥ parighairiva*; 1.17.16, *parighaiścāyasaiḥ*.

9 A wooden club is mentioned in Mbh. 1.167.19.

10 Ibid., 3.152.15, *mahāgadāṁ kāñcanapaṭṭanaddhāṁ*. Cf. 3.255.4, where his mace is described as made of *śaikya* iron and embossed with gold.

11 Ibid., 8.23.27.

12 Ibid., 5.50.28, *catuṣkiṣkuṁ ṣaḍasrimamitaujasaṁ*.

13 Rām. Bāla, 27.7.

14 Mbh. 1.62.12; see n. 12 on p. 283 of *Ādi parva*, Cr. Ed.

explained by the commentator as *prakṣepa* or hurling at the enemy from a distance, *vikṣepa* or close fight at the weapon's point, *parikṣepa* or brandishing it around in the midst of foes, and lastly *abhikṣepa* or hitting the opponent in front. The *maṇḍalas* or circling manoeuvres associated with club-fighting are repeatedly mentioned.[1] A warrior often rushes away from his broken chariot with his mace in his hand; it is Bhīma's favourite pattern of behaviour. The fate of a kingdom after a victorious war is again staked by Yudhiṣṭhira on a single duel with the mace between Bhīma and Duryodhana. The *Śalya parva* [2] affords us a vivid description of this thrilling fight; the entire repertoire of tricks is here in evidence. The end, though, belies the rules; Duryodhana is struck on his thighs despite the fact that a blow below the navel is taboo.

The club is often hurled at the enemy like any other missile, and there are a few weapons which must be explained as clubs or bludgeons of one kind and another. The *sthūṇa* of black iron,[3] and the *laguḍa* of stone,[4] belong to this category in general. And the *bhuśuṇḍi* [5] may also be a heavy club, perhaps shaped like the trunk (*śuṇḍa*) of an elephant. The *mudgara* is probably a heavy tapering club, flung like the other weapons.[6]

We must not forget to consider the nature of the *yantras* so ostentatiously displayed on the city walls, repeatedly mentioned but relatively ineffectual in the Epic descriptions of battle. The word *yantra* [7] is of ancient usage, dating back to the *Ṛgveda*, where it occurs in the sense of 'any instrument for holding or restraining or fastening, a prop, support, or barrier'. In the *Ma-*

---

[1] Mbh. 1.1.152, Cr. Ed.; 9.57.17ff., Cal. Ed.

[2] Ibid., 9.55.ff.; 9.57.17ff., Cal. Ed. One binds up his hair, and puts on a breastplate and helmet in order to fight with a club. See 9.32.60ff., Cal. Ed. In 3.12.39ff., Cr. Ed., Bhīma and a Rākṣasa fight with uprooted trees.

[3] Ibid., 7.154.37.

[4] Ibid., *aśmalaguḍa*.

[5] Ibid., 3.21.32; 3.166.15. The St. Petersb. Dic. and Monier Williams only describe it as a kind of weapon. The word *śuṇḍa* also means to 'break' or 'crush'; see Monier Williams' Dic., s.v. A few scholars take the *bhuśuṇḍi* to be a firearm on the authority of very late texts; but the meaning is clearly impossible for the Epic, where it occurs as an ordinary projectile weapon with many more.

[6] Mbh. 3.268.5; 5.19.3. *Mudgara* is given by Hopkins, op. cit., p. 291, and Monier Williams as meaning a hammer; In Hindī, however, it denotes a heavy tapering club, a pair of which are used for exercise. These are the 'Indian clubs' of the Western museums.

[7] Cf. Monier Williams' Dictionary, s.v.

hābhārata, too, it has a variety of connotations, as for instance, 'a fetter, band, tie, thong, rein, trace, any instrument or apparatus, a bolt on the door, or oars or sails in a boat'. More specifically, however, *yantra* appears as a concomitant of fortfication, where it must be construed as a weapon of offence and defence. *Yantras* protect the cities of Indraprastha,[1] Dvārakā,[2] Ayodhyā [3] and Laṅkā.[4] In the *Rāmāyaṇa* we are told of stones hurled by *yantras*, which are also used for raining arrows on the enemy.[5] The noise produced by the *yantras* in action is a subject of special notice.[6] The tenacity of the *yantra* tradition in Indian literature is proof alike of its real existence and its value. But the utmost that can be reasonably claimed for it points to its being either a catapult, ballista or a huge bow which threw stones and heavy arrows at the enemy. Some of these *yantras* must have been strung like bows,[7] and their noise can be explained as the ringing flap of the string, the whizz of stones and missiles, and the crash and disorder in the ranks opposite. Whatever the exact nature of these contrivances, they were doubtless of simple construction and could not quickly cast many stones or arrows around, which may account for their comparative ineffectiveness.

That elephants and chariots also carried *yantras*, is proved by a few references;[8] but *yantras* in open battle seem to signify weapons in general. King *Ajātaśatru* of Magadha, a contemporary of the Buddha, used a new engine of war against the Vajjis, called the *mahāsilākaṇṭaga*,[9] which must have been a stone-hurling contrivance like those denoted by the Epic *yantras*.

An interesting weapon figuring in the Epics is called *śataghnī*.

---

1 Mbh. 1.199.33.

2 Ibid., 3.16.5.

3 Rām. Bāla, 5.10.11.

4 Ibid., Yuddha, 3.12ff.; Mbh. 3.268.4.

5 Rām. Yuddha, 3.12. Compare the Bible, 2nd Book of Chronicles, ch. 26, v. 15, which speaks of king Uzziah who 'made in Jerusalem engines, invented by cunning men, to be on the towers and upon the battlements, to shoot arrows and great stones withal.' The king is assigned to c. 766-740 B. C.

6 Cf. Mbh. 3.268.4, *karṇāṭṭayantradurdharṣā*.

7 Cf. Ibid., 15.23.9, Cal. Ed., *sajjayantrāyudhopetaiḥ*. The sound of the bow is compared to that of a *yantra* in Mbh. 14.77.26, *vicakarṣa dhanuḥ. . . yantrasyeveha śabdo 'bhun mahānstasya*, Cal. Ed.

8 Mbh. 7.122.84, Cr. Ed.; 15.23.9, Cal. Ed.

9 Raychaudhuri, Political History of Ancient India, 1953, Sixth Ed., p. 213.

Literally, it means a 'hundred-killer'; but we must beware of poetic epithets; even an ordinary hook is sometimes called an 'all-killer'. An analysis of the relevant data reveals that *śataghnīs* belonged to two particular categories easily described as large and small. We find them on the walls and gates of cities beside the *yantras*;[1] they often have wheels and spikes and bells. These *śataghnīs* must have been columns of wood or stone or metal, girded with spikes and usually provided with wheels for easy movement, which were hurled on the enemy trying to storm and scale the walls of a city. Their crash must have produced a great noise accompanied by some damage. But though poets talk of hundreds, not many could easily be got on top of the walls; hence their negligible impression on the result of an operation, despite the attention attracted by their size and display.

The smaller variety of *śataghnī* was used as an ordinary missile on the field of battle, and was held in the hand, like clubs, swords, and other weapons.[2] In the *Karṇa parva*, *śataghnīs*, along with other weapons, form the equipment of a hero's chariot,[3] and are occasionally said to be adorned with bells.[4] Bhīṣma is pelted by the Pāṇḍavas with *śataghnīs*,[5] which are elsewhere hurled together with clubs, pikes and swords.[6] The *Droṇa parva* speaks of Karṇa being covered with a shower of arrows, so that he looks like a *śataghnī* with numerous spikes.[7] The reference is clearly demonstrative of the shape, and possibly also the size of the larger variety of a *śataghnī*.

We have thus seen that the so-called *śataghnīs* were projectiles, whether large or small, hurled at the enemy in open battle as well as in siege warfare. Presumably, the smaller variety was not furnished with wheels found helpful in the case of larger specimens. Yet, if we sometimes hear of wheeled *śataghnīs* being flung in battle like the other missiles, we must attribute this to the poet's love of the miraculous; for he seems to imagine the Epic warriors hurling these colossal *śataghnīs* with an ease associated with javelin-throwing. The *śataghnī* stands in a class apart from the *yantra*;

---

1 Mbh. 1.199.33; Rām. Sundara, 2.21; yuddha, 3.14.23.
2 Mbh. 9.45. 109-10, Cal. Ed.
3 Ibid., 8.7.8, Cr. Ed.
4 Ibid., 8.10.32, *sakiṅkiṇīḥ*.
5 Ibid., 6.114.2.
6 Ibid., 3.22.2; cf. 7.131.34; 7.154.27.
7 Ibid., 7.108.40.

while the latter propels stones or arrows, the former is itself hurled as a missile.[1]

It is interesting to note a number of other objects used for purposes of offence and defence, even though some of them can hardly be classed as weapons. *Huḍa* as an implement of war is often associated with fortified defence,[2] and may have been a rod of metal used as a projectile.[3] Stones and firebrands of dry grass were also thrown on the enemy from the walls of a city.[4] And *śṛṅgikas* mentioned in the same context along with liquids and other substances, appear to have been hollow horns full of burning oil and other ingredients such as pepper(?) flung at the besiegers.[5] The ramparts of Laṅkā are protected by warriors equipped with earthen pots full of poisonous snakes and resinous powders, presumably burning.[6] Elsewhere, soldiers are armed with oil, treacle and sand,[7] presumably hot, and linen steeped in oil and clarified butter,[8] to be used clearly for hurling firebrands. They also carry crude instruments for seizing the hair of their opponents,[9] and ropes and nooses to add to their terror.[10] This strange assembly of rough and ready weapons only serves to remind us of the antiquity of the Epic tradition.

Warriors, in fact, fight with whatever they can lay their hands on. Sugrīva and Vāli fight with wood and stones;[11] and Arjuna attacks Kirāta with trees and rocks.[12] Stones as weapons are indeed fairly common, frequently heaped on the walls of cities,[13] and we hear of torrents of rocks in battle.[14] The *Droṇa parva* speaks of mountaineers, adepts in the art of fighting with stones, producing a thick shower of missiles.[15] Stones must have been both slung and

---

[1] Date, The Art of War in Ancient India, pp. 36,42, erroneously supposes that both *yantra* and *śataghnī* were used for hurling stones at the enemy.
[2] Mbh. 3.16.5; 3.268.4.
[3] See Monier Williams' Dic., s.v.
[4] Mbh. 3.16.6, *solkālātāvapothikā*.
[5] Ibid., 3.16.8, 9, *dravyairanekairvividhaiḥ*.
[6] Ibid., 3.268.4.
[7] Ibid., 5.152.5.
[8] Ibid., 5.152.7.
[9] Ibid., 5.152.5, *kacagraha*.
[10] Ibid., 5.152.4, *rajju* and *pāśa*; cf. 7.35.25.
[11] Ibid., 3.264.30.
[12] Ibid., 3.40.42.
[13] Ibid., 3.16.6; 3.268.4.
[14] Ibid., 3.23.10.
[15] Ibid., 7.97.29ff.

thrown by the hand. Balls [1] (*guḍa*) of metal or stone, to which the Epics refer, were hurled, presumably with the help of a sling.

It is needless to discuss the formidable list of the so called divine weapons, mere figments of the poet's imagination. The Epics, however, reveal a popular faith in the efficacy of magic and incantations; amulets designed to confer victory are worn, and weapons are often enlivened with charms and *mantras*. Though they help little in point of fact, it is interesting to note the practice of these tricks of faith.

The use of shields and protective armour is throughout in evidence. It is doubtful if the ordinary soldier of an army could afford an elaborate armour, though knights of rank almost invariably appear armed with a cuirass or breastplate, and arm-and-finger protectors.[2] Cuirasses or breastplates of copper, iron, silver and gold are not infrequently referred to as enriched with gems and diamonds.[3] It is most unlikely that cuirasses were made entirely of a metal so soft as gold, though, of course, as we learn, they were adorned or sometimes plated with gold.[4] Indeed, poetic flirtation with the precious metals makes them utterly commonplace. Armour of black iron decorated with gold is specifically mentioned.[5] In the *Virāṭa parva*, the Matsya king's armour is described as impenetrable, and 'decked with a hundred suns, a hundred circles, a hundred spots, and a hundred eyes'.[6] Despite, however, such epithets as 'impenetrable' or 'invulnerable', no armour is proof against the well shot shafts of a warrior. Much too often in the Epic, we find the coat of mail loosened, cut off and bored by powerful arrows, spears and other weapons.[7]

Chain-armour was also known and worn by both men and animals.[8] Poetic fancy, as usual, depicts it as made of gold. Reduced to reality, it must have been iron or copper, occasionally adorned with gold or silver.

---

1 Mbh. 7.154.37 has *aśmaguḍāḥ*.

2 *Sannaddhaḥ kavacī khaḍgī baddhagodhāṅgulitravān.*

3 Ibid., 1.26.41, *kavacāni vicitrāṇi vaidūryavikṛtāni*; 4.57.4; 4.57.7, *kavacānāṁ . . . tāmrarājatalohānāṁ*.

4 Ibid., 4.30.13 has *suvarṇapṛṣṭhaṁ sūryābhaṁ*.

5 Ibid., 4.49.15, *suvarṇakārṣṇāyasavarmanaddhā*; 4.30.10 has *savajrāyasagarbhaṁ tu kavacaṁ taptakāñcanaṁ*.

6 Ibid., 4.30.12; cf. 4.30.14.

7 Cf. 4.57.4; 6.44.30.

8 Ibid., 5.154.10, Cal. Ed., *rukmajālapraticchannā*; 6.19.31, Cal. Ed., *hemamayair jālair dīpyamānā ivācalāḥ*; mailed horses in 3.18.1; 4.30.16, Cr. Ed. Also see above, p. 42.

The arm-guard and the finger protector were worn by archers to protect their hands and fingers from the friction of the bow-string. Warriors also wore some kind of a helmet, called *śirastrāṇa* or 'head-protector', of metal, sometimes studded with precious stones, the exact shape of which it is not possible to visualise. They also often wore turbans of cloth, known as *uṣṇīṣa* [1] or *veṣṭana,* which must have effectively deadened the blows of weapons. Crowns or head-gears adorned with diamonds and garlands are also mentioned,[2] and Arjuna is called *kirīṭamālī.*[3] We do not know if the *kaṇṭhatrāṇa* or 'neck-protector' occasionally referred to, was part of the cuirass or the helmet, or a separate piece attached to one or both of them. At any rate, it seems to have served little practical purpose, if we are to draw any conclusion from the numberless heads so easily lopped off, often at one blow. The warriors also revelled in a jealous exhibition of their personal adornments, such as ear-rings, bracelets and armlets of gold, diamonds and garlands.[4] The ear-rings could possibly be seen dangling below the turban, but it appears that the hand-guard left that portion of the arm bare where bracelets and other ornaments were fastened to be displayed.

Tiger-skins covered and protected chariots,[5] but were also occasionally worn by men to serve as extra protection.[6] The *Śānti parva* mentions defensive armour of ox and serpent hide for elephants.[7] Many folds of ox-hide may have been used to protect the elephant's body; but the serpent-skin seems to be intended only for decorative purposes. Shields of leather called *carma* were popularly used. The sword and shield invariably go together in the descriptions of battle. A knight siezes his sword and shield when his bow fails him and his chariot is rendered useless. It seems as though the shield awaits its turn lying in the chariot, until he gives up the bow and arrow that must have occupied both his hands. It is possible, though we have no definite evidence, that a small shield was fastened to a warrior's fore-arm while he used

---

1 Mbh. 4.57.11.

2 Ibid., 3.170.35; 4.49.18.

3 Ibid., 4.19.18.

4 Ibid., 3.170.35; 4.49.18; 4.57.11; 6.17.17, *kāñcanāṅgadakeyūraiḥ*.

5 Cf. Ibid., 5.81.18.

6 Ibid., 4.50.4.

7 Ibid., 12.101.6.

the bow and arrow. *Śarāvara*, literally 'that which protects from arrows', is used specifically of a shield in the *Bhīṣma parva*,[1] but in connection with a sword. Shields of tiger-skin and ox-hide are often referred to as decorated with such devices as the sun, moon and stars.[2] *Phalaka*, presumably signifying a shield of wood or metal, distinguished from *carma* in the *Śānti parva*,[3] is described as held in the left hand elsewhere.[4]

Evolved through the tedious toil of many millennia, all these aids to early strife led to man's conquest of man and the spread of techniques and civilization, at a price paid in suffering associated with war.

---

[1] Mbh. 6.86.36, *nikṛṣya niśitaṁ khaḍgaṁ gṛhītvā ca śarāvaraṁ*; cf. 6.56.17, *suvarṇatārāgaṇabhūṣitāni śarāvarāṇi*; 7.13.66.

[2] Cf. Ibid., 6.83.30.

[3] Ibid., 12.101.8.

[4] Ibid., X. 8.55, *savye sa phalake bhṛśaṁ*. Hopkins, curiously enough, takes it to mean a sword in these passages. *Phalaka*, signifying a tablet or slab in general, is more naturally rendered as a shield. See St. Petersb. Lexicon and Monier Williams' Dic., s.v.

CHAPTER SIX

FORTS AND FORTIFICATIONS

In the history of defence and warfare, fortified sites played a role of key significance, until the invention of the aeroplane and the modern engines of destruction reduced their efficacy; but they yet remain, great and grim reminders of bygone battles. Forts sheltered towns and villages and all that they contained, commanded roads and rivers as well as the adjacent territory, and served as refuge against pressure of raiders and invaders. Even non-military people and those unfit for the field could help man the defences of a fort, while the enemy needed double the strength of the garrison to invest it. The beginnings of fortification in India can be traced as far back as the prehistoric age. At Kot Diji, fifteen miles south of Khairpur and 25 miles east of Mohenjodaro, a fortified town of pre-Indus date has been laid bare by recent excavation, 'with a strongly walled citadel armed with rectangular towers of stone and mud-brick'.[1] A burnt layer crowns the 'Kot Dijian' strata, a reminder, perhaps, of the site's destruction about 2400 B.C., when it was surmounted by an unfortified settlement of the Harappan type.[2]

At Kohtraṣ Buthi, in Sind, N. G. Majumdar [3] discovered a fortified site of the Amri culture, slightly earlier than the Harappan. The ruins occupy the top of a hill steep and inaccessible on three sides, but gradually sloping down to only ten feet above the surrounding plain on the south. As one goes up the southern slope, he comes across first a low rampart wall, and next a second wall, larger and stronger than the first. This latter wall is made of cyclopean masonry, and shows traces of four ruined bastions with an entrance on the south-east. Professor Piggott [4] likens the site to a 'promontory fort', and compares it with the fortifications on the Tharro hill, also in Sind. Here, too, the fortifications 'take the

---

[1] Wheeler, Early India and Pakistan, pp. 106-7; The Indus Civilization p. 15.

[2] Ibid.

[3] Majumdar, ASI., Annual Report, 1930-34, p. 102.

[4] Piggott, Prehistoric India, p. 77.

form of double walls, curved and of massive construction and 250 feet apart, cutting off the southern headland of the hill in true promontory-fort manner'. Amri Ware was found on the surface, but plain red ware allied to that of Harappā, was also in evidence.[1] Yet another Amri settlement in Sind, called Dhillanijo Kot, shows traces of a defensive wall surrounding the site.[2]

At Toji and Mazena-damb in South Baluchistan, two sites probably of the Kulli culture, Stein noted the indications of a possible defensive wall around the settlement, and similar walls probably stood at the Siah-damb of Jhau.[3] And at Mughal Ghundai, too, there are traces of a defensive wall to the settlement.[4]

Not long ago, Sir Mortimer Wheeler's fieldwork and excavation at Harappā and Mohenjodaro proved the existence of lofty citadels at the two sites. 'We now know that each of them was dominated by a massively fortified citadel, and must therefore have been subjected to autocratic or bureaucratic 'citadel rule', its precise form at present unknown and unlikely to be known until perhaps some happy discovery unlocks the Harappā script'.[5]

The defences at Harappā[6] fell roughly within the limits of a parallelogram, 460 yards by 215 yards, and there was a complex western gate-system with terraces designed for ceremonial purposes, and provided with guard-rooms at the outer angles. The main entrance was perhaps represented by the gateway on the northern side.

The great rampart of mud and mud-brick was designed as an embankment against the inroads of the flood water. Ten to twenty feet high, it helped raise the base of the defences proper above flood level. On the bund stood the main wall of mud-brick battered externally and internally, with a basal width of 40 feet and a height of about 35 feet. It was revetted with a facing of baked brick on the outside, battered back to a slope of 23-31 degrees from the vertical, and reinforced by rectangular towers or salients, some of which were carried higher than the main wall, as suggested by the surviving masses of mud-brick core.

---

[1] Piggott, op. cit. p. 78.
[2] Ibid.
[3] Ibid., p. 97.
[4] Ibid., p. 124.
[5] Wheeler, Ancient India, no. 3, p. 59.
[6] Ibid., pp. 64ff.; pl. XV; The Indus Civilization, pp. 20ff., and fig. 4 and plan facing p. 20.

A long period of wear and tear necessitated the reconstruction of the original baked brick revetment, which was considerably thickened in some places. This rebuilding with complete bricks instead of brick-bats was done in perfect fashion at the height of Harappā's glory. But in the next and the last phase of reconstruction, an additional salient was added to the north-west corner, and the two entrances of the western gate-system were wholly or partially blocked. The Harappans, as Wheeler said, were on the defensive.

The westernmost mound at Mohenjodaro was surrounded by similar defences.[1] It is actually surmounted by a Buddhist stūpa of the second century A.D., which has hindered a proper excavation of the site. The artificial platform of the citadel, built of mud-brick and mud, dates from the phase to which great public buildings such as the Bath and the Granary also belong. At or near its south-eastern corner the citadel mound includes a system of solid burnt-brick towers, yet to be fully explored.[2] The brickwork of the earliest of these towers, 31 x 22 ft., contemporary with the platform, was originally reinforced by horizontal timbers; it tended to crumble as the wood decayed, and was partially repaired with bricks. The Great Granary, also contemporary with the citadel mound, was the only other building so constructed. The later builders of the adjacent towers did not repeat the mistake. 'It would almost appear that the mound and its buildings are the work of a new immigrant regime accustomed to the traditions of mud-brick rather than of baked-brick architecture'.[3]

Two of the rectangular bastions at the south-eastern corner seem to have flanked a postern gate, which was later blocked and replaced by a platform with a parapet. About a hundred baked-clay missiles were found in the débris on this platform.[4] The towers, together with other foundations to their east yet uncovered, may be found to belong to a small fort or strong-point.

A baked-brick tower or salient, still standing 10 feet high, has been partially exposed on the west side of the citadel, to the south of the Granary. A small postern has also been identified to the north of this tower. The citadel platform had defences throughout its circuit, even though they were not as uniform as those of Harappā.

---

1 See Wheeler, The Indus Civilization, pp. 27ff., and fig. 6.
2 Ibid., pl. VI B.
3 Ibid., p. 30.
4 Ibid.

A small site of the Harappan culture, Ali Murad in Sind, was surrounded by a stone wall three to five feet thick, which enclosed an irregularly rectangular area including houses and at least one well.[1] It is not far from the Phusi Pass, opening from the Kirthar range on to the lowland, and the fortification seems to have been a normal provision for safety from enemies and robbers.[2]

At Sutkagen-dor in Makran, Stein found massive fortifications enclosing an area about 170 yards by 125 yards, in association with Harappan pottery.[3] The wall was built of roughly squared stone blocks in courses, 30 feet wide at the foot and with a vertical inner face, while the outer face was battered at an angle of 40 degrees. It must have been originally 20 to 25 feet high, and the whole site was indeed very strongly fortified. In the south-western corner, there were traces of a gateway only 8 feet wide, with probable flanking towers or guard-houses; buildings once stood both inside and outside this gateway. Sutkagen-dor must have been an important trading post, as providing contact with the sea-borne trade of the Persian Gulf and the Arabian Sea.[4]

Recent excavations at Kālībangan on the left bank of the Ghaggar in Northern Rājasthān have brought to light an important centre of the Harappan Civilization.[5] The larger mound revealed successive remains of ordinary houses. But the smaller mound contained a massive mud-brick platform, over which stood the relevant buildings. The latter mound perhaps represents a citadel, the location of which facing the general habitation area reminds one of both the Harappā and Mohenjodaro citadel-mounds. And

---

[1] N. G. Majumdar, Explorations in Sind, MASI., no. 48, 1934, pp. 89-90.

[2] Wheeler, op. cit., p. 48; Piggott, Prehistoric India, p. 173.

[3] Stein, An Archaeological Tour in Gedrosia, MASI., no. 43, 1931, pp. 60ff.; Archaeological Reconnaissances in North Western India and South Eastern Iran, London, 1937, pp. 70-71.

[4] Piggott, Prehistoric India, pp. 174, 210; cf. also Wheeler, The Indus Civilization, p. 48. George F. Dales, Jr., and his colleagues recently made a 500 mile survey of the Makran coast on behalf of the Pennsylvania University Museum, and confirmed that Sutkagen-dor was a port. Another Harappan site discovered by them, Sotka-koh or 'Burned Hill' about nine miles north of Pasni in the Shadi Kaur valley 'would have been in the ideal strategic position to control traffic between the coast and the interior.' It stood on top of a jagged natural outcrop and a 1600 ft. stone wall was traced along the eastern edge of the rock. The rest of the site is badly eroded. Cf. Antiquity, June 62, pp. 86-92; Sankalia, Prehistory and Protohistory in India and Pakistan, pp. 174-5.

[5] Indian Archaeology 1960-61, pp. 31-32; cf. The Illustrated London News, March 24, 1962, pp. 454-457.

if these two cities were the provincial capitals of a big empire, it is not impossible that Kālībangan also enjoyed a metropolitan status in the Sarasvatī valley.[1]

Walter A. Fairservis, Jr., asserts that religion was the intensifying factor that created and gave form to the Harappā civilization; Mohenjodaro was almost purely a ceremonial centre;[2] and the fortifications at Mohenjodaro and Harappā were presumably defences against floods only.[3] But his hypothesis does not bear scrutiny. The prehistoric fortifications at the two famous sites and elsewhere cannot be explained away as mere defences against floods. A man in his house is safer than a man in the open, and it does not require a great stretch of the imagination to seek safety behind a wall against an enemy's onslaught. That the walls also guarded against floods, does not by any means disprove the contemporary appreciation of their military value. Religion has been a vital factor in Indian life across the centuries, but it has always sought harmony with the political authority; the one could not fashion the pattern of existence without the other. Lofty citadels such as those of Harappā and Mohenjodaro, including great gateways and watchtowers, clearly bespeak authority as well as the need for defence against an alien enemy. The astonishing organisation and efficiency of urban life, well planned streets and drainage system, great granaries and coolies' barracks, alike betoken the whip of a coercive power that formulated the laws of civic life and ensured their observance. A certain measure of autocracy is plainly manifest in the scheme of affairs, and the citadels presuppose a regular organisation of defence, despite the poor quality of the Harappan weapons. Large round balls of baked clay and sling pellets of round and ovoid shape found in and around the enclosed area at Mohenjodaro,[4] leave little doubt that the fortifications stood as bulwarks of defence against the contingency of human invasion.

The numerous references to forts and fortifications in the *Ṛgveda* and the later Vedic literature were dismissed by earlier scholars

---

[1] Indian Archaeology 1960-61, pp. 31-32.

[2] Walter A. Fairservis, Jr., American Museum Novitates, published by the American Museum of Natural History, New York. No. 2055, November 17, 1961, The Harappan Civilization—New Evidence and More Theory, p. 18.

[3] Ibid., p. 15.

[4] Marshall, Mohenjodaro and the Indus Civilization, II, pp. 465, 466; Wheeler, The Indus Civilization, p. 30.

as being either mythical or at best referring to primitive earthworks reinforced by palisades or possibly rarely by stone. The later discovery, however, of prehistoric fortifications, lent a character and reality to the Ṛgvedic *purs* and *durgas* that had never been visualised before. And the gap that yawned between Harappā and the later fortified sites, has been considerably narrowed by the archaeological labours of recent years. The advent of the Aryans in India synchronises with the death or destruction of the cities of the Indus valley. Some of the inhabitants of these cities were probably the Dasyus and Dāsas of the *Ṛgveda*, proto-Australoids with dark skins and flat noses, worshippers of the phallus—natural enemies of the Aryan intruder.

Indra, the Aryan battle-god, goes on 'from fight to fight intrepidly, destroying fort after fort with strength'.[1] He overthrows the non-Aryan kings and rends their forts 'as age consumes a garment.'[2] He is the great leveller of the Dāsas' towns;[3] and all the circumstantial evidence, as Sir Mortimer Wheeler remarks, seems to brand him as the author of the destruction of great cities of the Harappan epoch. A verse of the *Ṛgveda*, describing how he slays the noseless Dasyus, and in their home overthrows the hostile speakers,[4] reminds one of people massacred in their homes and streets at Mohenjodaro. And Hariyūpīya, mentioned in the *Ṛgveda* as the scene of an Aryan victory, may be none other than Harappā itself.[5] This, though, is a mere conjecture, and proof is yet distant. Agni, too, like Indra, figures as a fort-destroyer,[6] and indeed helps him reduce ninety castles of the Dāsas.[7] And the myth of Indra killing a demon to free the pent-up waters may probably signify the destruction of the river dams constructed by the Indus people, so that the waters turned against them.[8]

---

[1] RV. I.53.7; cf. I.32.6; I.33.12; I.61.5; I.63.7; I.130.7; I.131.4; I.174.2; II.20.7, 8; III.34.1; IV.30.20, etc.

[2] Ibid., IV.16.13; cf. I.53.8, 9; I.54.6; II.14.6.

[3] Ibid., I.103.3. The word *pur* in the *Ṛgveda* definitely connotes a fortified site, but for the sake of literary style, we occasionally render it as 'castle', 'town' or 'city' in our text.

[4] Ibid. V.29.10.

[5] Ibid., VI.27.5; Wheeler, The Indus Civilization, p. 20; cf. B. B. Roy, JBORS., March 1928, pp. 129-30; R. C. Majumdar and others in 'An Advanced History of India', London, 1946, p. 26; Kosambi in JBBRAS., 26, p. 56.

[6] RV. VI.16.39; VII.6.2.

[7] Ibid., III.12.6.

[8] Piggott, Prehistoric India, p. 262; Kosambi, loc. cit., p. 49.

We can now understand the nature of the forts and strongholds (*pur, durga*) [1] described in the *Ṛgveda* as made of *ayas* [2] and of stone.[3] The epithet *āmā* [4] may sometimes refer to unbaked (literally 'raw') brick walls. The word *dehī* [5] is used in the *Ṛgveda*, in the sense of ramparts or defensive walls, with palisades and a ditch. And the *Atharva Veda* uses *vapra* [6] for 'rampart'. Forts are described as 'broad' (*pṛthvī*) and wide (*urvī*),[7] or as consisting of a hundred walls,[8] even in the *Ṛgveda*; and the term *mahāpura*, 'great fort', occurs in the *Yajur Veda Saṁhitās* and the *Brāhmaṇas*.[9] The view of Pischel and Geldner[10] that there were towns with wooden walls and ditches in the Vedic period, like Pāṭaliputra of a later day as known to Megasthenes and the Pāli texts, does not appear altogether improbable.

The significance of the autumnal forts mentioned in the *Ṛgveda*,[11] is somewhat difficult to explain. They must have served to guard the people against floods and human attack during autumn. But, as floods do not constitute a regular feature of the autumn, the forts presumably served their primary purpose of defence against man during the cool season of campaigns and predatory activity. This possibly explains the epithet 'autumnal' as applied to the Vedic fortifications.

The *Ṛgveda* mentions the *pūrpati*, 'lord of the fort'.[12] He may have been a ruler or governor,[13] or a regular officer, like the *grāmaṇī* at another level.[14] Macdonell and Keith hold that he was the chief of a fort under attack.[15] It was, as we know, a time of troubles and insecurity; sudden attacks and regular raids presented a permanent source of anxiety; and we should not be surprised if the *pūrpati*

---

1 Both these words are common in the RV. For full list of their occurrence see Grassmann, Wörterbuch, s. vv.
2 Ibid., I.58.8; II.20.8; X.101.8.
3 Ibid., IV.30.20.
4 Ibid., II.35.6.
5 Ibid., VI.47.2; VII.6.5; Vedic Index, I, pp. 379, 539.
6 AV. VII.71.1.
7 RV. I.189.2.
8 Ibid., I.166.8; VII.15.14, *śatabhuji*.
9 TS. VI.2.3.1; KS. 24.10; MS. 3.8.1; AB. I.23.2; Gopatha Br. 2.2.7.
10 Vedische Studien, I.22, 23.
11 *Śāradīḥ*, RV. I.131.4; I.174.2.
12 Ibid., I.173.10.
13 Muir, OST. V, p. 456.
14 See below, p. 142.
15 Vedic Index, s.v.

was the commander of a permanent garrison, the custodian of the fort's defence.

Forts were reduced by siege (*upasad*) and effective blockade,[1] and sometimes finally captured by breaching the walls (*prabhid*) and assault. The *pur-cariṣṇū* of a Ṛgvedic passage may have been some kind of a battering ram used in assaulting a fort.[2] Fire doubtless played an important part in siege operations.[3] Arrows tipped with flame [4] must have been used to set fire to enemy strongholds. The *Taittirīya Saṁhitā* speaks of the three citadels of the Asuras cleft by a shaft, whose point was Agni.[5] Agni is not infrequently described as a destroyer of forts. The role of fire in war is well illustrated in a Ṛgvedic passage cited below:

> 'Transfix the fiends with darts that burn most fiercely.
> Forth go in rapid flight thy whirling weapons:
> follow them closely, glowing in thy fury.
> Spread with thy tongue the winged flames, O Agni;
> unfettered, cast thy firebrands all around thee'.[6]

And again:

> '. . . in kindled fire he [Indra] burnt up all their weapons,
> And made him rich with kine and carts and horses'.[7]

The *Atharva Veda* similarly speaks of 'tongues of fire' and 'tufts of smoke' left in the trail of a conquering army.[8]

That all the forts referred to in the Vedic literature were not Dāsa strongholds, is proved alike by the internal evidence of the

---

[1] TS. VI.2.3.1; ŚB. III.4.4.3-5; AB. I.23; Gopatha Br. II.2.7.
[2] cf. Vedic Index, II. p. 417.
[3] RV. VII.5.3.
[4] Ibid., I.66.4.
[5] TS. VI.2.3.1, 2; cf. KS. XXIV.10; XXV.1; Kapisthala KS. XXXVIII. 3.4; MS. III.8.1, 2; ŚB. III.4.4.3-20, 26, 27; AB. I.23, 25.
[6] RV. IV.4.1, 2; cf. TS. I.2.14.1.
[7] RV. II.15.4.
[8] AV. XI.9.19; cf. TS. I.4.46. The Assyrians and the ancient Greeks also made use of fire for both attack and defence, as we learn from old bas-reliefs and the tales of Homer. At the siege of Plataea in 429 B. C., the Plataeans covered the woodwork of their fortifications with hides and skins in order to lessen the effect of the flaming missiles of the Peloponesian attackers. The Spartans on the same occasion piled large bundles of wood against the city walls, saturated them with a mixture of sulphur and pitch, and set them on fire. (W. Y. Carman, A History of Firearms, London, 1955, pp. 1, 2.)

Vedas and the spadework of the archaeologist. The *Ṛgveda* contains repeated prayers to Agni to preserve the faithful with 'forts of *ayas*',[1] and to 'be unto us a wide, broad ample castle'.[2] The excavations at Kauśāmbī have brought to light the impressive fortifications of the town famous in antiquity. The mounds of the ancient rampart describe a peripheral circuit of roughly four miles, and, girdled by a moat, form a semi-circle with the Yamunā as the base.[3] Eleven gateways, five of which were the principal ones, pierce the eastern, northern and western sides of the rampart, which was reinforced by a series of towers and salients at regular intervals.[4] Incidentally, a passage of the *Kāṭhaka Upaniṣad*[5] uses *ekādaśa-dvāra* as an epithet of *pura*. Macdonell and Keith[6] point out that the passage in question is metaphorical like another in the *Śvetāśvatara Upaniṣad*;[7] the number of gates depends on the nature of the body, and does not indicate the shape or size of cities. They seem to forget that the metaphor would become inept and inaccurate, if the cities had invariably one gate only. The passages of the *Śatapatha Brāhmaṇa*[8] cited in their support do not necessarily prove that the city had one gate alone; they simply refer to an open or closed gate of the stronghold, and do not by any means preclude the possibility of more gates than one.

The first defences at Kauśāmbī came into being in SP. I.3, two structural periods before the arrival of the Painted Grey Ware. 'A rampart of mud with sloping sides, revetted with a burnt brick wall battered back to about 30 to 40°, of which the courses are laid in the so called English bond, leaving footings in successive courses, reinforced by bastions and towers square in plan, are elements of construction strongly reminiscent of the Harappan citadel'.[9] The earliest moat was dug in SP. II.5, before the N.B.P. Ware made its appearance.[10] We may note here that the *Śatapatha Brāhmaṇa*[11]

---

[1] RV. I.58.8.
[2] Ibid., I.189.2; cf. TS. I.1.14.4; VII.16.10.
[3] G.R. Sharma, The Excavations at Kauśāmbī, 1957-59, p. 24; pl. 5.
[4] Ibid., The text of the book does not clearly specify the exact periods of the gates' construction.
[5] Kāṭhaka Up., II.5.1.
[6] Vedic Index, I, p. 540, n. 13.
[7] Śvetāśvatara Up. III. 18, *nava-dvāra-pura*, 'the citadel of nine gates'.
[8] ŚB. XI.1.1.2, 3.
[9] G. R. Sharma, loc. cit., p. 41.
[10] Ibid., pp. 29, 39.
[11] ŚB. VII.1.1.13.

knows of the moat as part of the defence architecture. The defences from SP. I.3 up to SP. III.12, followed a similar pattern, but during SP. III.11, a curved entrance was constructed, enclosing a corbelled underground passage.[1] The changes effected in the subsequent periods of rebuilding do not form part of the present study. The latest excavations at the site have, however, led to the discovery of a stone fortress-palace of the old kings of Kauśāmbī.[2] Standing on the Yamunā in the south-west corner of the ancient walled city, the palace occupied an area of 1033 feet x 492 feet. The level of the area was raised by building a 8¼ ft. high platform of mud-blocks and mud-bricks. The northern wall, about 427 feet in length and 19 feet in width, was built of stone set in lime of very fine quality.[3] The core consists of random rubble with well-dressed stones providing the facings of the two sides. This wall was joined at its eastern and western ends by two return walls,[4] and had a circular tower at each junction, with a rectangulai one in the middle. The circular stone towers had a diametei of about 26 feet, and the central oblong tower, added later, measured about 15 feet in width and depth.[5]

Three main stages of architectural evolution are discernible. The earliest building has nearly the same plan as the later ones, but the walls are built entirely of random rubble, huge stones being laid in line.The sides ot the wall were poss'bly plastered. Dıessed stones mark the second phase of constructional activity; and bıick core and stone facings characterise the rebuilding of the third phase after an extensive destruction of the palace. The first structure antedates the N. B. P. Ware, and has been tentatively dientified with the palace of king Udayana and his descendants.[6]

We must not fail to recall here the famous fortifications of Rājgir. The remains of the fortress may easily date back to the sixth century B.C., if not earlier still.[7] Local tradition identifies

---

1 G. R. Sharma, op. cit., pp. 32, 33, 44.

2 Indian Archaeology 1960-61, pp. 33-35, reports on the discovery of the fortress palace.

3 Ibid,, pl. LV. A.

4 Ibid., pl. LV. B.

5 Ibid., pl. LVI. A.

6 Udayana was a contemporary of the Buddha.

7 Limited excavation within the very big site has yielded the N. B. P. Ware at the lowest level at one point, and a preceding layer of 'a medium to coarse red ware mixed with a few fine black sherds' at another. See Indian Archaeology, 1953-54, p. 9, and 1954-55, p. 16.

the site with Girivraja, the capital of king Jarāsandha according to the *Mahābhārata*.[1] And the Buddhist texts tell us how king Bimbisāra left the old city in order to build a new one at the foot of the hills. Girivraja, no doubt, belongs to the pre-Bimbisārian epoch of Indian history. The town nestled in the lap of an uneven valley with hills that served as walls on all sides. And this natural defence was further strengthened by artificial fortifications. Two lines of walls run round the city; the inner line measures 4¼ miles in length, while the outer line goes up and down the Vaibhāragiri, Sonagiri, Udayagiri, and along the southern range of the hills to Giriyak, and then back at intervals over Śailagiri, Chaṭhāgiri, Ratnagiri and Vipulagiri. 'The faces of the walls are built of massive undressed stones between three and five feet in length, carefully fitted and bonded together, while the core between them is composed of smaller blocks carefully cut and laid with chips or fragments of stone, packing the interstices between them'.[2] 'On the west of Sonagiri, and on the Vaibhāragiri, Vipulagiri and Ratnagiri, the walls are much ruined and seldom rise higher than 7 or 8 feet. From the fact that whenever the height of between 11 and 12 feet is reached, the walls are invariably finished off with a course of small stones, and that there are no fallen blocks of stone lying near, we may assume that this was the original height of the massive masonry described above. Above this sub-structure, there was no doubt a superstructure composed either of smaller stone-work or of bricks baked or unbaked, or possibly of wood and stone or brick combined'. The thickness of the fortifications on the various hills varies from 14 feet to 17 feet and 6 inches. Bastions were added to the outside of the walls to reinforce them at important points. Sixteen of them have been discovered, but there may have been more. They are solid rectangular structures measuring in plan 47 to 60 feet long by 34 to 40 feet broad. Rising to the same height as the wall, they were doubtless provided with superstructures that have vanished with time.[3] The outer walls are also characterised by stairs or ramps built in the thickness of the wall along its inner face, to

---

[1] Mbh. 2.18.30; 2.19.2ff., describes how Kṛṣṇa, Arjuna and Bhīma see the city of Girivraja from the Gorathagiri hill. The city is said to be protected by the hills of Vaihāra, Varāha, Vṛṣabha, Ṛṣigiri and Caitya-giri, connected with one another, besides fortifications.

[2] ASI. Annual Report, 1905-6, pp. 88-89.

[3] Ibid., pp. 89-90.

provide access to the top. The nine ramps discovered so far measure roughly 5 feet 6 inches wide and 15 feet long.

Separate watch-towers erected at various prominent points on the hills, add to the efficacy of the defences. Two of these stand on the Vaibhāra hill, four on the Vipula hill, and one on the easternmost peak of the Ratnagiri.[1] The defences of old Rājgir cannot fail to remind one of the chalcolithic fortresses of North-western India and testify to the sagacity and strategical considerations of the ancients in the choice of a suitable site. Was the prehistoric tradition continuous? The discoveries of the future will furnish a definitive answer.

G. R. Sharma explored the site of Unchadih between 20 to 30 miles east of Allahābād. He found clear traces of a fortified habitation, 170 x 110 feet, with corner-towers—a miniature model of Kauśāmbī. The rampart was 30 feet high and faced with bricks on the outer side. There were signs of a moat about 25 feet wide, with watch-towers on its outer side. Unchadih has Painted Grey Ware of the Kauśāmbī type, and a few specimens are identical with those associated with the early periods of the Kauśāmbī defences.[2]

Eighteen miles to the south of Allahābād is the little fortified site of Bhītā, about 400 yards square, which may have been the Vichi or Vicīgrāma mentioned on certain sealings found there.[3] The presence of the N. B.P. Ware points to the antiquity of the site.

In the Bareilly district of U.P., the ruins of Ahicchatrā, the capital of North Pāñcāla in antiquity and mentioned in the *Mahābhārata*, dominate the plain around with lofty ramparts 3½ miles in circuit. Excavations in 1940-41 revealed two successive earthen ramparts below a stout wall of baked brick. Painted Grey Ware was found both below and within the earlier rampart, which can easily be placed earlier than the fifth century B.C.[4]

Excavations at the Garh Kālikā mound on the outskirts of Ujjain have laid bare the mud fortifications of the ancient town, flanked by a moat on two sides, and by the river Śiprā on the other two. The colossal rampart is contemporaneous with the first period of the site's occupation, ascribed to c. 700-500 B.C.[5] A sherd of Painted

1 ASI., Annual Report, 1905-6, pp. 89-90.
2 Indian Archaeology 1959-60, p. 46.
3 Wheeler, Early India and Pakistan, p. 128.
4 Ibid., pp. 131-132.
5 Indian Archaeology 1957-58, p. 34.

Grey Ware found in the core of the rampart points to its possible associations with the users of that type.[1] The rampart encloses an area measuring roughly 1 x 3/4 mile, and has a maximum extant height of 42 feet.[2] Built of yellow and black earth with a gentle slope on the inner side, it was 245 feet broad at the base.[3] And a moat, excavated on the east and south, connected with the river on the north and west, provided a girdle of water as a further barrier.[4] The western or river-side wall was reinforced with wooden logs and sleepers during Pd. I itself, the fortifications there measuring more than 350 feet in breadth.[5]

Though the early Aryans were not used to city life, towns must have soon sprung up, nestling under the protection of their forts; we hear of Āsandīvant,[6] Kāmpīla,[7] Ayodhyā[8] and Kauśāmbī;[9] and Pāṇini refers to town-planning, forts and ramparts, moats, gates and watch-towers.[10] The evidence of archaeology allied to that of literature, proves beyond doubt the great burgeoning of civic life with regular defence structures in the Ganges valley and beyond, between c. 1000-300 B.C.

The *Nikāyas* furnish a further corroboration of the Vedic and archaeological evidence. Walled and battlemented towns are now and then referred to in the discourses of the Buddha to provide glimpses of fortified defence lulling kings and their subjects into a repose of fancied security. The *Dīgha Nikāya* alludes to a border city defended by strong ramparts and towers, and provided with a single gate; a clever and expert watchman stationed by the king admits men only when they are well known, and refuses entry to all strangers.[11] One gathers the impression that strategic towns on the border were usually fortified, for they held the key to the interior of a kingdom. The *Saṁyutta Nikāya* speaks of a city with iron walls,[12] while the *Aṅguttara* specifies the seven requisites of

---

1 Indian Archaeology., 1956-57, p. 20.
2 Ibid., fig. 9 on p. 21, sketch plan.
3 Ibid., 1957-58, p. 34.
4 Ibid., 1956-57, p. 20.
5 Ibid., 1957-58, p. 34.
6 Vedic Index, I, p. 72.
7 TS. VII. 4.19; MS. III.12.20.
8 AB. VII.3.1.
9 ŚB. XII.2.2.13; Gopatha Br. I.2.24; AB. VIII.14.
10 V. S. Agravala, India as known to Pāṇini, p. 137.
11 Dīgha, II.146; cf. Aṅguttara, V.194, 195, *dovārika*.
12 Saṁyutta, II. 182, implying strength.

a fortress, as also the four kinds of supplies necessary for its maintenance.[1] A pillar aloft in a king's citadel symbolises strength and stability; a road and a moat around the citadel make it more unassailable still;[2] while an armoury of swords and spears ensures the supply of weapons to the garrison, including elephant-drivers, horsemen, charioteers, bowmen, standard-bearers, billeting officers, soldiers of the supply corps, the king's sons, storm troops, warriors in cuirasses, and home-born slaves. The intelligent and resourceful gate-keeper keeps out all strangers; the rampart is high and wide, and covered with a coat of plaster. And great stores of grass, wood and water, rice and corn, sesame, beans, vetches and cereals, and medicines, including *ghee*, fresh butter, oil, honey, sugar and salt, are vital to withstand the rigours of siege.

The Epics too, as one would expect, support and supplement the information derived from other sources. The *Mahābhārata* refers to fortifications not infrequently, while the Rāma-Rāvaṇa story revolves round the siege of Laṅkā. Both *vapra* and *caya* occur in the Epic in the sense of earthen ramparts,[3] but more elaborate citadels are not wanting. Thus the *Ādi parva* [4] describes the town of Indraprastha, surrounded by a wide moat, lofty walls and numerous gates, each furnished with a couple of doors. An abundant stock of weapons promises a stout defence; the battlements bristle with sharp hooks and *śataghnīs* and other machines (*yantra*) of war; and the walls are manned along their length. Elsewhere,[5] Nārada asks Yudhiṣṭhira if his forts are provided with treasure, food, water, weapons and other contrivances of defence, as also with masons and bowmen.

The *Āraṇyaka parva* furnishes an interesting account of defence against siege.[6] Gateways and pennons, walls and watch-towers, characterise the town of Dvāravatī, fully provided with stocks of food, weapons and other devices for hurling fire and stone on the enemy. The tramp of the approaching enemy rouses the inmates to a sense of danger; all the mimes, dancers and singers are driven

---

[1] Aṅguttara, IV.106, 107.

[2] The moat and road are both attested by archaeology; cf. Kauśāmbī and Ujjain; see above, pp. 127-28, 130.

[3] Hopkins, op. cit., p. 175.

[4] Mbh. 1.199.29ff.

[5] Ibid., II.5.25, *dhanadhānyāyudhodakaiḥ, śilpidhanurdharaiḥ*. Cf. also Rāmāyaṇa, Ayodhyā, 100.53, where Rāma asks Bharata a similar question.

[6] Mbh. 3.16.3ff.

out of the city, and drinking is prohibited by proclamation in a bid to stamp out carelessness and frivolity. Bridges (*saṁkrama*) are destroyed and boats forbidden to ply; trenches around the town are spiked with poles at the bottom, and the surrounding area rendered uneven and difficult of access. No one leaves or enters the town without giving the requisite sign (*mudrā*). Such precautions are impressive even by modern standards. The enemy replies with a blockade of all the roads and passages leading to the town.

The *Rāmāyaṇa* speaks of the firm gates of Ayodhyā secured by cross-bars (*argala*).[1] Kiṣkindhā's golden gates, moat and citadel are also described.[2] And the fortifications of Laṅkā are repeatedly mentioned.[3] Hanumān tells Rāma how Rāvaṇa's soldiers defend the city furnished with four huge gates and four bridges across the moat running round the town.[4] The gates and bridges are provided with the usual *yantras* and *śataghnīs*. Hanumān adds that he has broken the bridges, covered the moat, set fire to Laṅkā, and dragged down the citadel. The use of fire in siegecraft is very important, and thatched roofs were often plastered with mud to make them reasonably proof against that danger.[5]

We must make a due allowance for the exuberance of the poet and possible additions to the little details of the various passages; but the view that all the descriptions of solid walls and watchtowers to be found in the Epics are late interpolations, justifiable perhaps when it was formulated,[6] has clearly had its day. Hopkins says that the *Rāmāyaṇa* contains not exact descriptions of fortifications, but standing epithets and set formulae applied to the various towns in the text with but slight modifications.[7] It may indeed be perfectly true that the poet followed a fixed pattern in describing the cities figuring in a story; but it does not follow that a model never existed, and that solid walls and bastions found

---

[1] Rām. Bāla, 6.28; cf. Ayodhyā, 100.40, *dṛḍhadvārām*.

[2] Ibid., Kiṣkindhā, 14.5, *taptakāñcanatoraṇām*; 31.27, *prākāra* and *paridhā*.

[3] Ibid., Araṇya, 48,11, *prākāreṇa parikṣiptā*; yuddha, 39.21, *gopurairuccaiḥ*; Sundara, 2.14ff.

[4] Ibid., Yuddha, 3.6ff. Compare Mbh. 3.268.2ff., where the Laṅkā fortifications are described. The warriors guarding the walls hold earthen pots full of poisonous snakes, resinous powders and other combustible material.

[5] Cf. Hopkins, op. cit., p. 178, n.

[6] Ibid., p. 175. n.

[7] Ibid., p. 174, n.

their way into the Epics only at a later day. Words are superfluous; the evidence of archaeology brooks no refutation. We now know that both earthwork fortifications and masonry walls defended the Indian towns of old, long before the rise of the Epics, and indeed continued to do so right into the modern period.[1]

Elephants were used for battering down walls and gateways, as we know from their epithet *purabhettāraḥ*.[2] The *yantras* so often described were presumably arrow-and-stone scattering contrivances.[3] While some of these *yantras* were furnished with bowstrings, others may have been catapults. In the Epics, however, these mechanisms do not seem to play any significant part commensurate with their prominence in the accounts of fortifications. They do not inflict damage serious enough to deserve specific mention or affect the outcome of battle.

---

[1] Two early fortified sites of the 3rd and 2nd century B. C., later than those described earlier, Jaugada (Indian Archaeology, 1956-57, pp. 30, 31), and Śiśupālgarh (Ancient India, no. 3, pp. 62ff.; Wheeler, Early India and Pakistan, pp. 134, 135, fig. 29, pl. 29.) have been brought to light in Eastern India.

[2] Mbh. 2.54, 10.

[3] See above, pp. 112-13.

CHAPTER SEVEN

ORDER AND ORGANISATION—THE EVIDENCE OF GROWTH

The discovery of impressive citadels at the centres of the Harappan civilization suggests the presence of a ruling aristocracy whose functions must have included the inevitable burden of defence. Increase in wealth leads to the formation of classes within a community, while the threat of outward looking neighbours with expanding populations makes the emergence of war leaders essential and even unavoidable. The vast extent and singular uniformity of the Harappan culture itself owed something to aggressive excursions. If it was an empire, it must have had the requisite backing of force; the citadels must have guarded both against internal strife and external invasion.[1] Though more palpable proof is lacking, we can nevertheless imagine the existence of some kind of a fighting order.

The literature of the Aryans testifies to the evolution and growth of a military hierarchy, which also determined, to no mean extent, the nature of their secular administration. The Vedic evidence proves beyond doubt that the office of the king, the supreme commander in battle, grew out of warfare. Indra is the divine prototype of the idolised leader of war, the saviour and conqueror, who rises to kingship. Says the *Ṛgveda*:

> 'See this abundant wealth he possesses, and put your trust in Indra's hero vigour.
> He found the cattle and he found the horses, he found the plants, the forests and the waters'.[2]

Is it unreasonable, therefore, if they elevate him to royalty, 'the hero who in all encounters overcomes, most eminent for power, destroyer in the conflict, fierce and exceeding strong, stalwart and full of vigour'? [3] The *Taittirīya Saṁhitā* speaks of the conflict

---

1 See Wheeler, The Indus Civilization, pp. 57, 101.

2 RV. I.103.5.

3 Ibid., VIII.35.17; cf. SV. IV.II.4.1; AB. VIII.4.12. For Indra as the prototype and guardian of kingship, see R. N. Dandekar, Vṛtrahā Indra, ABORI, vol. 31, 1950, p. 53, f. n. 2.

between the gods and the Asuras, wherein the former held on to Indra, the strongest, as their leader.[1] The *Aitareya Brāhmaṇa* mentions the defeat of the gods at the hands of the Asuras. 'Through our lack of a king they conquer us', said the gods, 'let us make a king'. They made Soma king, and with him as their leader, they conquered all the quarters.[2] True, 'the kingship originates in military necessity, and derives its validity from consent'.[3] Another passage in the *Taittirīya Saṁhitā* describes 'the strong who is dread in battle contest', to whom 'all the people bowed in reverence'.[4] And the *Atharva Veda* [5] records the king's prayer that he may be

> 'A rival-destroying bull, conquering royalty, overpowering, that I may bear rule over these heroes and the people'.

The king is here a great hero, and there is a clear distinction between the warriors and the people. In another text, a Brāhmaṇa is expressly stated to be unsuitable for kingship.[6] The king is the summit of the *kṣatra*;[7] he is the protector of his people.[8] The clashing interests of the people were harmonised by the surrender of all to an independent authority less ethereal than a mythical deity; and the mortal king succeeded better with his priestly advisers in ensuring the security of his followers.[9] The Aryan invasion of India led to the growth of the monarchic element, just as it did also in the case of Greece.[10]

The most important function of the king, therefore, was to fight in order to protect his own people as well as to retain and enhance his own position. Thus, the *Atharva Veda* addresses the monarch: 'of lion-aspect, do thou devour all the clans (*viś*); of tiger-aspect, do thou beat down the foes; sole chief, having Indra as companion, having conquered, seize thou on the enjoyments of them that play the foe'.[11] That the king fought and led his army in person,

---

1 TS. II.4.2.1.; cf. KS. X. 10; MS. II.5.10.
2 AB. I.14.
3 Beni Prasad, Theory of Government in Ancient India, 1927, p. 15.
4 TS. III.4.4.1.
5 AV.I.29.6 . . . *vīrāṇām virājāni janasya ca.*
6 ŚB. V.1.1.12.
7 AV. IV.22.2.
8 RV. III.43.5, *gopājanasya*; IX. 35.5, *janasya gopatiḥ.*
9 Cf. AV. VI.98.2; MS. IV.12.2.
10 Vedic Index, II, p. 210. Cf. also the German invasion of England.
11 AV. IV.22.7.

is amply demonstrated by the famous battle of the ten kings in the *Ṛgveda*, and the warlike deeds of monarchs like Divodāsa, Sudās, and Trasadasyu. According to the *Kauṣītaki Upaniṣad*, King Pratardana met his death on the field of battle.[1] In the *Rājasūya* ceremony the king is called 'the sacker of forts.'[2] The *Taittirīya Brāhmaṇa* refers to the Kuru-Pañcāla kings carrying out raids in the season of dews, i.e. in winter after the rains.[3] The terms *udāja* and *nirāja* point to the Vedic king's share of the booty of war.[4]

War thus led to the growth of states and governments. Even peace was armed; military preparedness was imperative to avoid or resist an enemy's strike. The king became the keystone of the military and administrative arch. He rose from power to power and even assumed despotic airs,[5] while the semblance of popular choice and acceptance was yet retained. The concept of universal conquest was perhaps born with the battle of the ten kings, in which the victorious side was led by Sudās. The horse-sacrifice begins as early as the *Ṛgveda*[6] and becomes the symbol of paramountcy in later literature. The universal ruler is described in the *Aitareya Brāhmaṇa* as sole ruler (*ekarāṭ*) and possessed of the whole earth (*sārvabhauma*) bordered by the ocean.[7] The *Śatapatha Brāhmaṇa* reveals the struggles for suzerainty among the monarchs of old, when they delighted in arresting the progress of each other's sacrificial horse.[8] 'Indra shall conquer, he shall not be conquered; overlord among kings shall he rule; in all conflicts shall he be a protector, that he may be reverenced and honoured'.[9] That is how overlordship arose out of war, with its corollaries, heredity and despotism.

---

[1] Kauṣ. Up., 3.1.

[2] *purāṁ bhettā*; Vedic Index, s.v. *rājan*. In RV. X.75.4, we have the simile of a warrior-king leading his army's wings. Cf. ŚB. XIII.2.2.2.

[3] TB. I.8.4.1-2. The Hittites, for example, campaigned in spring and summer. Gurney, The Hittites, p. 108.

[4] Cf. Vedic Index, II, pp. 212, 418. There are many references to the distribution of booty; cf. RV. VII.32.7; AV. VI.66.3. An epigraph from a relief depicting the conquest of Lachish says that Sennacherib, the king of Assyria, sat upon a *nimedu* throne and passed in review the booty taken from Lachish. Some such review may be conjectured for the Vedic period.

[5] Cf. RV. IV.42, the boast of Trasadasyu, 'I am Indra, I am Varuṇa'. For the king's divinity, see ŚB. V.3.3.12.

[6] RV. I.162; 163.

[7] AB. VIII.15.

[8] ŚB. XIII.5.4.19-22.

[9] TS. II.4.14.2.

The requirements of a conquering people evoked not only the monarch, but also a whole military aristocracy. As smaller principalities coalesced into growing kingdoms, the dispossessed potentates joined the ranks of this aristocracy, and made war and government their chief occupation. The Ṛgvedic battle of the ten kings was the end of the so-called pure Aryan; it was presumably won by a faction of the Aryans and earlier Indians together, and serves to demonstrate the acceptance and absorption of the nobles and princes of local extraction into the new order. And the addition of the king's chief retainers, with military duties, to the ranks of the princely nobility, helped to stem the tide of enemy attacks as well as attempts at local rebellion. All this is not to say that the people did not fight; but they constituted only the rank and file, leaving the leadership with the members of the nobility. Even in the *Ṛgveda* the people are once described as averse to war, peace being their normal rule.[1] The generality of their order soon became too immersed in trade and agriculture to feel inclined to take up arms in defence of their kingdom, much less for aggression. The aristocracy aggrandised itself at their expense, in return, of course, for the protection it afforded them; and in this it was helped by the collaboration of the priests, who also stood to gain by such an arrangement. The growing specialisation of functions is clearly discernible in the *Ṛgveda*, where the three higher orders are specified,[2] and the famous though late *Puruṣa-sūkta* contemplates the division of society into four orders of men.[3] Faith in the divine origin of the four orders must have taken root before the end of the Ṛgvedic period, but there is little or no indication of an inflexible hereditary caste. *Rājanya*, the general term for royal families, mentioned first in the *Puruṣa-sūkta* of the *Ṛgveda*, must have included other nobles too, not members of a royal family. In the *Śatapatha Brāhmaṇa*, the *rājanya* is distinct from the *rājaputra*, the son of the king.[4] *Kṣatriya* was the general term originally applied to all the nobles irrespective of the kingly power. The early use of the term in the *Ṛgveda* is connected with royal

---

[1] RV. VI.41.5; cf. Vedic Index, I, p. 204, n. 9.

[2] RV. VIII.35.16-18.

[3] Ibid., X.90, 12. Compare the patrician gentes of Rome, the Eupatridae of Athens, the nobles of early Germany, the eorls of the Anglo-Saxons, and the Athravas and Rathaesthas of ancient Iran. Cf. CHI, I, p. 125.

[4] ŚB. XIII.4.2.17; XIII.1.6.2.

or divine authority.[1] But the association of the *kṣatriya* in these passages with words like *rāṣṭra* or *sāmrājya* seems to point to a member of the warrior community.[2] Another Ṛgvedic passage implies a distinction of professions between the *ṛṣi* (seer) and the *rājan* (king).[3]

That the *kṣatriyas* included those princely families of earlier settlers who managed to retain their status despite defeat, is also borne out by the testimony of the Epics and the Buddhist literature.[4] The *kṣatriyas* later clearly denoted the royal house and its branches, and nobles and their families. The *rājanya* and the *Kṣatriya* were practically identical, despite an occasional reference to mutual differences.[5]

In return for the services rendered to protect the people and give them peace to ply their trade and agriculture, the *kṣatriyas* earned the right to live on them and at times even oppress them. The king made grants of conquered land and slaves to his nobles;[6] 'rule these villages or those', says the monarch to his officials.[7] The king, who himself represents the *kṣatriya* class, takes possession of whatever he likes; the people pay tribute to the *kṣatriya*, who says whenever he pleases 'Hello *vaiśya*, just bring to me what you have stored away'.[8] The people go down before a noble as he approaches, crouching down by him on the ground.[9]

Indeed, an aristocracy had no other excuse for its existence, if it was not military. Essentially proud as it was, it would otherwise have lacked confidence. Its desire to rule and dominate was the quintessence of its very being; it ruled by war and it desired war at regular intervals. There is not much to show that the nobles did anything else in particular, except attending to military and

---

1 RV. IV.42.1; VII.64.2; VIII.25.8; X.109.3; VIII.67.1.

2 See V. M. Apte, Were castes formulated in the Ṛgveda?, BDCRI, vol. II, p. 47.

3 RV. V.54.7. Cf. Muir, OST., I, p. 247.

4 Vedic Index, s.v. *kṣatriya*.

5 KS. XX.I; AB. VII.20; PB. XXIV. 18.2. In the later dogmatic literature, we find the *brāhmaṇa*, *kṣatra* and *viś* identified with Agni, Indra and the viśve-devāḥ respectively. The arrangement of the hymns in the RV., as far as the leading deities are concerned, foreshadows according to Eggeling, the social gradation of the Hindu community. See SBE., 12, Introduction, p. xix.

6 CHI, I, p. 128.

7 Praśna Up. III.4.

8 ŚB. I.3.2.14, 15.

9 Ibid., III.9.3.7.

administrative matters. To borrow a phrase from Tacitus, they were, like the Germani, at once haters of quiet and lovers of indolence.

The *Atharva Veda* [1] speaks of the bow as a special attribute of the *kṣatriya*; and the *Aitareya Brāhmaṇa* [2] adds the horse-chariot and the corslet to the arms of the lordly power. The *aśvamedha* ceremony contains the prayer that the *rājanya* should be heroic and skilled in archery, sure of his mark, and a great chariot-warrior.[3] The *Chāndogya Upaniṣad* mentions *kṣatra-vidyā*, which perhaps means the science of the bow, besides training in the use of other weapons.[4] And the *Aitareya Brāhmaṇa* speaks of the proper age when a *kṣatriya* is fit to bear arms.[5]

The term *kṣatriya* was never applicable to all the warriors in an army even in the Epics or the Buddhist literature. There are unambiguous references to the people fighting in the *Ṛgveda*;[6] and the *Atharva Veda* [7] designates the people as *balaṁ* or 'force', a regular term for an armed force in later literature. The *Śatapatha Brāhmaṇa* tells of Indra, a representative of the nobility, entreating the aid of the Maruts, symbolising the people, against his enemy Vṛtra.[8] And it was not impossible for a *vaiśya* to become a *kṣatriya*.[9]

Notwithstanding the people's participation in war, the bulk of an agricultural community must have peace to live and last. The warrior in the *Ṛgveda* and the later *Saṁhitās* is called the disturber of the people.[10] And yet wars, against both earlier settlers and fresh invaders, were a matter of necessity. Kings arose and kingdoms grew; their retinues and their nobility provided the leadership as well as the nucleus for standing armies; grand alliances were formed and fateful battles fought.[11] The *Atharva Veda* categorically refers to the army (*senā*) as a permanent institution of

1 AV. XVIII.2.60; KS. XVIII.9; XXXVII.1; ŚB. V.3.5.30; TA. VI.1.3.

2 AB. VII.19.

3 TS. VII.5.18.1; MS. III.12.6; KS. Aśvamedha, V.14; VS. XXII.2; ŚB. XIII.1.9.2.

4 CHU. VII.1.2,4; 2.1; 7.1.

5 AB. VII.14. Compare Germania, ch. 13, p. 283; 'No one takes arms until the state has endorsed his competence: then in the assembly one of the chiefs or the father or a relative equips him with spear and shield . . . .'

6 RV. IV.24.4; VI.26.1; VII.79.2; VIII.18.18; 96.15.

7 AV. IX. 7 9.

8 ŚB. IV.3.3.6,7.

9 Vedic Index, I, p. 207; cf. RV. VII.104.13.

10 RV. X.103.1; TS. IV.6.4; AV. XIX.13.2.

11 Cf. RV. VII.18.

the state.[1] The growing complexity of life and the division of functions explain the rise of the warriors as a class distinct from the patient tillers of the soil pictured in the pastoral hymns of the *Ṛgveda*,[2] who increasingly left to the *kṣatriya* the burden of defence and aggression.

The interdependence of the nobility and the priesthood is stressed time and again in the Vedic literature.[3] The priest, called the *purohita*, accompanies the king and his army to the field of battle, and prays with charms and spells to ensure his master's success.[4] In the *Ṛgveda* the Bharata army is enabled to cross the Vipāś and the Śutudrī only when the priest Viśvāmitra propitiates the rivers with his prayers.[5] Viśvāmitra and Vasiṣṭha assist the opposing factions in the battle of the ten kings.[6] That much reliance was placed on the priest's ability to undo the designs of the enemy through divine aid and magic, is clear from the vast array of the Atharvanic hymns. 'I perfect their kingdom', says the priest, 'their might, their vigour, and their strength. With this oblation I cut off the arms of their enemies.... Go forth, you men, and conquer; may your arms be terrible'.[7] The *purohita* of king Divodāsa rescues him from trouble.[8] He is indeed the flaming fire guarding the kingdom.[9] Occasionally, though rarely, a *purohita* serves even two kings at the same time.[10] He also figures as one of the king's nine jewels (*ratnins*) in the *Brāhmaṇa* literature.[11]

The *senānī*, appearing in the *Ṛgveda* and the later *Saṁhitās*, was a general appointed by the king.[12] He must have assisted the king on the battlefield, and also led expeditions too trivial to demand the monarch's personal attention. The office of the *senānī* evidences the stability of the Vedic military organisation. The

---

1 AV. XV.9.2.
2 RV. IV.57.
3 Cf. Bloomfield, The Atharva Veda, p. 75; TS. V.1.10; AB. VII.26; VIII.27; ŚB. IV.1.4.1ff.
4 RV. VII.18.13; AV. III.19.
5 RV. III.33.3ff.
6 Cf. Hopkins, JAOS, XV, p. 260 et seq.; RV. VII.18.
7 AV. III.19.
8 PB. XV.3.7.
9 AB. VIII.24.25.
10 ŚB. II.4.4.5.
11 Ibid., V.3.1.2.
12 RV. VII.20.5; IX.96.1; X.84.2; VS. XVI.17; KS. XVII.11; MS. II.9.4; TS. IV.5.2.1; VS. XV.15; ŚB. VIII.6.1.21; cf. CHI, I, p. 94.

standing armed force of the king must have been organised and commanded by the *senānī*, besides the contingents led by the *grāmaṇīs*. In battle he commanded the front where the chiefs stood.[1] The *Aitareya Brāhmaṇa* calls him the *senāpati*, commander of the army.[2] The *senānī*, too, is one of the king's *ratnins*.[3]

Next in importance to the *senānī* was the *grāmaṇī*.[4] Not infrequently in the *Ṛgveda*, *grāma* denotes a clan with ties of kinship, rather than a single settled village. Sāyaṇa too at one place explains *grāmaṇī* as *grāmāṇām netā*, which would mean that the *grāmaṇī* was a subordinate chieftain in charge of many villages.[5] A passage in the *Atharva Veda* suggests the association of the *grāmaṇī* with vigour, riches and plenty, in other words, with authority and prosperity.[6] His office may have been subject to royal appointment, or hereditary, or even sometimes elective for all that we know; he was often a *vaiśya*,[7] and a member of the royal entourage.[8] There must have been many *grāmaṇīs* in a kingdom, but presumably the one living near the royal headquarters was the most prominent. That the *grāmaṇī* had important military duties, is clearly borne out by his association with the *senānī*. Zimmer regards his functions as essentially military.[9] He seems to have led his contingent in war under the overall command of the *senānī* and the king. The *vrājapati*, mentioned elsewhere, appears to be more or less equal in status to the *grāmaṇī*.[10]

The *pūrpati* of the *Ṛgveda*, literally 'the lord of the fort', seems to have been the commander of a garrison.[11]

The *sūta*, or the charioteer, was an important official. He figures

---

1 SVB. 3.6.1.10.

2 AB. VIII.23.10.

3 TS. I.8.9.1; TB. I.7.3.4; MS. II.6.5; IV.3.8; KS. XV.4; ŚB. V.3.1.1.

4 RV. X.62.11; 107.5; AV. III.5.7; XIX.31.12; TS. II.5.4.4; MS.6.5; KS. VIII.4; X.3; VS. XV.15; TB. I.1.4.8; ŚB. III.4.1.7; V.4.4.8; BU. IV.3.37.38.

5 See Eggeling, SBE, 41, pp. 60-61, n. J. W. Spellman, Aspects of kingship in ancient India, Ph. D. Thesis, 1960, University of London, pp. 207-208. For example, the kings of Ceylon used *gāmaṇi* as a title; Cf. A. L. Basham, Prince Vijaya and the Aryanisation of Ceylon, Ceylon Historical Journal, vol. I, no.3, p. 169.

6 AV. XIX.31.12-13; cf. U. N. Ghoshal, Kingship and kingly administration in the Atharva Veda, IHQ, 20, 1944, p. 112.

7 ŚB. V.3.1.6.

8 AV. III.5.7.

9 AL., p. 171.

10 CHI, I, p. 94; RV. X. 179.2.

11 RV. I.173.10. See the chapter on forts and fortifications, p. 125.

as one of the king-makers in the *Atharva Veda* and other texts.[1] In the *Pañcaviṁśa Brāhmaṇa*, he holds his place among the eight *vīras* or dignitaries of the king,[2] while elsewhere he is designated as a *ratnin*.[3] Presumably, he had to beguile the tedium of long hours of marching or journeying with anecdotes and stories to keep his royal master interested and amused.[4] A man of wit and wisdom, the royal charioteer was soon obliged to discharge many more functions; he often acted as a herald, bard or minstrel, or even as a messenger or envoy, as we also learn from the Epics.[5] He is also occasionally described as unslayable,[6] which seems to denote his character as a herald or envoy besides that of a charioteer, who should also not be molested or killed according to the Epic moralist.[7]

The *saṁgrahītṛ*, who also denotes a charioteer in many passages, appears as a *ratnin* of the king.[8] The *kṣattṛ* too appears to be a charioteer in certain passages,[9] and the *Vājasaneyi Saṁhitā* mentions the *anukṣattṛ*, who is an attendant on the charioteer.[10] The *Atharva Veda* mentions two forerunners (*puraḥsarau*) and two footmen (*pariṣkanda*) running beside the Vrātya's chariot.[11]

We also come across such terms as *aśvapa*,[12] *aśvapati*,[13] or a horse-keeper, *aśva-nāya*,[14] or a horse-leader, and *aśvasāda*,[15] or a horse-rider. The elephant-keeper is also present, called *hastipa* in the *Yajus* texts.[16]

Varuṇa's spies, of frequent occurrence in the *Ṛgveda* and elsewhere,[17] testify to the early organisation of state intelligence. The

---

1 AV. III.5.7; ŚB. XIII.2.2.18; 3.4.1, 7-8.

2 PB. XIX. 1.4.

3 KS. XV.4; MS. II.6.5; IV.3.8; TB. I.7.3.1; TS.1.8.9.1; ŚB. V. 3.1.5.

4 Cf. The Vedic Age, p. 431; the role of the charioteer in the Bhagvadgītā.

5 Cf. Vedic Index, s.v. *sūta*. VS. XXX.6 mentions the *sūta* as a dancer.

6 TS. IV. 5.2.1; MS. II.9.3; KS. XVII.12. VS.XVI.18. Cf. Vedic Index, s.v. *sūta*; Wilhelm Rau, op. cit., p. 108.

7 See the chapter on the ethics of war, p. 161.

8 Cf. Vedic Index, s.v.; Gonda, Ancient Indian kingship from the religious point of view, Numen, III, p. 125. TS. I.8.9.2; KS. XV.4; MS. II.6.5; VS. XVI.26.

9 VS. XVI.26; TB. III.4.7.1.

10 VS. XXX.11; cf. XXX.73; TB. III.4.9.1.

11 AV. XV.2.1. et seq., *pariṣkanda* also in VS. 30.13.

12 VS. XXX.11; TB. III.4.9.1.

13 VS. XVI.24; KS. xvii.13.

14 CHU. VI.8.3; VI.8.5.

15 VS. XXX. 13.

16 Ibid., XXX.11; TB. III.4.9.1.

17 RV. 1.25.13; IV.4.3; VI.67.5; VII.61.3; 87.3; X.10.8; AV.XVIII.1.9.

Atharva Veda refers to the thousand-eyed spies (*spaśaḥ*) of Varuṇa looking over the earth beneath them;[1] Soma's rays are compared to omnipresent and unwinking spies, ready with fetters for tying the offender.[2] That these spies and their work had military significance, cannot be doubted. The *Ṛgveda* speaks of spies, or presumably reconnoitring troops, going forward in an unambiguous context of war, and this is corroborated by another passage.[3] As the opposing armies approach each other, the spies try to find the exact position of the enemy [4] and messengers keep the king informed of the latest happenings.[5]

We have already referred to the functions of the *sūta* as an envoy or messenger. We find the regular term *dūta* for an envoy even in the *Ṛgveda*.[6] The story of Saramā as a female envoy (*dūtī*) on a peace mission has been discussed elsewhere.[7] Presumably, the envoys visited the enemy camps to explore the possibility of peace before the actual outbreak of hostilities.

The *prahita* is mentioned in the *Taittirīya Saṁhitā* as a simple envoy carrying messages.[8] The *pālāgala*, one of the *ratnins* in the *Śatapatha Brāhmaṇa*, is a courier or messenger, a forerunner of the later *dūtas*.[9]

In several passages the *samiti* stands together with *senā* or the army; it may have then functioned as a council of war, where the deliberations of the nobility took place.[10] The *vidatha* is confined mainly to the *Ṛgveda*. In many passages it clearly seems to be a body taking decisions in matters pertaining to war.[11]

In the *Nikāyas* and the *Vinaya*, as in the earlier Vedic literature, the king commands his army not infrequently, and remains an active participant in battle. He usually belongs to the warrior

---

1 AV. IV.16.4.

2 Ibid., V.6.3.

3 RV. IV.4.3; cf. TS.1.2.14.1; RV. VIII.47.11.

4 ṢVB. 1.1.24.

5 JB.1, 234.

6 RV. III.3.2; VI.8.4; VII.3.3; X.14.12; AV. VIII.8.10; ŚB. III.5.1.6; Kauṣ. Up. II.1, etc.

7 RV. X.108.2, 3. See below, p. 155.

8 TS. IV.5.7.1.

9 ŚB. V.3.1.11.

10 Ibid., VIII.6.1.16. In KS.37.14, a council of war of the gods is mentioned. Whether *samiti* signifies a 'council of war' or 'battle' in JB. 1, 234, is not very clear; cf. also JB. 1.338; Wilhelm Rau, op. cit., p. 82.

11 cf. RV. I.166.2; 167.6; V.59.2; Vedic Index, s.v.; R.S. Sharma, Aspects of Political Ideas and Institutions in Ancient India, pp. 68,69.

class,[1] and is duly trained in the art of handling an elephant, horse and chariot, and weapons such as the bow and the sword.[2] Courage and leadership are the prerequisites of royalty. We hear of kings such as Brahmadatta of Kāsī marching on Kosala,[3] and Ajātasattu of Magadha advancing into Kāsī.[4] The latter is, however, beaten and taken prisoner by king Pasenadi of Kosala who also confiscates the four divisions of his army. Thus the king protects, but does not fail to aggrandise himself at the expense of an effete neighbour. Members of the royal family all specialise in warfare, and we find the sons of a king among the defenders of a fort.[5]

The *khattiyas* or noble warriors are repeatedly described as the best of men by the Buddha, who places them even higher than the *brāhmaṇas*.[6] The inexorable logic of military might and secular authority places them in a position of command that in fact grows increasingly impatient of interference. The *brāhmaṇa* claim to superiority lay in matters religious and spiritual, where, too, it was successfully challenged by men like the Buddha and Mahāvīra.

Next to the king, the *senāpati* or the commander of the army is the most important military official.[7] The king's chief ministers also occasionally march with the army.[8] In the *Vinaya* king Bimbisāra asks his generals and chief ministers to go and search the borderlands after the outbreak of some disturbance.[9] The king's army is a standing organisation and doubtless the mainstay of his power and authority.[10]The four divisions of an army, chariotry, elephants, cavalry and infantry, are represented by the *yodhājīva gāmaṇi*,[11] the *hatthāroha gāmaṇi*,[12] the *assāroha gāmaṇi*[13] and the *asibandhakaputta*[14] respectively. It appears that they were all warriors by profession, living together in organised village com-

---

1 Aṅguttara, III.76, *khattiya muddhābhisitta*; III.152, *raññaṁ khattiyānaṁ*.
2 Majjhima, II.69, 94; Aṅg. III.152.
3 Vinaya, I.342; cf. Aṅg. III. 397.
4 Saṁyutta, I.83,84.
5 Aṅguttara, IV. 107.
6 Dīgha, I.99, *khattiyā va seṭṭhā hīnā brāhmaṇā*; Aṅg. V.328.
7 Aṅguttara, III.76.
8 Ibid., III.397; Vinaya, I.241.
9 Ibid., I.73, *senānāyake mahāmatte*.
10 Aṅguttara, III. 151; also see above, p. 16.
11 Saṁyutta, IV. 308; also see above, p. 36.
12 Ibid., IV.310; also see above, p. 80.
13 Ibid., IV.310; also see above, p. 67.
14 Ibid., IV.312, 314; also see above, p. 16.

munities headed by *gāmaṇis*. Elephant and horse trainers are elsewhere specifically mentioned.[1]

An important list of army personnel occurs where the requisites of a fort are described in some detail. Among them are *hatthārohā* or the elephantry, *assārohā* or the cavalry, *rathikā* or the chariotry, *dhanuggahā* or the archers, *celakā* or the standard-bearers, *calakā* or the billeting officers, *piṇḍadāyikā* or the soldiers of the supply corps, *rājaputtā* or the king's sons, *pakkhandino* or the storm-troops, *cammayodhino* or the warriors in cuirasses, and *dāsakaputtā* or the home-born slaves. The last but not the least is the *dovārika* or gate-keeper, who is an intelligent and responsible officer.[2] He opens the gate only to people trusted and well known and keeps out strangers and men of dubious credentials.[3] Thus forts were protected by permanently stationed garrisons with a proper division of their functions.

We also hear of spies and the important part they play in peace and war. In one of his talks with the Buddha king Pasenadi speaks of his spies and informants,[4] and on another occasion refers to the counsellors at his court and the weavers of spells aimed to arrest the advancing enemy.[5] Magic and sorcery helped to prop the morale of the credulous king and his army.

The Epics emphasize the central position of the monarch in the scheme of warfare. He retains his military duty together with his right to command. The military function is indeed inseparable from the royal obligation to protect the people from the threat of invasion or anarchy. Kings and princes undergo strenuous courses of military training and control their armies more by example than command. The rulers in Kurukṣetra are renowned warriors who lead their respective armies ranged on the two sides, under the nominal over-all command of a superior elected by popular choice. Almost all the famous heroes of the Epic, with rare exceptions, come from the ranks of the ruling nobility. Royal status is claimed by men of blue blood, generals of armies and warriors of distinction,[6] for might is the prime qualification of a kṣatriya.[7]

---

[1] Majjhima, III.132-133, *hatthidamaka*; Aṅguttara, III.161, *hatthidammasārathi*; Majjhima, I.446, *assadamaka*.

[2] Aṅguttara, IV.107.

[3] cf. Ibid., V.194; Dīgha, II,146.

[4] Saṁyutta, I.79, *purisā carā ocarikā*.

[5] Ibid., I.102.

[6] Mbh. 1.126.34.

[7] Ibid., 1.127.11.

In the *Mahābhārata* we come across the significant practice of the chief commander's selection by the kings and warriors present, ratified by the shouts and acclamation of the whole army. A leaderless army, even though powerful, is easily routed in battle; a chief is needed to weld the different commanders into a team capable of concerted action. Duryodhana, therefore, requests Bhīṣma to assume the burden of command;[1] the old warrior becomes the *senāpati*; drums, conches and the shouts of the assembled host signify the popular approval and acceptance of the chosen general.[2] The commander is well versed in military strategy, in the marching of troops and their disposition, and also their withdrawal from the field of battle.[3] He exhorts the assembled warrior chiefs to fight bravely and to prefer death to inglorious defeat.[4]

In the Pāṇḍava camp, too, there is a council of war, where the leaders present name the persons of their choice for the office of the commander. There is little or no unanimity in the views expressed, and the decision is referred to Kṛṣṇa, who names Dhṛṣṭadyumna. Once more, the din of approval betokens the popular acceptance, clearly reminiscent of days gone by, when the choice was more broadly based on the active selection of the whole army.[5]

The status of *senāpati* is much coveted. If one is honoured, the others naturally feel disgruntled;[6] indeed, Karṇa refuses to fight under the command of Bhīṣma.[7] The choice therefore falls on one who enjoys universal esteem as much by dint of his prowess and leadership and ability, as by age and temperament and social status. Droṇa is installed when Bhīṣma falls; the joy of the army expresses itself in shouts and the sound of drums and other musical instruments. The brāhmaṇas, gratified with presents, chant hymns to invoke divine favours; bards sing their songs of praise and the mimes dance; the chosen chief is duly honoured.[8]

Droṇa's fall is followed by the election of Karṇa as the new generalissimo. Aśvatthāmā proposes his name, and Duryodhana praises him.[9] He stands up with all the kings present to honour the new

---

[1] Mbh. 5.153.1ff.
[2] Ibid., 5.153.26-28.
[3] Ibid., 5.162. 7-11.
[4] Ibid., 6.17.7ff.
[5] Ibid., 5.149.1ff.
[6] Ibid., 7.5.15.
[7] Ibid., 5.153.25.
[8] Ibid., 7.5.38ff.
[9] Ibid., 8.6.5ff.

senāpati, who is properly invested.[1] The election of the commander and the ceremony of his installation at once reminds one of a royal consecration; it seems to be a relic of an earlier day when the king was chosen by his followers on account of his military ability, and invariably shouldered the burden of command. The complexities of an alliance led to the separation of the two offices. This points again to the origin of kingship from the necessities of warfare as attested by the Vedic testimony; the practice is undoubtedly earlier than the Buddhist times and indicates anew the antiquity of the Epic tradition.[2]

The commander's hold on the armies from the various kingdoms loosely knit together is necessarily far from stringent. He cannot do more than dictate general tactics and order the formation of the army. The arrays usually employed are the *makara* [3] or a double triangle with apices joined; the *śakaṭa* or a wedge, once with a wheel addition;[4] the *krauñca*,[5] *śyena*, *garuḍa* [6] (names of birds) or a rhomboid; the *maṇḍala*, *cakra*,[7] or a wheel; the *ardhacandra* [8] or a crescent. The shape of the *śṛṅgāṭaka* or a horned array is difficult to determine.[9]

The commander's personal bravery is lauded more than his strategic ability. His deeds kindle the courage of his army and inform their effort with an added intensity of purpose. His fall precipitates the rout of his forces; for an army without a leader (*nāyaka*) cannot stay in battle any more than a boat in water without a helmsman.[10]

The *senāpati*, *senāpraṇetṛ* and *camūpati*, all denote the commander. We also find terms such as the *sarvasenāpati*[11] and the *senāpatipati*,[12] signifying the commander-in-chief.

The necessities of a coalition apart, the king normally had a commander under him appointed by himself, a man of good birth,

---

1 Mbh. 8.6.35ff.
2 Also see Hopkins, JAOS, 13, p. 215.
3 Mbh. 6.71.4; 8.7.13ff.
4 Ibid., 7.53.27; 7.63.21ff.
5 Ibid., 6.46.39; 6.47.1.
6 Ibid., 6.52.2ff.
7 Ibid., 7.63.21ff.
8 Ibid., 6.52.10ff.
9 cf. Hopkins, loc. cit., pp.210-211.
10 Mbh. 7.5.8.
11 Ibid., 5.154.12.
12 Ibid., 5.154.13.

devoted to him and competent.[1] *Balamukhyas* or captains of the army are also referred to.[2] And many leaders are chosen on the eve of a war.[3]

An important office, mentioned in the *Śānti parva*, may be likened to that of a quarter-master general. King Yudhiṣṭhira entrusts his younger brother Nakula with the charge of keeping a register of the forces, giving them their food and pay and supervising the other affairs of the army.[4] That the core of the army, necessarily enlarged on the eve of a great battle by haphazard recruitment and the accession of volunteers, must have been a permanent establishment, there can be no doubt whatsoever. Repeated stress is laid on the importance of regular and punctual payment of wages and rations to the army;[5] irregularity in this may lead to disaffection or even rebellion.[6] In the *Sabhā parva* Nārada asks Yudhiṣṭhira if he pays his troops in advance before he marches,[7] and if he supports the wives and children of men who lay down their lives for him, or undergo misery on his account.[8]

While the chariot-warriors usually represent the nobility, or rarely the brāhmaṇa teachers, such as Droṇa, Aśvatthāmā and Kṛpa, the cavalry is perhaps drawn from the ranks of the other warrior classes not so well off. The body of the infantry is recruited from the commonalty, from among the *vaiśyas* and even *śūdras* and adventurers of foreign extraction.

Among the miscellaneous office-bearers mentioned in the Epic, we hear of the *sūta*, the *sārathi* or charioteer,[9] the *aśvādhyakṣa*, *aśvabandha* or stable-master,[10] the *purohita* or priest,[11] the *amātyas* or ministers.[12] Body-guards of kings,[13] and sentinels and door-keepers are also referred to.[14] The *sabhāpāla* or the keeper of the assembly

---

1 Mbh. 5.154.13; cf. 2.5.36; Rām. Ayodhyā, 100.30.
2 Mbh. 2.5.37.
3 Cf. Ibid., 5.154.9.
4 Ibid., 12.41.11.
5 Ibid., 3.16.21, 22; 2.5.38; cf. 3.17.6; Rām. Ayodhyā, 100.32, 33.
6 Ibid.; Mbh. 2.5.39.
7 Ibid., 2.5.48.
8 Ibid., 2.5.44.
9 See above, pp. 44-48.
10 See above, p. 45.
11 Mbh. 5.20.1.
12 Ibid., 2.5.26; Rām. Bāla. VII.11.
13 Mbh. 2.5.77.
14 Ibid., 7.58.31.

blows his conch to call the Vṛṣṇi warriors to arms.[1] The bellman riding on an elephant proclaims a king's victory in his capital.[2]

Spies are usefully employed to ascertain the nature of a hostile country, its army and fortified places.[3] The *Virāṭa parva* refers to spies sent by the Kurus to trace the whereabouts of the Pāṇḍavas.[4] Spies are always present in the camp and the army. Yudhiṣṭhira places his spies (*cārapuruṣā*) in the Kuru camp and army.[5] From them he learns everything about Droṇa's intention to capture him alive.[6] And the Kuru spies, presumably in the Pāṇḍava camp, apprise Jayadratha of Arjuna's vow to kill him.[7]

The *Rāmāyaṇā* also teems with references to military espionage. We repeatedly hear of Rāvaṇa's disguised spies sent to the Rāma camp to discover the nature, number and disposition of the enemy troops.[8] They are often caught and belaboured, but spared. And Vibhīṣaṇa's spies bring news of Laṅkā's plans of defence.[9]

The *dūta* functions as an important intermediary between two opposing factions. Such ambassadors are often sent before the actual outbreak of warfare to convey messages and the terms of a possible agreement. Missions of such an onerous nature are sometimes entrusted to envoys of royal status. Kṛṣṇa goes to the Kaurava camp to propose the Pāṇḍava terms of a peaceful settlement and to point to the calamitous consequences of war in the event of failure. He marches on his embassy with an impressive escort of ten charioted knights, 1,000 foot-soldiers and 1,000 horsemen, and other attendants.[10]

The person of the envoy is traditionally inviolable.[11] King Dhṛtarāṣtra receives Kṛṣṇa outside the city, which is adorned in honour of his arrival.[12] And in court, the blind monarch stands up to receive

---

[1] Mbh. 1.212.11.
[2] Ibid., 4.63.25, *ghaṇṭāpaṇavakaḥ*.
[3] Ibid., 3.149.40; cf. 2.5.27; 5.189.18; 12.138.40.
[4] Ibid., 4.24.5; 4.25.8-12.
[5] Ibid., 5.195.2.
[6] Ibid., 7.12.2.
[7] Ibid., 7.52.1.
[8] Rām. yuddha, 25.1ff.; 29.24ff.
[9] Ibid., 37.6ff. Spies are also mentioned in Sundara, 4.15ff.; Kiṣkindhā, 15.16ff.
[10] Mbh. 5.82.1, 2. Prince Aṅgada goes to Rāvaṇa as Rāma's envoy, cf. 3.267.54.
[11] Cf. Mbh. 5.86.13-18.
[12] Ibid., 5.87.3ff.

the royal ambassador.[1] It is interesting to learn from a remark of Kṛṣṇa that an envoy accepts the food and worship of his hosts only after the success of his mission.[2] The ambassador tries to sow dissension in the ranks of the enemy, and Kṛṣṇa goes to the extent of suggesting the capture of Duryodhana and his lieutenants to the elder Kurus.[3] And when his mission fails, he asks the Kauravas to begin the battle in a week's time.[4]

Purohitas or priests are also sent as envoys. King Drupada of Pāñcāla sends his priest to the Kauravas on behalf of the Pāṇḍavas.[5] Trusted charioteers are also called upon to discharge this function. Thus Sañjaya, the charioteer and friend of Dhṛtarāṣtra, goes as the Kaurava envoy to the Pāṇḍavas to impress upon them the futility of a war.[6] And Ulūka, the charioteer of Duryodhana, conveys to the Pāṇḍavas the Kaurava challenge to fight.[7]

A *dūta*, says Yudhiṣṭhira, speaks according to his instructions. If he does otherwise, he should be slain.[8] The *Rāmāyaṇa* prescribes a few punishments for visiting envoys who infringe the conventional rules of behaviour, such as the amputation of limbs or whipping, shaving the head or branding the forehead of the offender.[9]

The Epic also affords a peep into the camp-life of old. Words such as the *skandhāvāra*, *śibira* and *senāniveśa* denote the army camp, which never encroaches upon burning grounds, shrines and any other sacred spots.[10] The ground, preferably level and abounding in grass and fuel,[11] is properly measured for an encampment;[12] a moat is dug around to protect it, and guards are stationed at important posts.[13] Door-keepers and sentinels keep watch outside the tents of the chief heroes and princes.[14] Stocks of arms and armaments, food and water and fodder are in evidence,[15] and physicians and mechanics form part of the establishment.[16]

1 Cf. Mbh. 5.87.13.
2 Ibid., 5.89.18.
3 Ibid., 5.126.47.
4 Ibid., 5.140.16ff.
5 Ibid., 5.5.18; 5.6.1ff.; 5.20.1ff.
6 Ibid., 5.23; 24; 5.25; 5.27.
7 Ibid., 5.158.1ff.; 5.157.3.
8 Ibid., 5.70.7. Compare Plato, Laws, 941.
9 Rām. Sundara, 52.15.
10 Mbh. 5.149.67-69.
11 Ibid., 5.153.34, 35.
12 Ibid., 5.149.72.
13 Ibid., 5.149.73, 74.
14 Ibid., 7.56.6; 7.58.31.
15 Ibid., 5.149.79-81.
16 Ibid., 5.149.78.

In the camp, too, we notice the prevalence of various democratic processes that govern and guide the course of action. It is there that the chief commander is chosen. And there, too, the other leaders are selected and strategy discussed.[1] We find Jayadratha on his way to the assembly (*samiti*) of kings in the Kaurava camp to seek their protection from Arjuna's murderous vow.[2] Councils of war are common on both sides.

In the evening after a bloody battle the heroes nurse their wounds and bathe in diverse waters.[3] Brāhmaṇas perform the propitiatory rites, and the bards hymn their praises; vocal and instrumental music helps to abate the agony of wounds and war.[4] The soldiers also sing and clap together;[5] the human spirit, buoyant as ever, forgets its suffering.

---

[1] Mbh. 5.155.37, 38; 5.157; 6.42.2ff.

[2] Ibid., 7.52.3. In Rām. yuddha, 17, 18, Rāma asks the Vānaras what to do with Vibhīṣaṇa.

[3] Mbh. 6.82.53.

[4] Ibid., 6.82.54.

[5] Ibid., 7.50.10ff.

CHAPTER EIGHT

ETHICS OF WAR

Warfare has often had such ecological functions as the expansion of populations and an increase in the extent of environment being exploited by man. A community does not usually wait to colonise until its existing territories attain a maximum carrying capacity. A slowly diminishing food supply begins to exert pressure for escape from the approaching equilibrium at noticeably lower levels. And if the time and effort needed for finding and clearing virgin land is appreciably greater than the difficulties of conquering previously used land for cultivation, violent aggression rather than peaceful dispersion is the rule. It was indeed true of the past, when the more arduous task of forest clearance was left to the helpless and beaten enemy, deprived of his possessions by the right of might. The Aryans thus needed little apology for waging war on their enemies; only fire and sword could furnish the key to 'land, sunlight, water and life',[1] as swarms of invaders fell upon the earlier settlers of the soil. No qualms of the later-day Epic morality deterred the early Aryan; and not a few hymns of the *Ṛgveda* tell of the devastation that accompanied his progress. Smouldering fires testify to the exploits of Agni, thus invoked by the poet:

> 'Rise up O Agni, spread thee out before us: burn down our foes, thou who hast sharpened arrows'.[2]

Great battles were fought and thousands done to death,[3] or sometimes drowned in rivers.[4] The famous battle-hymn of the *Ṛgveda* speaks of arrows smeared with poison,[5] not allowed by the later code of ethics, and goes on in the same implacable strain:

> 'Loosed from the bowstring fly away, thou arrow, sharpened by our prayer.
> Go to the foemen, strike them down, and let no one be left alive'.[6]

---

[1] RV. I. 100.18; VI.25.4; VI.46.4.
[2] Ibid., IV.4.4.
[3] Ibid., II.14.7; IV.16.13; IV.30.21.
[4] Ibid., VII.18.12.19; Louis Renou, Vedic India, p. 6.
[5] RV. VI.75.15; cf. AV.IV.6.6, 7, 8.
[6] RV. VI.75.16.

The concept of a supreme sovereign and universal conquest takes root as early as the *Ṛgveda*, which recognises the *aśvamedha*,[1] and becomes well developed in the later *Saṁhitās* and the *Brāhmaṇas*. The *Atharva Veda* says: 'May Indra conquer, may he not be conquered; may he king it as overking among kings: be thou here one to be famed, to be praised, to be greeted, to be waited on, and to be reverenced'.[2] Ceremonies and sacrifices like the *rājasūya*, *vājapeya* and *aindramahābhiṣeka*, were meant for the glorification of the all-conquering king and *kṣatra*. The *Aitareya Brāhmaṇa* says of the lordly power: '. . . the breaker of citadels has been born, the slayer of the asuras has been born, the guardian of the holy power has been born, the guardian of the law has been born'.[3] The same *Brāhmaṇa* mentions the names of kings like Janamejaya Pārikṣita, Sudās Paijavana, Bharata Dauḥṣanti, and many more, who went conquering in every direction and performed the horse-sacrifice.[4] They campaigned primarily perhaps to exact homage, and secondarily only to annex territories nearer home. These are the beginnings of the ideal of 'righteous conquest', which 'is evident, though not explicitly stated in later Vedic literature.'[5] It acted as an especially effective means of promoting social cohesion in that it provided an occasion when the members of the society united and submerged their factional differences in the pursuit of a common purpose. Prosperity depended on solidarity; warfare promoted it and thus had indirect economic and ecological consequences.

Notwithstanding the fierceness of spirit and unabashed prayers for cattle and booty,[6] an incipient moral consciousness appears as early as the *Ṛgveda*; it is a war on the unbeliever where it is not a struggle with another Aryan; and gods like Indra and Agni are invoked to destroy the heathen with maledictions and aggressive deeds.[7] This perhaps provides the first crude attempt at a moral justification of warfare; the extermination of the non-Aryan is sought because he does not worship the Vedic gods.

---

[1] RV. I.162; 163.
[2] AV. VI.98.1.
[3] AB. VIII.12.
[4] Ibid., VIII.21; 23.
[5] A. L. Basham, The Wonder that was India, p. 124.
[6] RV. I.7.4; I.8.1; I.16.9; I.31.6; I.36.8; X.84.2.
[7] Ibid., I.51.8; I.100.18; I.103.3; I.130.8; III.12.6; III.29.9; III.30.17.

> 'Root up the race of Rākṣasas, O Indra, rend it in front and crush it in the middle.
> How long hast thou behaved as one who wavers?
> Cast thy hot dart at him who hates devotion'.[1]

But sectarian rancour goes hand in hand with more mundane allurements; Indra slays the phallus-worshippers (*śiśnadevāḥ*) and wins the treasure of a 'hundred-gated' fort.[2] People fight in defence of the truth and their rights as they understand them; a faith in the ordeal of war, so characteristic of the ancient world, cautiously comes to the fore.[3]

One can detect the embryo of a few moral concepts of the Epics as early as the *Ṛgveda*. Like the *Mahābhārata*, it speaks of an envoy visiting the opposite party with a view to exploring the possibility of avoiding imminent hostility. Indra's messenger Saramā finds her way to the Paṇis to demand the return of stolen cattle and to threaten them with destruction in the event of failure. The latter try to induce her to stay with them; but the last verse seems to record the fulfilment of her prophecy.[4] The text of the hymn leaves no doubt that the person of an envoy was considered sacred. We learn from the later *Saṁhitās* that the *sūta*, who acted as charioteer, bard, herald or envoy, was regarded physically inviolable.[5]

That the sanctity of compacts and treaties was respected as early as the proto-Aryan and Ṛgvedic times, will appear both from the texts of the Mitanni-Hatti treaties and the *Ṛgveda*. The names of Mitra, Varuṇa, Indra and Nāsatya occur in the Hatti-Mitanni and Mitanni-Hatti treaties, significantly in the same order as they do in a verse of the *Ṛgveda*.[6] Do these gods then protect treaties, promises and oaths? And do they punish a breach of faith? 'It is quite natural that the list [of the Aryan gods of the Mitanni treaty] is opened by Mitra, the god of compacts and the personification of friendship'.[7] Mitra in the *Ṛgveda* causes people to make

---

[1] RV. III.30.17.

[2] Ibid., X.99.3; Macdonell, Vedic Mythology, Strassburg, 1897, p.155.

[3] RV. X.42.4, *tvāṁ janā namastyeṣvindra santasthānā vi hvayante samike*. . . ; compare Gurney, The Hittites, pp. 176-177.

[4] RV. X.108.

[5] MS. II.9.3; KS. XVII.12; TS. IV.5.2.1; VS. XVI.18.

[6] RV.X.125.1, *ahaṁ mitrā mitrā-varuṇā ubhā bibharmi ahaṁ indrāgnī ahaṁ aśvinā ubhā*. There are only two slight variations; *aśvinā* instead of *Nāsatyā*, and *indrāgnī* instead of Indra.

[7] Sten Konow, 'The Aryan gods of the Mitanni People', Kristiania Etnografiske Museums Skrifter Bind 3 Hefte 1; Kristiania, 1921, p. 38.

mutual arrangements conducive to peace.[1] This speciality of Mitra is also evidenced in the *Avesta*.[2] But Varuṇa, Indra and the Nāsatyas share this function with Mitra only in the *Ṛgveda*.[3] Varuṇa looks down on the truth and untruth of the people,[4] and Indra avenges the breach of covenants.[5] The *Ṛgeveda* repeatedly calls on Indra to destroy the ***amitra***, 'him who does not recognise the sacredness of contracts or treaties'.[6] The Nāsatyas are alike protectors of treaties; we find them (aśvins) slaying the enemies and keeping in agreement those who are connected by a contract or treaty.[7]

The later Saṃhitās similarly refer to compacts and agreements; we are told of an armistice and truce in one,[8] and of a one-year treaty in another.[9] The ***Pañcaviṁśa Brāhmaṇa*** speaks of a compact between the gods and the asuras; the cattle should belong to that party which vanquishes the other.[10] War thus becomes an ordeal, a mere tournament for winning a prize. But we also hear of bad faith on the part of gods like Viṣṇu and Indra; the latter violates his pledge and slays Vṛtra, while the former abets the crime.[11] Elsewhere, Indra and Namuci reach an agreement: " 'Of us two not [one] shall kill the other either by night or by day, either with [what is] wet or [what is] dry'. Indra cut off his head at dawn before sunrise with foam of water. . . . This head rolled after him calling: 'man-slayer, thou hast cheated, thou hast cheated'."[12] The *Mahābhārata* also moralises on the old story: 'that head of Namuci, after it had been cut off, followed after Indra shouting

---

1 RV. III.59.1, ***mitro janān yātayati bruvāṇaḥ***; cf. 3.

2 Paul Thieme, The 'Aryan' gods of the Mitanni Treaties, JAOS, 80, 1960, p. 306.

3 Ibid., p. 317.

4 RV. VII.49.3 *yāsāṁ rājā varuṇo yāti madhye satyānṛte avapaśyan janānāṁ* . . . ; cf. V.65.6; 72.2; Thieme, loc. cit., pp. 307, 308.

5 RV. X.89.9; Dumézil, Naissance d'archanges, p. 33ff.; Thieme, loc. cit., p. 309.

6 RV. 1.63.2; 63.5; 100.5; 133.1; III.30.16; VI.25.2; 33.1; 44.17; 46.6; 46.8; 73.2, 3; VII.18.9; 25.2; 32.25; VIII.16.10; X.103.4; 152.3.

7 Ibid., VIII.35.12 ***hataṁ ca śatrūn yatataṁ ca mitriṇaḥ*** . . . ***aśvinā***; Thieme, loc. cit., p. 314.

8 TS. 2.1.8.4.

9 MS. 2.1.2.

10 PB. XIII. 6.7.

11 TS. VI.5.1.1-3; cf. PB. XX. 15.6.

12 Ibid., XII. 6.8. ***Indraśca vai namuciśca asuraḥ samadadhātāṁ***. . . , 9; cf. TB. 1.7.1.7, 8.

close by: 'woe to you, wicked slayer of friends'.[1] A sacrifice on the advice of Brahmā, and a bath in the waters of the river Aruṇā, atones for Indra's guilt.[2] But an opposite, down to earth view is not difficult to find in the Epic itself; Duryodhana says that Indra made friends with Namuci, but, nevertheless, cut off his head; for, that is the usage among enemies.[3] The *Kauṣītaki Upaniṣad* actually tells us that Indra violated many treaties.[4]

The rule of law in personal and class relations amongst the Aryans was perhaps inapplicable to the unbelieving Non-Aryans. So we hear in the *Taittirīya Saṁhitā*:

> 'Swiftly [goes] the chariot of the worshipper like a hero in every contest;
> He who by sacrifice is fain to win the minds of the gods
> Shall prevail over those who sacrifice not'.[5]

Economics and religion do not part company; while the one demonstrates the necessity of aggression, the other extenuates its harshness in the eyes of the aggressors, and even justifies it. The *Atharva Veda* puts it very succinctly:

> 'I overpower the piśācas with power;
> I take to myself their property; I slay all the abusers [of the gods]; let my design be successful'.[6]

The same text elsewhere refers to the enemy being driven away from villages, while 'seizing those that are to be seized'.[7] Here then is an explicit reference to prisoners of war. Two AV. hymns are devoted to the tying up of enemies.[8] This leads us on to the treatment of the captured. AV. VIII.8.10 says: 'To death do I deliver those yonder; with fetters of death [are] they bound; the sad messengers that are death's—them I lead them to meet, having bound them'. The following verses speak of the 'fetters of death, from which once you have stepped into them you are not released';[9]

---

1 Mbh. IX.43. 36ff. (Cal. Ed.).
2 Ibid.
3 Ibid., 2.50.20 (Cr. Ed.)
4 Kauṣ. Up. III.1, *bahvī saṁdhā atikramya.*
5 TS. 1.8.22.
6 AV. IV.36.4.
7 Ibid., V.20.3,4.
8 Ibid., VI.103;104.
9 Ibid., VIII.8.16.

when the enemy army is caught in traps, it dies of hunger, exhaustion, slaughter and fear.[1] Thus, though prisoners were taken on the field of battle, a large number of them were only led away to death; but some must have been pressed into menial service. Another hymn in fact proves that some of the non-combatants were taken prisoner, while others were driven away.[2] The *Aitareya Brāhmaṇa* significantly refers to ten thousand female slaves brought from various countries, all daughters of wealthy men, given away to brāhmaṇas in celebration of all round conquest.[3] We are reminded of the ancient Hittites, king, lords and soldiers, who all brought back with them civilian captives at the end of their campaigns. So did the ancient Assyrians, who even transplanted whole populations from one place to another.

The *Upaniṣads* mark a momentous stage in the development of moral consciousness. Prajāpati instructs gods, demons and men with the syllable '*da*', which signifies for them respectively, *dama* or self-control, *dayā* or compassion, and *dāna* or charity.[4] All the three qualities run counter to violence. The *Chāndogya Upaniṣad* mentions *ahiṁsā* or non-violence together with austerity, charity and truth in speech.[5] Truth and non-violence are indeed inseparable; one is distant and unrealisable without the other. Elsewhere, we hear that truth alone is ultimately victorious, and not falsehood.[6] Truth is the quality of speech, and *dharma* or law and justice that of action.[7] That is why the *Bṛhadāraṇyaka Upaniṣad* places law and justice (*dharma*) higher than the *kṣatra* (power); dharma is the *kṣatra* of the *kṣatra*; therefore there is nothing higher than *dharma*. A weak man thus hopes to defeat a strong man by means of justice, as one does through a king.[8] The same *Upaniṣad* says that the *kṣatra* injuring a brāhmaṇa strikes at its own source.[9] The *Chāndogya Upaniṣad* similarly calls killing a brāhmaṇa a

---

[1] AV. VIII.8.18.
[2] Ibid., V.20.4.
[3] AB. VIII.22.
[4] BU. V.2.
[5] CHU. 3.17.4.
[6] MU. 3.1.6.
[7] TU. 1.11.1.
[8] BU.1.4.14. *dharmaṁ tadetat kṣatrasya kṣatraṁ yaddharmastasmāddharmātparaṁ nāsti atho abalīyān balīyāṁsaṁ āśaṁsate dharmeṇa, yathā rājñā evaṁ.*
[9] Ibid., 1.4.12.

crime.[1] These Upaniṣadic ideas provide the groundwork for the later growth of Buddhist morality as well as the Epic code of war and peace.

Buddhism appealed to the masses in general and the merchant class in particular because it made a passionate plea for lessening the misery inflicted by violence. Tradition has it that the Buddha himself stopped a clash of arms between the Śākyas and the Koliyas, and persuaded them to settle their differences without bloodshed.[2] Victory, says the *Dhammapada*, only breeds hatred, for the conquered sleep in sorrow; but tranquillity leads to a state of bliss above victory or defeat.[3]

In the *Saṁyutta Nikāya*, a *yodhājīva gāmaṇi* tells the Buddha of the popular belief in his community that a warrior dying in battle is reborn in the company of the *devas* of passionate delight.[4] The Buddha warns him, however, that it is a travesty of the truth; for the fighting man only gets purgatory after death, or else rebirth as an animal.[5] The *Aṅguttara Nikāya* condemns even hunters to purgatory.[6] The accent everywhere is on non-violence. This inner message of peace, added to the horrors of war as revealed to Aśoka in his Kaliṅga campaign, influenced that monarch to preach as well as practise non-violence and for ever abominate bloodshed. But human nature is not easily changed by the affirmation of great spiritual truths, and we hear of war even in the *Nikāyas* and the *Vinaya*. The use of poisoned arrows is attested;[7] and the rattle of the car of the 'wheel-rolling King' (*cakravartin*) echoes through the *Bālapaṇḍita Sutta* of the *Majjhima Nikāya*.[8] The Vedic doctrine of universal conquest has come to stay.

The Epics propound the ideal of righteous conquest (*dharmavijaya*) tacitly assumed in the later Vedic literature, with a clarity hitherto unknown.

> 'A King should not attempt
> to gain the earth unrighteously,

---

[1] CHU. 5.10.

[2] Jāt. V.412ff.; DA. II,627ff.; DhA. III.254ff.

[3] Dhammapada, 201.

[4] Saṁyutta, IV.308, *sarañjitānaṁ devānaṁ sahavyataṁ upapajjatīti*.

[5] Ibid., IV.308, 309; cf. The Buddha's dialogues with the *hatthārohogāmaṇi*, IV. 310; *assāroho gāmaṇi*, IV.310; *asibandhaka-putta*, IV. 312, 314.

[6] Aṅguttara, V. 289.

[7] Majjhima, II.216; 256.

[8] Ibid., III. 173ff.

for who reveres the King
who wins unrighteous victory?
Unrighteous conquest is impermanent,
and does not lead to heaven'.[1]

Righteous conquest is hence perfectly in order and there is no shrinking from warfare as such; but this is aggression without provocation, even though the aim is not necessarily the dethronement of the adversary and the annexation of his kingdom. The fruit of victory is tribute and homage to superior power pursued by many heroes of the Epic,[2] and later by rulers of undoubted historicity.[3]

It became part of kingly duty to attack one's neighbours in the normal course of events; warfare was reduced to the level of a large scale tournament and might even be something of a festive occasion. And yet the Epic itself is not wanting in passages vividly depicting the agony of war, instinct with a desire for peace. Victory creates animosity;[4] hostilities do not easily cease if there is even one alive in the enemy's family; for narrators are never needed to remind him of the past.[5] Success through war is the very worst of successes, involving as it does, slaughter and loss of lives.[6] The Pāṇḍavas, Bhīma and Arjuna, are averse to war; submission to the Kauravas is preferable to the destruction of the Bharatas.[7] Kṛṣṇa offers to go to the Kauravas in a bid to secure peace and avert the impending disaster.[8] And he adds that they would escape all blame for the war if his visit fails to yield any results.[9] This is symptomatic of a highly developed moral conscience; war is an evil and a crime; hence the desire to shelve the blame. A host of speakers impress upon Duryodhana the dire consequences of war and counsel peace.[10] But every speech is made to play upon his

---

[1] Mbh. 12. 97. 1-2. Basham, op.cit., p. 124.

[2] Mbh. 2.23; 24; 25; 26; 27; 28; 29 etc.

[3] Samudragupta is a famous example. Kālidāsa has stated the Hindu ideal of *dharmavijaya* in his *Raghuvaṁśa*: *gṛhīta pratimuktasya sa dharmavijayīnṛpaḥ śriyaṁ mahendranāthasya jahāra natu medinīṁ*

[4] Mbh. 5.70.59.

[5] Ibid., 5.70.62.

[6] Ibid., 6.4.32. Strict non-violence is ordained for the brāhmaṇas; the highest morality is sparing life; a brāhmaṇa should never take any creature's life. Ibid., 1.11.12.

[7] Ibid., 5.72.1-23.

[8] Ibid., 5.70.79-81.

[9] Ibid., 5.70.88.

[10] Ibid., 5.121.20ff.; 5.122.1ff.; 5.123.1ff.; 5.124.

fears with exaggerated accounts of Pāṇḍava prowess; and Duryodhana is not short of a characteristic reply. Born in a noble Kṣatriya race, who would bow to an enemy from fear, covetous of life only? One should ever keep erect and it is better to break at the knots than to bend.[1]

Thus in a human society where strife is endemic, the old faith in the victory of the just still persists,[2] and so the rules of righteous warfare are enunciated and their observance insisted upon. Only equals should fight each other;[3] elephants should oppose only elephants; and so the chariots, cavalry, and infantry should attack only their opposite numbers.[4] A king should fight only with a king, and a commoner should not strike a monarch.[5] Similarly, a kṣatriya should fight an equal in battle, a man of his own order.[6] Karṇa is refused competition with Arjuna in a tournament on the ground that he is a man of lowly extraction.[7] Those indulging in wordy warfare should be fought only with words; and those who leave the ranks should never be slain.[8] One should strike another after giving due notice, only when justified in so doing by considerations of fitness, daring and might. No one should strike another who is confiding or unprepared or panic-stricken.[9] A foe engaged with another should never be struck, as also one without armour, or whose weapon is rendered useless.[10] Chariot-drivers and draught-animals, men engaged in transport of weapons, and drummers and buglers, should not be attacked.[11] A kṣatriya should not strike one who is fatigued and frightened, weeping and unwilling to fight; one who is ill and cries for quarter, or one of tender years or advanced age.[12] In the *Sabhā parva*, Nārada asks Yudhiṣṭhira if he cheris-

---

[1] Mbh. 5.125.18ff.

[2] Ibid., 6.21.11, *yato dharmas tato jayaḥ.*

[3] Ibid., 6.1.27.

[4] Ibid., 6.1.29.

[5] Ibid., 12.97.7.

[6] Ibid., 12.286.5.

[7] Ibid., 1.126. 30-33.

[8] Ibid., 6.1.28. The warriors in the Epic are enamoured of bragging, both on and off the field of battle, even though Bhīma once shows unusual humility when he calls it ignoble to talk of one's own prowess (5.74.6). But Karṇa finds no fault with the boast of heroes saddled with heavy responsibilities (7.133.24ff.).

[9] Ibid., 6.1.30.

[10] Ibid., 6.1.31.

[11] Ibid., 6.1.32.

[12] Ibid., 12.286.4.

hes with paternal affection the foe who has surrendered from fear, or who has sought asylum, vanquished in battle.[1] A kṣatriya should defend even his enemy if entreated with joined hands.[2]

A brāhmaṇa is declared unslayable, and so is an ambassador.[3] If a brāhmaṇa desirous of peace goes between two contending armies, they should at once desist from the fight. And if someone dares to wound or slay him, he violates a rule that is time-honoured.[4] We are reminded of the story of the Buddha's intervention in the strife between two tribes, referred to earlier; and of a brāhmaṇa's timely intercession, which avoided a war over the Buddha's Relics.[5] In the *Rāmāyaṇa*, Rāma spares the life of Paraśurāma because he is a brāhmaṇa.[6] But it is no sin to resist an attacking brāhmaṇa.[7] Thus, in the *Virāṭa parva*, Arjuna pays his regards to Droṇa and Aśvatthāmā on the field of battle, and tells his teacher that he will strike him only if he is first attacked.[8] And he cuts off Kṛpa's coat of mail without killing him.[9]

In the *Ādi parva*, Yudhiṣṭhira says that one should not slay a woman even though enraged, and restrains Bhīma from killing the demoness Hiḍiṁbā.[10] Bhīṣma refuses to strike a woman, or rather Śikhaṇḍī who had formerly been a woman and whose sex had changed.[11] In the *Rāmāyaṇa*, Viśvāmitra has to justify Rāma's

---

[1] Mbh. 2.5.45; cf. 8.49.22ff. According to 2.35.7, a kṣatriya becomes the master of his beaten adversary, if he sets him free.

[2] Ibid., 3.232. 10-12; cf. 5.12.19-21. In the *Āraṇyakaparva*, (3.19.13, 14), Pradyumna says that a Vṛṣṇi hero never turns his back from battle, or strikes a surrendering foe, a woman, a child or an old man, and a warrior deprived of his chariot and weapons.

[3] Ibid., 5.6.16. The rule was operative in early Greece. An ambassador was, however, punished for conveying false messages. (Plato, Laws, 941). Herodotus describes the divine retribution that overtook Sparta in the 5th century B.C., for slaying the Persian herald. (7.134).

[4] Mbh. 12.97.8.

[5] Dīgha, II.166. Doṇa the brāhmaṇa addresses the assembled Mallas: 'Hear, gracious sirs, one single word from me. Forbearance was our Buddha wont to teach. Unseemly is it that over the division of the remains of him who was the best of beings, strife should arise and wounds and war.'

[6] Rām. Bāla, 76.5ff.

[7] Cf. Mbh.1.181.6; The slaughter of a brāhmaṇa intent on fighting is allowed.

[8] Ibid., 4.50.7-8, 9-10; 4.53.17.

[9] Ibid., 4.52.13.

[10] Ibid., 1.143.2. ŚB. XI.4.3.2 also says that 'people do not kill a woman'.

[11] Ibid., 5.193.60ff. Elsewhere (6.103.73), he says that he hates to strike a woman, or one bearing the name of a woman, one who has a single son or none at all, and one who is a vulgar fellow.

killing of the demoness Tāḍakā as imperative for the benefit of the four orders of society.[1] He cites instances of Indra killing Mantharā, Viṣṇu killing the mother of Śukrācārya, and many other monarchs killing irreligious women.[2] Lakṣmaṇa angrily cuts off the ears, nose and breasts of the demoness Ayomukhī who wants to make love to him,[3] and similarly lops off the nose and ears of Śūparṇakhā, but does not kill her because she is a woman.[4] Slaughter would perhaps be preferable to such a sordid mutilation, dictated by Lakṣmaṇa's interpretation of the law according to his lights. Women were made prisoners of war, as we know from Hanumān's account of Rāvaṇa's harem; for many of its lovely ladies were brought as booty of war.[5] In the *Mahābhārata*, the Gandharvas carry off the Kauravas and their women as prisoners.[6] And in the *Mausala parva*, the Ābhīras attack Arjuna and abduct the Vṛṣṇi women.[7]

We are told, however, that male and female spectators were allowed on the field of battle, and evidently no harm was done them. The Kuru king makes proper arrangements for onlookers, including masons, bards, singers, and panegyrists, traders and prostitutes, spies and others.[8]

The warriors of the day were duly indoctrinated in the code of morality and duty. Thus the education of Dhṛtarāṣṭra, Pāṇḍu and Vidura includes lessons in morality, history, tradition, *Vedas* and the allied literature, apart from military exercises.[9] Nārada asks Yudhiṣṭhira if experienced teachers proficient in the scriptures have been appointed to instruct the princes and army chiefs.[10] It is a kṣatriya's duty to fight a just battle in order to right a wrong; happy are they who obtain such a fight, an open door to heaven.[11] But if a warrior turns away from a fight for justice, he reaps only

---

1 Rām. Bāla, 25.17.

2 Ibid., Bāla, 25.20-22.

3 Ibid., Araṇya, 69.17.

4 Ibid., Araṇya, 18.21.

5 Ibid., Sundara, 9.6, 69.

6 Mbh. 3.231.12.

7 Ibid., Mausala, VII.47ff. (Cal. Ed.). The law-books, however, lay down that courteous treatment should be accorded to female prisoners, and they should be duly returned to their families after some length of time.

8 Ibid., 5.196.18, 19. Tacitus in his *Germania*, p. 275, (chs. 7, 8), mentions the presence of female spectators on the battlefield: '. . . Close at hand, too, are their dearest, whence is heard the wailing voice of woman and the child's cry . . . they minister to the combatants food and exhortation.'

9 Mbh. 1.102.18; cf. 1.213.65, Abhimanyu's education.

10 Ibid., 2.5.23.

11 Ibid. 6.24.32.

sin by renouncing his duty and glory.[1] To die of disease at home is sin for a kṣatriya;[2] victory or death in battle is eternally ordained by the creator; and that is the goal of a warrior.[3] Unnerved by the lurking shadow of a bloody conflict, Kuntī reminds her children of the great occasion for which a kṣatriya mother bears a son.[4] And Kṛṣṇa exhorts Arjuna to fight because if slain he will obtain heaven; and if victorious he will enjoy the earth.[5]

A warrior must always answer a challenge. Suddenly challenged but not forgetful of his duty, king Jarāsandha lays aside his crown and braids up his hair.[6] To turn from the field of battle is disgrace for a kṣatriya.[7] Carried off the field while unconscious, Pradyumna recovers soon enough to tell his charioteer that he does not deem life worth much, having fled from battle like a coward, his back pierced with arrows.[8] The chariot is ordered back to the scene of action. Old Dhṛtarāṣṭra asks his charioteer whether his son Duḥśāsana was slain while flying away from battle, humbled and divested of all manliness. He hopes that his son did nothing dastardly, nothing to be ashamed of. Did he face his death as nobly as the other kṣatriyas? [9] These sentiments of a blind parent, his heart wrung with anguish, reveal not a little of the heart-beat of the kṣatriya, not a little of the ideals that animated him to do or die. Glory was dearer than life itself; victory was the root of right; and death was preferable to the humiliation of defeat.

We come across many tokens of generous chivalry in practice as in precept. Yudhiṣṭhira releases the gandharva Citraratha, saying: 'Who would kill an enemy defeated in battle, shorn of strength

1 Mbh. 6.24.33.

2 Ibid., 6.17.11; cf. 12.98.23-25.

3 Ibid., 5.71.4; cf. 1.194.18.

4 Ibid., 5.135.9, *Yadarthaṁ kṣatriyā sūte tasya kālo 'yamāgataḥ*. Tacitus, Germania, p. 275, ch. 7, says of the old German tribes: 'they take their wounds to mother and wife, who do not shrink from counting the hurts and demanding a sight of them . . . .'

5 Mbh. 6.24.37, 38.

6 Ibid., 2.21.6ff.

7 Ibid., cf. 2.11.63. One who deserts his comrades to save his own life, should be slain, according to the *Śānti parva* (12.98.21,22), with sticks or stones, or should be wrapped in dry grass and burnt to death. The injunction was rarely, if ever, translated into practice. Almost every hero of the Epic leaves the field at one time or another. Compare Germania, ch. 6, p. 273: 'many survivors of war ended their infamy with a noose.'

8 Mbh. 3.19.31; cf; Rām. Yuddha, 106.1ff., where Rāvaṇa rebukes his charioteer for taking him off the battlefield. See also above, pp. 46-7.

9 Mbh. 8.5.46, 47.

and fame, and protected only by his wives'?[1] Śikhaṇḍī does not wish to strike the chariotless Kṛpa from his car.[2] Similarly, Arjuna stops and waits for Kṛpa to regain his seat, when the latter reels from his chariot.[3] Rāma allows the fainting Rāvaṇa to leave the field and return refreshed with a new bow.[4] And Karṇa remembers his promise to Kuntī before the beginning of the Mahābhārata war,[5] when he spares the lives of four of the Pāṇḍava brothers. Dragged out of his hiding behind dead elephants, Bhīma is allowed to escape with the epithets of 'beardless eunuch, fool and glutton';[6] while fleeing Nakula[7] and Sahadeva[8] are admonished to fight only with their equals. And the beaten Yudhiṣṭhira is asked to follow brāhmaṇa practices and refrain from attacking his superiors in battle; but his life is likewise spared.[9] Proud kṣatriyas in fact disdain to choose weaker rivals in a trial of strength; Jarāsandha chooses Bhīma, the mightiest of the three challengers and his equal in prowess.[10] And so Duryodhana picks his own equal opponent, and his own weapon.[11]

The theoretical injunction, however, that chariots should oppose only chariots and so on, is utterly unworkable in battle and is inevitably flouted without apology. A king attacks anyone who crosses his path, and fights another king only by accident. Many attack one, and one attacks many, while fleeing armies are mercilessly slaughtered by the heroes. Bhīṣma says truly that the strong man's word is often construed as morality, while a weak man's opinion is easily ignored even though it be the highest morality.[12]

Despite the frequency of violations, the sense of morality is still high; whole passages are full of recriminations and painful

---

1 Mbh. 1.158.33. Compare the case of Manapa-Dattas' mother who fell at the feet of the Hittite king and implored that her son be taken into allegiance. The king showed kindness to the woman (Gurney, The Hittites, pp. 115, 116).

2 Mbh. 8.53.13.

3 Ibid., 4.52.10.

4 Rām. Yuddha, 59.138.

5 Mbh. 5.144. 20ff.

6 Ibid., 7.114.67ff.; 1.1.139.

7 Ibid., 8.17.90ff.

8 Ibid., 7.142.12ff.

9 Ibid., 8.33.36ff.

10 Ibid., 2.21.2-7.

11 Ibid., 9.32.27ff. (Cal. Ed.); 33.51ff.

12 Mbh. 2.62.15, *balavāṁstu yathā dharmaṁ loke paśyati pūruṣaḥ. sa dharmo dharmavelāyāṁ bhavatyabhihitaḥ paraiḥ.*

attempts at justifying reprehensible behaviour. Kṛṣṇa makes a tawdry bid to instigate the slaughter of the old Bhīṣma,[1] unrighteously committed by Śikhaṇḍī and Arjuna. Bhūriśravā while fighting another, struck unawares by Arjuna, reproves him for his unholy act, and men of the whole army join in the censure.[2] Arjuna meets the charge with an exercise in casuistry; he would have sinned, had he not saved the life of a friend, and so he cut off the arm of Bhūriśravā.[3] It is silly to talk about fighting with one person only; there would be no real war if one man were to fight but one at a time.[4] We are reminded of Vāli who reproaches Rāma for killing him while hidden like a snake, against rules of chivalry and righteousness.[5] Rāma's thin defence is that he kept his word given to a friend, who in need must be helped.[6] Sātyaki cuts off the head of Bhūriśravā sitting in *prāya* (yogic posture) and rebuts censure with the stock argument that Abhimanyu was also unfairly slain.[7] 'Tit for tat' is thought to be a valid apology. Yudhiṣṭhira and Bhīma lie to Droṇa that his son has been slain, and the grief-stricken, unresisting old man is dragged away and beheaded by Dhṛṣṭadyumna despite cries of shame and shouts to restrain him.[8] The death of Droṇa raises a fierce debate. Arjuna accuses Yudhiṣṭhira of lying and sinning for a kingdom's sake,[9] while Sātyaki reproaches Dhṛṣṭadyumna for slaying his own preceptor.[10] But the unrepenting Dhṛṣṭadyumna questions the propriety of Bhīṣma's slaugther and Bhūriśravā's murder; high morality and immorality are alike difficult to comprehend.[11] A clash of arms between him and Sātyaki is averted only by the intervention of others present.

In fact, none of the Epic heroes can stand in spotless white and point the finger of scorn and accusation at others; they are all alike human, alike time-serving. Arjuna slays Karṇa while he tries to extricate the wheel of his chariot from the earth. Forgetful of

---

1 Mbh. 6.103.95, 96.
2 Ibid., 7.117.62; 7.118.3-19.
3 Ibid., 7.118.23ff.
4 Ibid., 7.143.28 (Cal. Ed.) *ekasyai 'kena hi kathaṁ saṁgrāmaḥ saṁbhaviṣyati.*
5 Rām. Kiṣkindhā, 17.13ff.
6 Ibid., Kiṣkindhā, 18.3ff.
7 Mbh. 7.118.42ff.
8 Ibid., 7.165.46ff.
9 Ibid., 7.167.33ff.
10 Ibid., 7.169.8ff.
11 Ibid., 7.168.38; 7.169.20ff

Duryodhana's restraint when he was unconscious, Bhīma strikes him on his thighs with his mace in utter disregard of an ancient rule;[1] a blow should never be dealt below the navel.[2] To add insult to injury, he kicks the royal head of his fallen rival, though Yudhiṣṭhira rebukes him for his ugly impertinence.[3] A proud prince is laid in the dust; a basic rule of battle is violated. Furious Balarāma rushes at the culprit, but Kṛṣṇa, of course, restrains him.[4]

Aśvatthāmā, Kṛtavarmā and Kṛpa destroy the army of Yudhiṣṭhira at night, sleeping without suspicion of danger.[5] Aśvatthāmā cites some ancient verses in order to silence contemporary morality and justify the surprise attack and slaughter at night. The enemy's forces should be attacked even when they are tired or wounded, eating, retiring or sleeping, broken, confused or reft of commanders.[6]

The Epic code of ethics helped to soften the edge of conflict, even though the lofty ideals were often impracticable in action or at variance with human folly. The civilian population was allowed to pursue its labours unmolested;[7] temples and places of public worship were left undefiled.[8] That these rules were operative in the fourth century B.C., is fully supported by the testimony of Megasthenes.[9] 'It is doubtful if any other ancient civilization set such humane ideals of warfare'.[10]

---

1 Mbh. 9.58.45, 46. (Cal. Ed.).
2 Ibid., 9.60.6 (Cal. Ed.) *adho nābhyā na hantavyaṁ iti śāstrasyaniścayaḥ.*
3 Ibid., 9.59 (Cal. Ed.).
4 Ibid., 9.60.9ff. (Cal. Ed.) Kṛṣṇa suggested the blow to Bhīma ,cf. 1.1.152. (Cr. Ed.).
5 Ibid., 1.2.28; 9.1.13.
6 Ibid., 10.1.50ff.
7 Cf. Rām. Yuddha, 4.39, 40.
8 cf. Mbh. 3.17.3.
9 Megasthenes and Arrian, frag. 1.
10 A. L. Basham, op. cit., p. 126.

CONCLUSION

The instinct of self-preservation in the face of increasing competition generated the first pulsions of bloody strife in the world of men, involving slaughter and loss of lives. Fairly early in the story of India's past, men began to organise themselves for purposes of defence. They fought on foot with weapons of wood and stone until they discovered the use of metals. The nomadic horse-riding herdsmen of Rana-Ghundai domesticated the horse as early as the fourth millennium B.C. As settlements grew in size, fortifications came into being even before the advent of the Indus civilization. With the bloom of Harappā and Mohenjodaro, the Indus valley witnessed the rise of mighty fortifications proclaiming the authority of the state and the organisation of defence, the real form of which remains an elusive enigma to the historian. Weapons of copper and bronze were used; the elephant was domesticated as well as the horse, but there is little evidence of their use in war. The Harappan civilization was fully cognizant of the wheeled vehicle; but we have no proof of the battle-chariot before the advent of the Aryans.

The light horse-drawn chariot wrought a revolution in peace and war. It became the instrument of Aryan victories in the plains of India; the speed and shock of the new machine coupled with the superb archery of the charioted knight easily carried the day against the ill-equipped early Indian warrior on foot. Beyond the means of ordinary men, the chariot consolidated the authority of the king and the nobles who could alone afford it. The supremacy of the chariot in war and its association with the rich and the powerful is borne out alike by the Vedic literature and the Epics.

The Aryans also rode horses both in peace and war, and used the lance and the sword as their chief weapons on horseback. In the tortuous highways of the Khyber, in the fastnesses of hills and forests, horsemen must have played a part denied to the chariots by the ineluctable factors of geography. Poor kṣatriyas and many of the warriors from the ranks of the people must have ridden horses. But the Vedic cavalry was only a light irregular force useful in rounding up the booty of cattle and in pursuit of the enemy in difficult regions. The lack of stirrups, which appear in India earlier than anywhere else, did not deter the ancients from making use of the horse as a mount in war. The Epics testify to the growth of the cavalry which, however, proves unable to defy the might of the charioteer. The ancient cavalry could do comparatively little in really close fighting, whether in India or elsewhere; when man fought man, the riders not infrequently slipped from their saddle-cloths and grappled on foot. The *Nikāyas* furnish the first evidence of change in India; the importance of the chariot declines perceptibly; the horseman and the elephant come to the fore.

The Aryans made friends with the elephant soon after their arrival in India, and learnt the use of the animal from the people of the land. Before the end of the Ṛgvedic epoch, kings started riding on elephants whose strength was sometimes tried even on the field of battle. The later *Saṁhitās*, *Brāhmaṇas* and the *Upaniṣads* give evidence of the growth of easy familiarity between the new-comers and the elephant; and many references imply its use in war. The Indian army became fully fourfold before the end of the Vedic period, including infantry, chariots, elephants and cavalry. Chariots, however, retained their primacy as instruments of battle. The infantry was large in size but not in importance, and was invariably rated below the chariotry. The elephants were used only in small numbers and their efficacy in war was yet far from established. The Epics also hark back to the Vedic days and reinforce the idea. But the *Nikāyas* and the *Vinaya* attest a definite shift of emphasis from the chariot to the elephant.

That the early Indian armies were not merely multitudinous hordes of people devoid of order and organisation, is proved alike by the evidence of the Vedic literature, the Buddhist canon and the Epics. The imagination of the poet created the mêlée.

Copper and bronze were the earliest metals used for the maufacture of weapons in the Indus region, the Ganges valley and beyond. But the art of iron-smelting came to India from Anatolia about 1000 B.C., presumably through the agency of itinerant smiths. Iron appears in association with the P.G. Ware at a number of sites, and precedes the arrival of the N.B.P. Ware at a few others. By about 500 B.C., fully iron-using cultures flourished as far south as Amarāvatī. The Vedic testimony fully agrees with the discoveries of archaeology and appears conclusive on the point.

The Aryans were not slow to learn the value of fortified defence. The forts of their enemies added to the travails of their progress, and the lesson was not lost. The Vedic literature contains references to enemy as well as Aryan fortifications. Archaeology bears witness to the emergence of great cities in the Ganges valley and beyond in the early years of the first millennium B.C., nestling under the security of lofty citadels. The *Nikāyas*, the *Vinaya*, and the Epics fully bear out the evidence of archaeology and lend a life and a meaning to the dusty though impressive remains of the past.

Warfare led to the growth of states and governments. Out of war arose kingship with its corollaries, heredity and despotism. The army soon became a standing organisation, and new officers arose as the forces ramified. This steady development and division of functions is attested in the Vedic literature, the Buddhist canon and the Epics. The factors responsible for the rise of monarchy also created the warrior nobility of the *rājanyas* or *kṣatriyas*. The people continued to fight, but only constituted the rank and file, the bulk of the infantry. The growing necessity for specialisation in the art of war, and the needs of agriculture and other peaceful avocations, inevitably led to a separation of functions. The generality of the people began to be averse to war.

The growth of kingdoms and the need for coalescence in a land of limitless horizons prompted the doctrine of universal conquest and a universal ruler. It manifested itself in sacrifices like the *aśvamedha*; kings marched on their neighbours to exact obeisance as well as obedience; righteous conquest, as it was called, started as early as the later Vedic period.

Man's conscience sometimes troubled him at the sight of bloodshed; there were moments of revulsion; but the hard facts of economics and the grim struggle for power brooked no moral taboos on war. Yet he groped for extenuating circumstances and even persuaded himself that he fought for the sake of his faith. Struggle was unavoidable in the nature of things. He proceeded therefore to evolve and enunciate moral maxims to govern the conduct of warriors, to mitigate misery without abolishing war, to humanise rivalry without eradicating the consequent violence. The Vedic literature shows the germ of this uneasy morality that frets at its impotence. The Buddha from time to time raises his voice against war and its orgies of devastation, but to no avail. The Epics, however, recognise its inevitable character and therefore seek to ennoble and glorify it. An elaborate code of ethics is proclaimed, unexampled anywhere else in the ancient world, even though many of its tenets are impracticable in war.

The messages of men like the Buddha and Mahāvīra, and one victorious campaign, convinced an Indian monarch in the 3rd century B.C., that war was an evil and a crime. But the lesson was soon forgotten despite his rock and pillar inscriptions seeking to immortalise it; men fought men as they had done before; the story of later Indian warfare yet awaits its historian.

APPENDIX

ARCHERY IN MODERN INDIA

The tradition of ancient Indian archery is kept alive even today by a handful of display archers in the country. In the early years of the current century a famous archer from South India, nicknamed Kaliyugī Arjuna, shot a number of tigers and other wild beasts with his bow and arrows. Possessed of a powerful physique and an uncanny aim, he did great things with his favourite weapon, and for some time taught archery to the students of the Prem Mahā Vidyālaya, Brindāban. He could shoot four arrows simultaneously from the same bow and hit four difficult and different targets all at once. He made people put on spectacle frames fitted with silver rupees instead of glasses, which he shot down with two arrows of such an impeccably calculated force as to displace the little discs without injuring the men. He smeared exceedingly sharp arrow-tips with chalk dust and shot them at the bare backs of students with a perfect delicacy of control, so that they left only chalk marks on their tender targets without even grazing them. But he could also shoot powerful shafts that ripped through copper and iron plates. He could easily support a football in mid air for more than five minutes with a continuous shower of arrows. Imprisoned for seditious activities during the first world war, he died in jail.[1]

We have seen many of these feats repeated by another archer not many years ago. As well as performing many of the exploits of Kaliyugī Arjuna he could easily hit four thin sticks set upright in the ground at a fair distance with as many arrows discharged together from his bow. And he could also hit his target with his back turned to it, only by seeing its reflection in a mirror.

In antiquity, when almost every able-bodied man tried to learn the use of the bow, the standard of archery must doubtless have been high, with not a few outstanding masters of the great weapon.

---

[1] This account is based on the testimony of my father, who learnt a little archery from Kaliyugī Arjuna at Brindāban.

BIBLIOGRAPHY OF WORKS MENTIONED IN THE TEXT

A. *Sanskrit Texts*

Aitareya Āraṇyaka.
Ed. A. B. Keith, Oxford, 1909.

Aitareya Brāhmaṇa.
Ed. Theodor Aufrecht, Bonn, 1879. Ṛgveda Brāhmaṇas. The Aitareya and Kauṣītaki Brāhmaṇas of the Rigveda translated from the Original Sanskrit by A. B. Keith. HOS., vol. 25, Cambridge, Mass., 1920.

Atharva Veda.
Atharva Veda Sanhitā. Herausgegeben von R. Roth. . und W. D. Whitney. . . zweite verbesserte Auflage besorgt von Dr. Max Lindenau, Berlin, 1924. Translated with a critical commentary by W. D. Whitney . . . , revised and . . . edited by C. R. Lanman = HOS., vols. 7 and 8, Cambridge, Mass., 1905.
The Hymns of the Atharva Veda, tr. R.T.H. Griffith, 2 vols., Benares, 1916-17.

Bṛhadāraṇyaka Upaniṣad.
Ed. and tr. E. Röer, 3 vols., Bibliotheca Indica, Calcutta, 1849-1856.

Chāndogya Upaniṣad.
Ānandāśrama Sanskrit Series, vol. 14, Poona, 1902.

Gopatha Brāhmaṇa.
Herausgegeben von Dr. Dieuke Gaastra, Leiden, 1919.

Jaiminīya Brāhmaṇa.
Ed. Dr. Raghuvira and Dr. Lokesh Chandra, Nagpur, 1954 = Sarasvatī Vihāra Series, vol. 31.

Jaiminīya Upaniṣad Brāhmaṇa.
The Jaiminīya or Talavakāra Upaniṣad Brāhmaṇa: Text, translation and Notes, by Hans Oertel . . . New Haven, 1894 = JAOS XVI, 79-260.

Kāṭhaka Saṁhitā.
Kāṭhakaṁ. Herausgegeben von Leopold von Schroeder. 3 Bde. und Wort-Index von Richard Simon, Leipzig, 1900-1912.

Kauṣītaki Brāhmaṇa.
Herausgegeben und übersetzt von B. Lindner . . . I. Text, Jena, 1887.

Kauṭilya's Arthaśāstra.
Ed. R. Shamasastri. Revised Edn., Mysore, 1924.
Tr. R. Shamasastri, 5th edn., Mysore, 1956.

Mahābhārata.
For the first time critically edited by V. S. Sukthankar and others.
The Ādi Parvan, ed. V. S. Sukthankar, Poona, 1933.
The Sabhā Parvan, ed. F. Edgerton, Poona, 1944.
The Āraṇyaka Parvan, ed. V. S. Sukthankar, Poona, 1942.
The Virāṭa Parvan, ed. Raghuvira, Poona, 1936.
The Udyoga Parvan, ed. S. K. De, Poona, 1940.
The Bhīṣma Parvan, ed. S. K. Belvalkar, Poona, 1947.
The Droṇa Parvan, ed. S. K. De, Poona, 1953-58.
The Karṇa Parvan, ed. P. L. Vaidya, Poona, 1954.
The Śalya Parvan, Pt. I, ed. R. N. Dandekar, Poona, 1956.
The Sauptika and Strī Parvans, ed. Velankar and Paranjpe, Poona, 1956.

The Śānti Parvan, ed. S. K. Belvalkar, Poona, 1949-53.
(All the references in our text, unless otherwise stated, are to this Critical Edition of the Mbh.)

Śrīmahābhārataṁ.
Ed. P. C. Roy, 3rd Edn., Calcutta, 1809 Śaka.

Maitrāyaṇī Saṁhitā.
Herausgegeben von Dr. Leopold von Schroeder. 4 vols., Leipzig 1881-1886.

Muir, John.
Original Sanskrit Texts on the Origin and History of the People of India, their Religion and Institutions, 5 vols., II edn. London, 1872-74.

Pañcaviṁśa Brāhmaṇa, or Tāṇḍya Mahābrāhmaṇa.
Ed. Anandachandra Vedantavagisa. 2 vols. Calcutta, 1870, 1874 = Bibliotheca Indica.
Panchaviṃśa Brāhmaṇa. The Brāhmaṇa of twenty-five chapters, translated by Dr. W. Caland, Calcutta, 1931.

Rāmāyaṇa.
Śrīmadvālmīkīyaṁ Rāmāyaṇaṁ, 'Rāmābhinandinī' bhāṣāṭīkāsahitaṁ. Paṇḍit Pustakālaya, Kāśī, 1951.
(All the references in our text are to this edition of the Rāmāyaṇa.)

Ṛgveda Saṁhitā.
Ed. Śrīpāda Śarmā Dāmodara Sātavalekar, Oundh, 1940.
Der Rig-Veda, Aus Dem Sanskrit Ins Deutsche Übersetzt Und Mit Einem Laufenden Kommentar Versehen von K. F. Geldner. HOS., vols. 33, 34, 35. Cambridge, Mass. 1951.
The Hymns of the Rigveda, translated with a popular commentary by R. T. H. Griffith, II Edn., 2 vols., Benares, 1896-97.
(The versified English translations of Ṛgvedic passages in our text have been borrowed from Griffith, with emendations wherever necessary.)
Ṛgveda, English translation with notes by Wilson. New Edn. 6 vols. Bangalore, 1925-28.

Sāma Veda.
Ed. Śrīpāda Dāmodara Sātavalekar, 3rd edn. Oundh, 1956.
The Hymns of the Sāmaveda, translated with a popular commentary by R. T. H. Griffith, Benares, 1907.

Sāma Vidhāna Brāhmaṇa.
Ed. and Tr. A. C. Burnell, Vol. I. Text and Commentary with Introduction, London, 1873.
Das Sāmavidhāna Brāhmaṇa. Ein altindisches Handbuch der Zauberei. Eingeleitet und übersetzt von Sten Konow. Halle, 1893.

Śatapatha Brāhmaṇa.
Ed. A. Weber, Berlin-London, 1855.
The Śatapatha Brāhmaṇa according to the text of the Mādhyandina School, tr. Julius Eggeling, 5 vols. Oxford, 1882-1900. (SBE., vols. xii, xxvi, xli, xliii, xliv.)

Taittirīya Āraṇyaka.
Ānandāśrama Sanskrit Series, no. 36, 2 vols. Poona, 1898.

Taittirīya Brāhmaṇa.
Ānandāśrama Sanskrit Series, no. 37, 3 vols. Poona, 1898.

Taittirīya Saṃhitā.
The Sanhitá of the Black Yajurveda with the commentary of Mádhava Ácárya.

Ed. Dr. E. Roer and E. B. Cowell, vol. I; vol. II, ed. E. B. Gowell; vols. III, IV, V, ed. Maheśachandra Nyáyaratna; vol. VI, ed. S. Sámaśrami. Bibliotheca Indica, Calcutta, 1860-1899.
The Veda of the Black Yajus School entitled Taittirīya Saṁhitā. Tr. A. B. Keith, 2 vols. Cambridge, Mass., 1914 = HOS., vols. 18 and 19.
Upaniṣads.
The Principal Upanishads. Edited with introduction, text, translation and notes, by S. Radhakrishnan, London, 1953.
The Thirteen Principal Upanishads. Tr. R. E. Hume, Second Edn., Oxford, 1931.
The Upanishads, tr. Max Müller, SBE. I, Pt. I, 1879; SBE. XV, 1884.
Vājasaneyi Saṁhitā.
Ed. Śrīpāda Śarmā Dāmodara Sātavalekar, Oundh, Vikrama S. 2003.
Tr. R. T. H. Griffith, The Texts of the White Yajurveda . . . , II edn., Benares, 1927.
Yāska.
Nirukta, 2 vols., Ānandāśrama Sanskrit Series, no. 88. Poona, 1921-26

B. *Pāli Texts*

Aṅguttara Nikāya
Ed. R. Morris and E. Hardy, 5 vols. PTS. London, 1885-1900.
Tr. F. L. Woodward and E. M. Hare, The Book of the Gradual Sayings, 5 vols., PTS. London, 1932-36.
Dhammapada.
With introductory essays, Pāli text, English translation and notes by S. Radhakrishnan, London, 1958.
The Minor Anthologies of the Pāli Canon, Part I, SBB, vol. 7, Dhammapada etc. Ed. and tr. Mrs. Rhys Davids, London, 1931.
Dīgha Nikāya.
Ed. T. W. Rhys Davids and J. Estlin Carpenter, 3 vols., PTS. London, 1890-1911.
Tr. Ṭ. W. and C. A. F. Rhys Davids, Dialogues of the Buddha, 3 vols., PTS. London, 1899-1921.
Jātaka.
Ed. V. Fausböll, 6 vols. and index. London, 1877-97.
Tr. by various hands, ed. E.B. Cowell, 6 vols. and index. Cambridge, 1895-1907.
Majjhima Nikāya.
Ed. V. Trenckner and Lord Chalmers, 3 vols., PTS. London, 1888-99.
Tr. I. B. Horner, The Collection of the Middle Length Sayings, 3 vols., PTS. London, 1954-59.
Saṁyutta Nikāya.
Ed. L. Feer, 6 vols., PTS. London, 1884-1904.
Tr. C. A. F. Rhys Davids and F. L. Woodward, The Book of Kindred Sayings, 5 vols., London, 1917-30.
Vinaya Piṭaka.
Ed. H. Oldenberg, 5 vols. London, 1879-83.
Tr. I. B. Horner, The Book of the Discipline, 5 vols., SBB. London, 1938-1952.

C. *Miscellaneous Sources*

Archives Royales De Mari, vol. VI, Paris, 1954.
Arrian,
  Anabasis of Alexander, Loeb Edn. London, 1933.
The Bible.
Budge, E. A. W., and King, L. W.,
  Annals of the Kings of Assyria. The Cuneiform texts with translations, transliterations, etc., from the original documents in the British Museum, London, 1902.
Dangin, F. Thureau,
  Une relation de la huitième campagne de Sargon, Paris, 1912.
Herodotus.
  Ed. T. E. Page and others, Loeb Edn., 4 vols., London, 1928.
Homer.
  Iliad.
Plato.
  Laws. Tr. R. G. Bury, Loeb Edn. London, 1926.
Polybius.
  The Histories, Loeb Edn., vol. II, London, 1922.
Pritchard, J. B.
  Ancient Near Eastern Texts relating to the Old Testament, Princeton University Press, 1950.
Quintus Curtius.
  History of Alexander. Tr. J. C. Rolfe. 2 vols., Loeb Edn. Cambridge, Mass., 1946.
Tacitus.
  Germania. (Dialogues, Agricola, Germania) William Heinemann, London, 1932.
(All the references in our text are to this edn.)

D. *Reference Books, etc.*

Ancient India.
  Bulletin of the ASI., New Delhi.
ASI.
  Annual Reports, Calcutta and Delhi.
Böhtlinck, O. and Roth, R.,
  Sanskrit Wörterbuch. 7 vols. St. Petersburg, 1855-75.
Grassmann, H.,
  Wörterbuch zum Rig-Veda, Leipzig, 1873.
Hastings, J., ed.,
  Encyclopaedia of Religion and Ethics, 12 vols. Edinburgh, 1908-26.
Indian Archaeology.
  A Review (Annual).
Macdonell, A. A., and Keith, A. B.,
  Vedic Index of Names and Subjects, 2 vols. London, 1912.
Malalasekera, G. P.,
  Dictionary of Pāli Proper Names, 2 vols. London, 1937-38.
Monier Williams, M.,
  Sanskrit-English Dictionary, new edn., Oxford, 1960.
Rhys Davids, T. W., and Stede, W.,
  The PTS. Pāli-English Dictionary, London, 1921.

E. *Monographs*

Agravala, V. S.,
India as known to Pāṇini. A study of the cultural material in the Ashṭādhyāyī, Lucknow, 1953.
Bachhofer, Ludwig,
Early Indian Sculpture, 2 vols. Paris, 1929.
Basham, A. L.,
The Wonder That Was India, . . . London, 1954.
Beni Prasad,
Theory of Government in Ancient India, Allahabad, 1927.
Bhandarkar, D. R.,
Aśoka, III Edn., Calcutta, 1955.
Bloomfield, M.,
The Atharvaveda. Strassburg, 1899.
Breasted, J. H.,
A History of Egypt, II Edn. London, 1951.
Carman, W. Y.,
A History of Firearms, London, 1955.
Chakravarti, P. C.,
The Art of War in Ancient India, Dacca, 1941.
Childe, V. G.,
New Light on the Most Ancient East, London, 1952.
What Happened in History, Harmondsworth, 1950.
Cunningham, Sir Alexander,
The Stūpa of Bharhut, London, 1879.
Date, G. T.,
The Art of War in Ancient India, Bombay, 1929.
Dikshitar, V.R.R.,
War in Ancient India, II Edn., Madras, 1948.
Dumézil, G.,
Naissance d'archanges: essai sur la formation de la théologie Zoroastrienne, 5 e édition, Paris, 1945.
Ebeling, E.,
Bruchstücke einer mittelassyrischen Vorschriftensammlung für die Akklimatisierung und Trainierung von Wagenpferden, Berlin, 1951.
Fairservis, Walter A., Jr.,
The Harappan Civilization—New Evidence and More Theory. American Museum Novitates, published by the American Museum of Natural History, New York. No. 2055, Nov. 17, 1961.
Forbes, R. J.,
Metallurgy in Antiquity; a notebook for archaeologists and technologists. Leiden, 1950.
Forrer, Les chars cultuels préhistoriques et leurs survivances aux epoques historiques, Paris, 1932.
Frankfort, H.,
More Sculpture from the Diyala Region. OIP. vol. LX, University of Chicago, 1943.
Ghate, V. S.,
Lectures on the Rigveda, ed. V. S. Sukthankar, II edn. Poona, 1926.
Gordon, D. H.,
The Prehistoric Background of Indian Culture, Bombay, 1958.
Gurney, O. R.,
The Hittites, Harmondsworth, 1952.

Held, G. J.,
The Mahabharata, An Ethnological Study. London, 1935.
Hunter, G. R.,
The Script of Harappa and Mohenjodaro and its connection with other scripts. . . . London, 1934.
Jayaswal, K. P.,
Hindu Polity, A Constitutional History of India in Hindu Times. III Edn. Bangalore, 1955.
Lundholm, Bengt,
Abstammung und Domestikation des Hauspferdes, Zoologiska Bidrag Fran Uppsala, 1949, 27: 1-289.
Macdonell, A. A.,
History of Sanskrit Literature, London, 1928.
Vedic Mythology, Strassburg, 1897.
Mackay, E. J. H., Chanhudaro Excavations, 1935-6, New Haven, 1943.
Further Excavations at Mohenjodaro, 2 vols. Delhi, 1938.
Maisey, F. C.,
Sanchi and its Remains, London, 1892.
Majumdar, B. K.,
Military System in Ancient India, 2nd edn. Calcutta, 1960.
Majumdar, R. C., and others,
Advanced History of India, London, 1946.
Majumdar, R. C., and Pusalkar, A. D., ed.,
The Vedic Age, . . . History and Culture of the Indian People, vol. I, London, 1951.
Majumdar, N. G.,
Explorations in Sind, MASI., no. 48, 1934.
Marshall, Sir John,
A Guide to Sanchi, Calcutta, 1918.
Marshall, Sir John, and others,
Mohenjodaro and the Indus Civilization, 3 vols. London, 1931.
Marshall, Sir John, and Foucher, A.,
The Monuments of Sanchi, vol. II, Calcutta (?), Date (?).
Mc Crindle, J. W.,
Ancient India as described by Megasthenes and Arrian; being a translation of the Fragments of the Indika of Megasthenes. . . and of the first part of the Indika of Arrian. London, 1877.
Picq, Ardant Du,
Battle Studies. Ancient and Modern Battle. Tr. J. N. Greely and R. C. Cotton. New York, 1921.
Piggott, Stuart,
Prehistoric India, Harmondsworth, 1950.
Ed. The Dawn of Civilization, London, 1961.
Pischel, Richard, and Geldner, K. F.,
Vedische Studien, 3 vols. Stuttgart, 1889-1901.
Prasad, B.,
Animal Remains from Harappa, MASI. 51, Delhi, 1936.
Rapson, E. J., ed.,
Cambridge History of India, vol. I. Cambridge, 1922.
Rau, Wilhelm,
Staat und Gesellschaft im Alten Indien . . . . Wiesbaden, 1957.
Raychaudhuri, H. C.,
Political History of Ancient India, sixth ed., Calcutta, 1953.

Renou, Louis,
Vedic India, Calcutta, 1957.
Saggs, H. W. F.,
The Greatness that was Babylon, London, 1962.
Salonen, Armas,
Die Landfahrzeuge des Alten Mesopotamien, Helsinki, 1951.
Hippologica Accadica, Helsinki, 1956.
Sankalia, H. D.,
Prehistory and Protohistory in India and Pakistan, Bombay, 1962-63.
Schrader, Otto,
Prehistoric Antiquities of the Aryan Peoples . . . tr. F. B. Jevons . . . from the second . . . edn., with the cooperation of the author. London, 1890.
Sharma, G. R.,
The Excavations at Kauśāmbī (1957-59), Allahabad, 1960.
Sharma, R. S.,
Aspects of Political Ideas and Institutions in Ancient India, Delhi, 1959.
Smith, Sidney,
Early History of Assyria to 1000 B. C. London, 1928.
Spellman, J. W.,
Aspects of Kingship in Ancient India (To c. 300 A. D.). Ph. D. Thesis, 1960, University of London.
Stein, Sir Aurel,
An Archaeological Tour in Waziristan and Northern Baluchistan, MASI., no. 37, Calcutta, 1929.
An Archaeological Tour in Gedrosia, MASI., no. 43, Calcutta, 1931.
Archaeological Reconnaissances in North Western India and South Eastern Iran, London, 1937.
Tschèpe, P. Albert,
Histoire du Royaume de Tch'ou, Changhai, 1903.
Vats, M. S.,
Excavations at Harappa, 2 vols. New Delhi, 1940.
Wheeler, Sir Mortimer,
Early India and Pakistan to Ashoka, London, 1959.
The Indus Civilization, II edn., Cambridge, 1960.
Winternitz, M.,
A History of Indian Literature, vol. I. Tr. Mrs. S. Ketkar, Calcutta, 1927.
Woolley, Sir Leonard,
Ur Excavations, ii, The Royal Cemetery, London, 1934.
Ur of the Chaldees, Harmondsworth, 1952.
Zimmer, H.,
Altindisches Leben, Berlin, 1879.

F. *Articles.*

Apte, V. M.,
Vajra in the Ṛgveda, ABORI, vol. XXXVII, 1956, pp. 292-295.
Were castes formulated in the Ṛgveda?, BDCRI., vol. II, 1940-41, pp. 34-49.
Arnold, W. R.,
Solomon's Horse-Trade, JAOS, 26, First Half, 1905, p. 104.
Banerjee, M. N.,
On Metals and Metallurgy in Ancient India, IHQ., III, pp. 121-133, 793-802.
Iron and Steel in the Ṛgvedic Age, IHQ., V, pp. 432-440.
A Note on Iron in the Ṛgvedic Age, IHQ., VIII, pp. 364-366.

Barnett, R. D., and Watson, W.,
Russian Excavations in Armenia, Iraq, vol. 14, pp. 139ff.
Basham, A. L.,
Prince Vijaya and the Aryanisation of Ceylon, Ceylon Historical Journal, vol. I, no. 3, Jan. 1952, pp. 163-171.
Bishop, C. W.,
The Elephant and its Ivory in Ancient China, JAOS, 41, pp. 290-306.
Chatterjee, S. K.,
Polyglottism in Indo-Aryan, Seventh Oriental Conference, Baroda, 1933, pp. 177-189.
Coomaraswamy, A. K.,
Horse-riding in the Ṛgveda and the Atharvaveda, JAOS, 62, 1942. pp. 139-140.
Dandekar, R. N.,
Vṛtrahā Indra, ABORI, vol. 31, 1950, pp. 1-55.
Downs, J. F.,
The Origin and Spread of Riding in the Near East and Central Asia, American Anthropologist, vol. 63, 1961, no. 6, pp. 1193-1203.
Gelb, I. J.,
The Early History of the West Semitic Peoples, JCS., XV, 1961, pp. 27-47.
Ghoshal, U. N.,
Kingship in the Ṛgveda, IHQ, vol. 20, 1944, pp. 36-42.
Kingship and Kingly Administration in the Atharva Veda, IHQ, 20, pp. 105-113.
Gonda, J.,
Ancient Indian Kingship from the Religious point of view, Numen, III.
Gordon, D. H.,
The Early Use of Metals in India and Pakistan, JRAI, vol. LXXX, 1952, pp. 55ff.
Hopkins, E. W.,
The Social and Military Position of the Ruling Caste in Ancient India as represented by the Sanskrit Epic, JAOS, 13, 1889, pp. 57-329.
Problematic passages in the Rigveda, JAOS, 15, pp. 252-283.
Konow, Sten,
The Aryan gods of the Mitanni People, Kristiania Etnografiske Museums Skrifter Bind 3 Hefte 1; Kristiania, 1921.
Kosambi, D. D.,
On the Origin of Brahmin Gotras, JBBRAS, 26, New Series, 1951, pp. 21-80.
Kronasser, H.,
Indisches in den Nuzi Texten, Wiener Zeitschrift für die Kunde des Morgenlandes, vol. LIII, 1957, pp. 181ff.
Lal, B. B.,
Excavations at Hastināpura and other explorations in the Upper Gangā and Sutlej Basins 1950-52. Ancient India, nos. 10 and 11, 1954 and 55, pp. 5-151.
Further Copper Hoards from the Gangetic Basin and a Review of the Problem, Ancient India, no. 7, 1951, pp. 20ff.
Protohistoric Investigation, Ancient India, no. 9, pp. 80ff.
A new Indus valley capital discovered: excavations at Kalibangan in Northern Rajasthan, The Illustrated London News, March 24, 1962, pp. 454-457.

Le Grain, L. L.,
Horseback riding in Mesopotamia in the IIIrd millennium B. C. Bulletin of the University Museum 11: (4) : 27-32, Philadelphia, University of Pennsylvania Press, 1948.
Macdonell, A. A.,
The Origin and Early History of Chess, JRAS, 1898, pp. 117ff.
Majumdar, N. G.,
Notes on Vajra, JDL., vol. XI, 1924, pp. 173-200.
Naik, A. V.,
A note on the copper swords from Kallur, BDCRI, vol. IV, no. 4, 1943, pp. 376-378.
Olmstead, A. T.,
The calculated frightfulness of Ashur Nasir Apal, JAOS, 38, pp. 209ff.
Parrot, André,
Les Fouilles dę Mari. . . . , Syria, XVI, 1935, pp. 117-140.
Piggott, Stuart,
Prehistoric Copper Hoards in the Ganges Basin, Antiquity, vol. 18, 1944, pp. 173-182.
Przyluski, J.,
Hippokoura et Satakarni, JRAS, 1929, pp. 273ff.
Satvant, Sātvata and Nāsatya, IHQ, IX, 1933, pp. 88-91.
Asses, Horses and Gandharvas, Indian Culture, vol. 3, 1936-37, pp. 613-620.
Raikes, R. L., and Dyson, R. H., Jr.,
The prehistoric climate of Baluchistan and the Indus Valley, American Anthropologist, vol. 63, no. 2, Pt. I, April 1961, pp. 265ff.
Ross, E. J.,
A chalcolithic site in Northern Baluchistan, with prefatory remarks by D. E. McCown, Journal of Near Eastern Studies, V, 1946, pp. 284-316.
Sastri, P. S.,
The Imagery of the Ṛgveda, ABORI, vol. 29, pp. 152ff.
Schoff, W. H.,
The Eastern Iron trade of the Roman Empire, JAOS, 35, pp. 224-239.
Sharma, Y. D.,
Exploration of Historical Sites, Ancient India, no. 9, 1953, pp. 116ff.
Sieg, Emil,
Bhṛgus, ERE., vol. II, pp. 558-560.
Singh, Sarva Daman,
The Elephant and The Aryans, JRAS, 1963, Parts 1 and 2, pp. 1ff.
Iron in Ancient India, Journal of Economic and Social History of the Orient, Vol. V, Part II, 1962, pp. 212ff.
Smith, V. A.,
The Copper Age and Prehistoric Bronze Implements of India, IA., 1905, vol. 34, pp. 230ff.
Thieme, Paul,
The 'Aryan' gods of the Mitanni Treaties, JAOS, 80, 1960, pp. 301ff.
Walhouse, M. J.,
Archaeological Notes, no. xxi—The Old Tanjor Armoury, IA., vol. 7, pp. 192-196.
Wheeler, Sir Mortimer,
Harappā 1946: The Defences and Cemetery R 37, Ancient India, no.3, 1947, pp. 58-130.
Whitney, W. D.,
On the main results of the later Vedic researches in Germany, JAOS, III, pp. 289-328.

INDEX